THE SEASON

THE SEASON

A SUMMER WHIRL THROUGH THE
ENGLISH SOCIAL SEASON

SOPHIE CAMPBELL

Aurum

First published in Great Britain
2013 by Aurum Press Ltd
74–77 White Lion Street
Islington
London N1 9PF
www.aurumpress.co.uk

A catalogue record for this book is available
from the British Library.

ISBN 978 1 84513 703 8

1 3 5 7 9 10 8 6 4 2
2013 2015 2017 2016 2014

Typeset in Berling by M Rules
Printed and bound by
CPI Group (UK) Ltd, Croydon, CR0 4YY

To my family
and to Max (1959–2012)

CONTENTS

STRANGE BEDFELLOWS

I t had been raining all day at Ascot. Fat drops rolled off the
leaves of the chestnut and lime trees and bowed the jaunty
striped roofs of gazebos. Puddles collected in the dips in the
gravel, forcing race-goers to hold on to their hats and hop from dry
spot to dry spot. In a brief lull the sun came out and a rainbow
appeared somewhere over Woking. In front of it, perfectly silhouetted, was a lone figure in top hat and tails. He was staring at
the sky, transfixed. I took a blurry picture of that moment and
every so often I look at it and wish it were more in focus, because
it captures so much about an extraordinary summer.

If you examine it closely, you can see the rain still sitting on his
expensively padded shoulders. He is immaculately, formally
dressed, as if he has stepped out of a Victorian miniature, and he
is wearing a uniform as sternly prescribed as any army or hospital
garb: fitted black tailcoat, striped grey trousers with a perfect break
above a pair of sodden black shoes, a black top hat with a black hat
band. Ideally it would be black silk plush, but even grey felt would

still be within the strictures laid down if you wish to attend the Royal Enclosure at Royal Ascot, the famous five-day flat racing meeting that takes place in southeast England every June.

We were not in the Royal Enclosure. We were in the Owners & Trainers' car park, 'Os & Ts', which is even cooler, and earlier I had seen the man arrive with an elegant woman in black. Each held a glass of champagne carefully aloft as they walked, so the liquid stayed level, as if the glasses were on gimbals. Suddenly, silently, without warning, she keeled over and lay at right angles to one of the tents, straight as a felled tree. He strolled on, unaware until alerted by a general buzz of concern, then turned, bent over – glass still level – and extended a hand, laughing, to help her up. 'Don't worry, she's a doctor,' drawled a voice from beneath a nearby awning, addressing the world in general. 'She'll know if she's hurt.'

So this was it. The most glamorous place to be (well, almost, because if there was one thing I learned that year it was that there is always somewhere else a little bit better) at the most glamorous race meeting of the summer, and the party was just about to begin. It was pouring, which gave a dreamy intimacy to the interior of the gazebo. People were friendly, considering I had parachuted in from nowhere. I was excited – I had never been to Ascot before and here I was, teetering just below the summit of the English social season – but I did wish someone was sober enough to answer one or two pertinent questions. What was going on, exactly? How had enclosures and dress codes survived into the early years of the twenty-first century? Why was flat racing smarter than jump racing? Who said? And how could there be a class system for car parks? These were the specifics, but I also wondered why Royal Ascot – admittedly a truly venerable event at 300 years old that year – had become the acknowledged summit of 'the season'. What 'the season' meant, precisely, was what I was trying to find out.

The word comes from the Latin *serere* – to sow, or a time of sowing – a period of assiduous labour, which, with luck and judgement, should result in a time of fruitfulness and plenty. Fertility, of crops and of people, has always been one of our earliest preoccupations. From Roman mosaics to medieval English manuscripts, the rhythms of the year have been beaten out in rituals and labours: tilling and sowing, fattening and slaughtering, salting and pickling. Hundreds of years later, in damp eighteenth-century England, a set of rituals began to crystallise that were also about fertility, obliquely speaking, and about preservation too, but this time of the status quo. The social elite began to have more leisure and they needed to meet and marry each other. They put an awful lot of work into doing so and having fun at the same time. They also created, perhaps unconsciously, a complex matrix of rituals and codes that would keep undesirables out. Those are the simple roots of it. The traditional English summer events that we know today – a core of around twelve – are just the survivors.

I always think of the social season with a capital S, because there are so many other seasons jostling in contemporary life: silly seasons, football seasons, awards seasons, festival seasons. Nobody would have done so in the past. The season was *the* season – there was no other, or no other that mattered, anyway. A world of confidence and assumptions resides in that small 's'. The concept encompassed not only the days whiled away *en fête* in the countryside but an endless round of dinners, parties and assemblies in London. There was a 'little season' in the autumn and a debutante season – the nursery slopes, as it were – for the young, which ran from spring to summer. The whole thing oiled the wheels of Society (which did seem to have a capital S), supplied endless gambling and sexual scandals and dovetailed neatly with the marriage market. It is also an English rather than British construct – southeast English in fact – because all these events still take place within seventy miles of London and by the end of the nineteenth century all were within reach of a train.

Many of us have participated, consciously or unconsciously, in the events of the season. One of their most distinctive features is that they are open to a remarkable range of spectators. Unlike a football match or a music festival, it's usually possible to get in free or pretty cheaply, so outside the enclosures anyone can go. Any apparent grandeur is often belied by eccentric ritual: I've been to the opera at Glyndebourne in the Sussex countryside and watched people drift across the lawns in clouds of tulle or cocktail dresses, only to fold themselves up on a mothy car rug for a picnic. I remember going to the polo at Smith's Lawn as a child and being shocked at the sight of smartly dressed grown-ups getting up halfway through the match, as if responding to an invisible signal, to mill about on the polo field, treading in chunks of turf thrown up by the ponies' hooves.

Every year I buy an evening ticket for the Chelsea Flower Show, though I don't have a garden, because I like the summery English atmosphere. I've even been to what I now know to be one of the most sought-after nights of the corporate year, its Monday night Gala Preview. It was a work invitation; I never even thought to be excited. I occasionally go to the Royal Academy Summer Exhibition to be rude about other people's paintings, and queue interminably for the tennis at Wimbledon every June, never being organised enough to enter the public ballot the year before.

They're all just things that are around, particularly if you live in London. They roll by, year after year, as much a part of the summer as sticky plane trees and postmen wearing shorts, boats on the Serpentine and drinkers spilling out onto the pavements. Posters go up on the Tube advertising the great race meetings – Royal Ascot, the Derby, Glorious Goodwood – or Chelsea, or Henley, or Wimbledon. For some reason these are not the same as other regattas or tournaments or flower shows, of which there are thousands across Britain. Mention at the office that you're going to, say, the Salcombe Regatta in Devon, and everyone will go 'How nice' and get back to work. Say you're going to Henley – or the Henley Royal Regatta, as it likes to call itself – and everyone will ask if your skirt is below the knee, in reference to its famously draconian dress code.

These particular events just have something different about them. 'The Derby is not an event,' a racecourse official once said to me crisply, 'it's an occasion.' At the time I thought him pedantic, but I've thought about it since: an event is just any old happening, but an occasion … an occasion is heightened, it has fizz and pizzazz and style. You have to step up to an occasion, make an effort and enter into the spirit of the thing. I had done lots of stepping up and making an effort and entering into the spirit of the thing, but I had never really connected them all, or thought of them as a collective entity, until asked to write a feature on the season by a national newspaper early one summer. They wanted to know how hard it was to get tickets and could anyone afford it and what did you have to wear.

I got on the phone and then started doing some reading. I was startled to find that racing at Ascot began when a Stuart monarch was still on the throne, and even more intrigued when the Derby turned out to have an encampment of Irish Travellers on its land for the ten days around the race meeting, their right to be there apparently enshrined in an Act of Parliament. I read descriptions of the Christie family's dream of building a European-style opera house in the English countryside in the 1930s, a time when the Royal Opera House in Covent Garden didn't even have its own full-time company, and marvelled at the arcane practices of the committee of Royal Academicians which annually battles through 12,000 submissions to select a thousand paintings for the Summer Exhibition.

All of a sudden, I was gripped. And like all these things, once you become obsessed with something it appears everywhere. The season turned up in conversation without my mentioning it. It appeared magically in books, paintings and radio programmes, often just as snippets, but they all added fuel to the fire. It popped up in the course of my work; I was sent to write about Newmarket, for example, where the first regular connection between racing and the movements of the court was established. I was also training in the evenings as a London tour guide and while reading novels about the city found that Thackeray, Trollope and Galsworthy came up trumps on the subject, often in the form of blistering literary attacks. An artist friend, a former student at the Royal Academy Schools doing his annual stint as a Summer Exhibition picture handler, came to stay on my sofa and regaled me with tales of paintings balanced on an ancient stool and the committee with its head in its collective hands, breaking for mid-morning beef tea. It was like lifting up a familiar old stone and finding all life seething beneath it.

When I decided to write about the season more thoroughly, though, it wasn't quite as simple as I'd thought. In fact, the closer I got the more fragmented it became, the whole shattering into dozens of glittering pieces so that I didn't quite know where to begin. Flowers, flat racing, opera and sailing made strange bedfellows. Furthermore, people reacted in such different ways when I said what I was writing about. Some muttered about 'toffs' and anachronisms, or thought I was writing a guide to dress codes and making picnics. Others thought it was a book about country sports: the operatic life cycle of the mayfly in fly-fishing rivers, say, or the intoxicating autumn whir of grouse on the northern moors.

People wanted to know if I was focusing on the debutante season, about which a great deal has been written and recorded already, often well and often by debs themselves. But instinctively I knew it wasn't the same thing. The events I was interested in seemed highly adult, sophisticated and public. The debutante season was effectively private, open only to those deemed suitable enough to be presented at court and therefore to 'come out' – at which point they were allowed to have a far racier time with the adults. There was also a Scottish season, based around stalking (the tracking and shooting of deer) and reeling, or country dancing. This began as the English season ended and grouse shooting began, causing an annual migration still undertaken by the Queen when she sets off to Balmoral late every summer. And finally, the modern season reared its complicated, colourful head: rock, pop and indie festivals, literary weeks, triathlons and marathons and, perhaps the most natural successor to flat racing, the motor racing season, with all its speed and glamour and noise.

I wondered idly if these newer, louder events would eventually drown out the rest, assuming the mantle of the English – or British – season of the future and leaving the old familiars to fade into rose-tinted obscurity. But before I could even begin to speculate on the subject, I needed to pin down a definition: what, exactly, was a traditional event of the season?

1

A TOE IN THE WATER

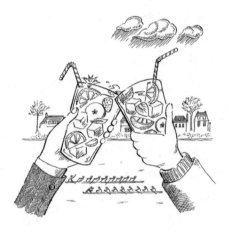

I n need of expert help, I rang Debrett's.

'Oh dear, yes, everyone does that,' said the person on the end of the phone, amiably enough, 'they always think we're some sort of social arbiter, but the only thing that interests Charles [Kidd – the editor] is the genealogy. That's his passion. He's really not into the parties.'

Debrett's Peerage & Baronetage[1] is the equivalent of the *General Stud Book* or the *Kennel Club Breed Register* for the British aristocracy and landed gentry, famously described by Oscar Wilde in *A Woman of No Importance* as 'the best thing in fiction the English have ever done'. It is a directory of inherited status, in descending order from royal duke to knight, published in its current form since 1864. Its origins are far older. John Debrett was an outsider: he came from French Huguenot stock and as a young man joined the firm of John Almon, a bookseller and stationer, opposite Burlington House on Piccadilly, then a centre of publishing. Almon, who had published his *New Peerage* for England, Scotland and Ireland in 1769, eventually handed the business to Debrett, who added the *Baronetage* in 1800. The two works later merged into one bumper volume: a meticulous guide to the background and bloodlines of anyone who was anyone. It still comes out every few years, at a cost of around £300, and prides itself on its measured, economical prose. Party guide it is not.

In the end I found Liz Wyse, who edits the website pages on the Modern Season, 'a well-loved round of events still regarded as highlights of the British social calendar'. She was at that time wrestling with a glamorous book on the Royal Wedding, to come out as Prince William married Kate Middleton; still, she kindly agreed to meet me for half an hour.

To my surprise, Debrett's does not occupy a basement in Mayfair or an attic in St James's, as you might expect, but an anodyne office reached via a lightweight front door and a vertiginous, dimly carpeted staircase on Hill Rise in Richmond. True, it's raised high over an elegant bend in the River Thames, with its passing rowing eights and pleasure cruisers, but somehow I was expecting more patina. I waited in an office with a blonde wood table, grey carpet, swivel chairs upholstered in royal blue and gold dust on the walls. There were rows and rows of past volumes of *Debrett's*, the earliest upholstered in buff calfskin with black spines. Only in 1838 did they switch to the distinctive red cloth binding, with a colophon of an English rose, Scottish thistle and Irish shamrock picked out in gold. It is printed, as it always has been, by Clowes in Beccles, Suffolk. Alongside were registers for Harrow, Clifton and Radley Colleges and Rugby School, the Eton School Roll, the Record of Old Westminsters: the evidence of a world entirely sure of itself, naturally hierarchical and neatly documented.

The door opened and Liz came in with a cup of coffee. I liked her at once but she didn't think she could help much. 'Because *Debrett's* is the definitive work of reference on all things social,' she explained, 'people are always trying to elicit from us a set of rules. We try really hard to get away from that. The modern social season is extremely difficult to define: we focus on events that were part of the traditional season and are still going – the Royal Academy Summer Exhibition, for example, is a very old event, though it's changed a lot – but we also include Glastonbury, the Big Chill, Latitude and so on. The main criterion is fun, but they need to have become established, they do need to have entered the country's DNA.'

As we talked, though, a picture began to emerge. At the end of the eighteenth century, Liz thought, for economic and cultural reasons the great landowning classes – who had immense political power and spent much time in Parliament – began to enjoy themselves as never before. On to the sporting calendar was grafted a new round of social imperatives: pleasure gardens, regattas, race meetings and balls. 'It all seems to flower at the end of the century under the great party man himself, the Prince Regent,' she said. 'That's when the determined pursuit of pleasure at spa towns, seaside resorts and so on became a recognisable circuit. There seems to be a great restlessness that emerges at this time.'

She pointed out that the elite was not impenetrable, but it was hard for anyone who didn't know exactly what was going on, because everyone else did. 'I don't think they would have talked about the season and what you did, it was a given: summer came and the events came around, as they always did, and you went, as you always did. It was like Christmas and Easter. It's extraordinary that it's all still going, when you think about it, that if you go to Clapham Junction during Ascot Week, you will still see the platform full of people in hats on their way to the Royal Enclosure.'

That night I found it difficult to sleep. Armorial bearings and absurd titles swam around in my head, bumping up against ghostly top hats and racecards. Did anyone ever do the whole thing, I wondered, the entire season? Even *Tatler* – one of the oldest magazines in Britain and the nearest thing we still have to a social almanac – no longer bothered with more than the key dates. Social columns in the newspapers now barely existed, though the Royal Household still issued a court circular every day, as it had done for over two centuries. No, it was absurd. Nobody would be that silly.

In the end, to shut me up, an acquaintance who likes racing suggested I cut my teeth on the Cheltenham Festival, the annual jump racing meeting held in the Cotswolds, which she saw as a warm-up for the summer season. 'Everyone's wrapped up in tweeds and stuff,' she said. 'It's pretty informal, but it's still got this amazing atmosphere. Racing people love it.'

Cheltenham is a Regency town in a bowl of hills – the source of its famous springs – on the edge of the Cotswolds escarpment. Its fortunes changed in the eighteenth century with the arrival of spa culture: this is where King George III came with his family to cure his madness, and Society followed. Its population exploded from 3,000 people at the turn of the nineteenth century to ten times that by 1850, which meant more spectators for its other great passion, steeplechasing. This eventually moved to a purpose-built racecourse in a stunning setting and is still home to the five-day jump racing festival, which includes the famous Grade 1 race, the Gold Cup, and draws around 130,000 race-goers to the Cotswolds every year.

Edward Gillespie, the manager of Cheltenham Racecourse, had an office near the main stand. It was the most spectacular mess.

On the floor were boxes of brochures, poster tubes, a kit bag and a box out of which stuck the blunt gold muzzle of a jeroboam of champagne. On his desk, amid piles of paper and a booklet commemorating Ascot's tercentenary ('marvellous job'), were a porcelain statue of a fine bay horse – Arkle, the Irish superstar who won the Gold Cup three times in the 1960s – a statue of Christ in Rio de Janeiro and a model of a jockey with a huge blue helmet, like a child on a bike. Edward is one of those people with almost too much energy for his medium-sized frame. He dashed in, sat down, got up, got coffee and sat down again. I asked if it was fair to see the Cheltenham Festival as a warm-up event for the summer season.

'It's very flattering that you think we're part of the season at all,' he said, not looking the least bit flattered, 'but we see ourselves as an antidote, really. Last year I did almost the whole classic season, not deliberately, I just happened to go to several events, and it made me realise the reason people love Cheltenham is it's unpretentious; it doesn't take itself very seriously. You've still got some good tweeds and lovely ladies wearing hats and men wearing their grandfathers' suits – and their children and grandchildren may do that too – but other people just come to relax, come in a smart jacket and jeans, or wear tweeds but don't wear a tie.'

He thought one of the reasons for this was the Irish. Eight thousand Irish spectators, jockeys, owners and trainers, plus their horses, come over for Cheltenham every year and the festival usually coincides with St Patrick's Day. 'The Irish element completely debunks the social hierarchy,' he grinned. 'It's fundamental to our atmosphere: you can't tell who you're talking to by the way they dress. Somebody really casually dressed could be in Fine Gael or be a major industrialist. Some of the most smartly dressed people may be the least wealthy. You just can't tell; it's very egalitarian.'

What did that say about our English events, I wondered? Irish, Scots and Welsh summer gatherings are generally just that: summer gatherings, with degrees of tradition attached. If there is formality involved you can bet your bottom dollar there is an English connection. We seem to have a talent for immaculate – some would say obsessive – organisation and a love of formality seen by everyone else as hilariously stuffy. There must be a reason why. When I say 'we', I'm not truly English myself. I am a Scots/Irish/English/Argentine hybrid from Surrey, and therefore despised by everyone. It seemed as good a qualification as any to investigate further.

We strolled the course, which traces the contours of the tussocky plateau, and saw the pressroom with its bird's-eye views and utilitarian rows of desks and sockets. We leaned over the railings above the parade ring to admire the full-size statues of Arkle and the legendary champion Golden Miller. Then Edward said something intriguing: 'It's very close to theatre, racing,' he mused, 'it's like an unscripted drama. I worked in the theatre as a young man. A lot of racing people are involved in theatre or the High Church. They know their sport, as they know their parts in the theatre or in church – it's just with racing nobody knows what the outcome will be.'

Jump racing, he told me, was less glamorous than the flat, partly because it took place in the winter, when the ground is softer. This put less strain on the horses' legs, but meant the spectators were bundled up against the weather, which was not conducive to high fashion. But the real reason was money. The winner of a great flat race commands colossal stud fees, or is sought after as a brood mare, so is worth a fortune. Jump horses, on the other hand, were usually gelded, partly to give them, let's say, a more streamlined silhouette for getting over the fences and partly to stop them fancying any fillies in the same race. So they had no breeding value, or not in the same way. It was all about prize money and betting. My mouth dropped open. Not only was it absurdly simple – obvious, when you thought about it – but I hadn't actually realised they used different horses for jumps and flat. I'd never given it a thought. If I had, I'd have assumed that racehorses, like barristers, had to take whatever job came along.

I did return for the Gold Cup and almost everything about it surprised me: the 'Cheltenham Roar' at the start, the unbridled jumping on benches and waving of umbrellas when people won, the visceral groan when they didn't, the lugubrious press photographers running lumpily along on the far side of the railings with howitzer-sized cameras on spikes. The Gold Cup itself was so fast, and finished so quickly, that I barely had time to understand what was going on. But I did see Long Run thunder to victory, ridden by Sam Waley-Cohen, the first amateur jockey to win the Gold Cup in thirty years. He would later come second in the Grand National. I also tasted the bitter aloes of gambling defeat: a lovely old lady on the bus gave me a tip for Long Run, but I switched at the last minute to Kauto Star because someone in my first cousin's office swore he would win.

Cheltenham piqued my curiosity sufficiently to send me off to the River Thames a week later, on a bitter day in late March, to watch the annual waterborne battle between Oxford and Cambridge, the Boat Race. A vindictive wind cornered the milk-chocolate curves of the river, sending spectators scuttling into pubs and beer tents. Helicopters puttered. The bank was thronged with students, their faces daubed with stripes to show which side they were on: dark blue for Oxford, light blue for Cambridge. We hunkered down among the weeds on the bank beyond Barnes Bridge, nursing plastic glasses of the first freezing Pimm's of the year.

You couldn't question the Boat Race's pedigree as a London

event, though it actually started upriver in Henley-on-Thames. It was the result of a friendly rivalry between two alumni from the north London public school Harrow: one went to Oxford, one to Cambridge, and in 1829 they staged a rowing race between the two universities. Fifteen years later the event relocated to south-west London, where it takes place on a northward loop of the River Thames, starting at Putney and ending at Mortlake. Every year a staggering quarter of a million people turn up to watch, walk the course and celebrate or drown their sorrows in the pubs afterwards. All over the world, millions more peer at their TVs, unaccountably fascinated by the spectacle of two crews of burly young Varsity men in flimsy boats, half-killing themselves to row a distance of four miles 374 yards.

The race began and after a long, cold hiatus we could hear the cheering downstream, faint at first, then getting louder as they approached. We all craned to see them come around the corner, jerking madly at their oars as they flew under the bridge, Oxford half a length ahead. We shouted our heads off until they had passed and kept shouting until they zoomed out of sight. Shortly afterwards, the news came through: Oxford had won, against the odds. Cambridge, the favourites, were gutted. And that was it.

All the students started swapping plans for south London pub-crawls and chilled families made for home. The rowing fraternity was ensconced in clubhouses all the way down the river: we could hear the parties under way as we strolled down to see the finish, which is marked by a rough stone wedge emblazoned with 'UBR', for University Boat Race. The BBC crew was rolling up its cables and dismantling its cameras. The post-race interviews had been heroically old-fashioned. 'They had the strength, character and went for it. We just let them slip,' said Cambridge, stoically. 'They put up a good fight initially but we just started inching away,' said Oxford, modestly. It all sounded incredibly English – and yet it didn't feel like a season event. It felt like a London event, and a university event, but not a social occasion. Something, I wasn't sure what, was missing.

I was still puzzling over this when I contacted Lady Celestria Noel, a journalist who was for some years 'Jennifer' on the famous social column 'Jennifer's Diary' for *Harpers & Queen* magazine and had written several guides to the season. Charles Kidd at Debrett's had suggested I contact her: 'She was a deb but she also went to Oxford,' he said courteously, 'and she will have a good overview of the whole thing.' Celestria agreed to an interview, so I asked casually what she thought made an event an event of the season. 'Oh, there are a few things,' she said, 'but the key one is the element of *passagiato*, that feeling that people are going to see and to be seen. I think that's what makes them different from ordinary events.' Suddenly it all made sense. That's why it happened during the summer. You couldn't do the *passagiato* in a howling gale. You needed to feel expansive, in display mode: it was not about winter camouflage (tweeds), but summer plumage (picture hats). It was the English, most uncharacteristically, showing off. No wonder alcohol was so crucial.

Of course, I decided to do it. I decided to follow the round of events that Edwardians would have recognised, with one or two additions absorbed later in the twentieth century. It began with the Chelsea Flower Show in London and ended with Cowes Week in the Isle of Wight. It would take me from late May to early August, a frothy two-and-a-half-month summer. This was the full schedule:

RHS CHELSEA FLOWER SHOW (late May)
Chelsea, London SW7

THE GLYNDEBOURNE FESTIVAL (May to August)
Nr Lewes, East Sussex

INVESTEC DERBY FESTIVAL (early June)
Epsom Downs, Surrey

ROYAL ACADEMY SUMMER EXHIBITION
(June to August)
Piccadilly, London W1

ROYAL ASCOT (mid-June)
Ascot Racecourse, Berkshire

ETON–HARROW MATCH, LORD'S (mid-June)
St John's Wood, London NW8

WIMBLEDON LAWN TENNIS CHAMPIONSHIPS
(late June to early July)
Merton, London SW19

HENLEY ROYAL REGATTA (late June/early July)
Henley-on-Thames, Oxfordshire

SECRET GARDEN PARTY (July – the 'Modern Season')
Abbots Ripton, Cambridgeshire

CARTIER (NOW AUDI) INTERNATIONAL POLO
(late July)
Guards Polo Club, Smiths Lawn, Windsor Great Park, Egham,
Surrey

GLORIOUS GOODWOOD (late July)
West Sussex

ABERDEEN ASSET MANAGEMENT COWES WEEK
(early August)
Cowes, Isle of Wight

Many weeks later, after my day in the Os & Ts at Ascot, I caught the late train back to London with a man from the same gazebo. 'Always good to have a bit of company on the train,' he said, eyeing our merry, alcohol-burnished fellow race-goers with suspicion as they piled into the nearby seats. 'You never know when someone's going to have a go at the topper.'

I tried hard to imagine if there was anywhere else in the world that you would hear that sentence. And I really couldn't.

2

GETTING IN

I t was the middle of May and everything was out of kilter. The spring was too hot, the sky was too smeary and a spiteful wind was building. The year before a volcano had erupted in Iceland, sending a plume of ash tens of thousands of feet into the atmosphere and causing global consternation. Could that be the reason for this year's weird weather, the newspapers wondered? The climatic conditions seemed to mirror the uncertain economy – and both affected the flowers that were being groomed like world-class athletes for their appearance at the annual floral Olympics, the Chelsea Flower Show. It was Chelsea that would kick off the season later that month. To add to the anxiety, one of the Thames bridges was closed for repairs, what felt like 2,000 miles of Victorian water pipes were being dug up and replaced, and real Olympic preparations were in full swing. Traffic around the show site at the Royal Hospital Chelsea would be even worse than usual, said the regulars gloomily. They always say that, though. It's a Chelsea tradition.

I was quite out of kilter myself, having raised my head in early March after months of slogging away at my London tour guiding exams to realise that if – as I had rashly decided – I was to write about and therefore attend all the events of the traditional English season I was leaving my planning perilously late. For most things it wouldn't be a problem, you could just buy a ticket. It was the enclosures that worried me. These elite access areas, entered with a coveted badge or invitation, existed only at a handful of events. While you no longer needed to be socially well connected, as such, it helped to know someone who went regularly or was involved in whatever world it was – opera, rowing, art – in some way. There were hurdles to be got over, and hurdling takes time. I embarked upon a series of hasty phone calls. The first, to my brother, who sometimes goes to the Royal Enclosure at Ascot, was unpromising:

'Can you do my sponsor thingy for the Royal Enclosure?' I asked.

There was a long pause.

'Do you mean for next year?' he said.

'Next year? No, this year. It's for my book.'

There was another pause, this time shorter.

'Well, I could have if you'd asked me before Christmas,' he said witheringly. 'You can't just do these things at the last minute.'

'But it's months away! I thought that was the 1950s. Can't I just pretend to be to be Arabee?'

Arabee is my sister-in-law. Even down the phone I could sense a chill in the air. You don't mess with Royal Enclosure badges. If you are caught doing so your membership can be rescinded and you will be cast out of the enclosure and into the wilderness of the next-door Grandstand or, even worse, the Silver Ring. The

Silver Ring is the undeniably jolly, 'more relaxed' area at the other end of the course, where there is no dress code. Horror stories circulate of Royal Enclosure attendees in times past, guilty of supplying undesirables with vouchers, who have been tapped on the shoulder by a gloved hand and firmly escorted into obscurity. Whether it's true or not doesn't matter: the point is if you want to get in you have to play it straight. And while I was annoyed with myself for not getting on to it earlier, I was also grudgingly impressed. I quite liked the Royal Enclosure being difficult to get into.

Enclosures, I discovered, are rarely permanent. They pop up like palely glamorous fungi in time for an event, usually in the form of pavilions, marquees or lawns. There is always some form of discreet barrier to keep everyone else out, but it is also essential that they can see in, in order to realise exactly what they are missing. In Victorian times, Ascot's Royal Enclosure was fenced in with hooped iron railings like a zoo, as if its exotic occupants might assemble at certain times to be thrown canapés by the general public. These days it is a less threatening white picket fence, but the procedures for becoming a Member during the Royal Meeting, as it is archly referred to, are still rigorous. Not as rigorous as the old hands would like, of course, but nonetheless an effort.

'It was one of those lovely things in the spring,' sighed one woman I spoke to, wriggling her shoulders against her sofa. 'A tiny notice would appear in *The Times* or the *Telegraph* in February and you had to apply by the end of April. You wrote to Her Majesty's Representative at the Ascot Office, which was at St James's Palace then, of course, and you put: "Miss Whatever-Your-Name-Was presents her compliments to Her Majesty and begs leave to apply for vouchers for Royal Ascot this year." That was what was expected of you. Everything was in the third person. Then you swapped the vouchers for your badge on the day. And you could reserve parking, so people always applied for the same spaces.'

That was because she went every year and probably had done since her early twenties. Those who had not needed to find two sponsors to sign their application, both of whom had attended the Royal Enclosure four times consecutively. The applicant then had to be vetted – socially – by the Ascot Office, which was (and still is) headed by an official known as Her Majesty's Representative. Viscount Churchill took over this role from the Master of the Buckhounds – it was by then a political rather than sporting appointment – in 1901. Legend says he had wire baskets for applications labelled 'Certainly', 'Perhaps' and 'Certainly Not'.

If all were well the applicant would receive a voucher allowing them to buy a racecourse badge for as many days as they wished to attend. This allowed some flexibility as social life became busier. The badge had your name and title on it in beautiful handwriting. It still does, actually; mine says 'Miss Sophie Campbell' in firm black italics.

Things had got easier in the twenty-first century, it turned out: in 2002 a simple application form and badges sent in the post replaced the voucher system and, better still, new applications could now be submitted a few weeks before the meeting and you needed just one sponsor who had been four times, and not even consecutively. Standards were clearly slipping, which was a great relief.

In the end my brother signed the form and I didn't have to impersonate my sister-in-law, but it was a warning. I began applying to other events in earnest, occasionally getting press accreditation but mostly just buying tickets online. I identified the trickiest ones to get into and rang everyone I could think of who might know a regular. I spent an agonising £235 on a ticket to the

Royal Academy Summer Exhibition Preview Party and found Chelsea's Gala Preview had been sold out for months. My calendar began to look like a paintball target. I don't have a car, which meant more planning was required. Clothes and shoes were a nightmare I couldn't begin to contemplate. And some things required a social leverage I didn't possess.

So I rang the ferociously well-connected Victoria Mather, the travel editor of British *Vanity Fair* and for many years author of the wickedly accurate 'Social Stereotypes' column in the *Telegraph Magazine*. She commissioned me every so often. I took her out to lunch, partly to find out if there was an outside chance of me getting into the exclusive Royal Yacht Squadron Ball at Cowes at the end of the season, which I knew she attended, and partly because I wanted to know if it was true she had streaked at Queen Charlotte's Ball as a 1970s deb. She sidestepped the streaking adroitly, opined that Cowes Week had survived partly because it had 'kept its Corinthian values' – amateurs, she explained, still competed at the highest level, unusually for a modern sporting competition – and added crisply that the season was now driven far more by celebrity than royalty.

We then entered delicate negotiations about yacht club balls. Her husband, she said, happened to be one of the rear commodores at the Squadron that year, so she would ask but thought it highly unlikely, me not having any sailing connections – or, in fact, being able to sail at all. But I was welcome to attend the Bembridge Sailing Club Ball as her guest. Bembridge is one of two pretty Edwardian sailing towns on the Isle of Wight's east coast – the other being its deadly rival Seaview, which of course has its own yacht club, regatta, shore sports and ball – and she said that was probably more exclusive, in a way, if not as famous. So I opted for Bembridge, hoping the Royal Yacht Squadron bash might come through later. I didn't think I could quite take the strain of doing both.

After all that it was a relief to set off to the West Country, leaving handwritten badges, invitations and e-tickets chugging quietly through a dozen or so booking systems. I wanted to see some of the frenzied preparations that take place every year before the Chelsea Flower Show explodes on to the world's consciousness – and before my season began.

3

THE LAST TRUCK TO CHELSEA

In a hot, shallow valley on the Somerset Levels the peonies were in bloom. More than in bloom: tightly packed balls of petals, each cupped in a star of green, were exploding into enormous heads of billowy pink and white frills. They looked like can-can dresses that, once unpacked, would never fold up again. Some were absurdly large – one variety, called Dinner Plate, was six inches across – while others were distressingly overblown, almost blowsy. And blowsy is not what you want for the greatest flower show on earth.

The 250-square-mile flatland of the Levels sits between two ridges of hills, the Mendips to the north and the Blackdowns to the south. In early times this was flood plain and Neolithic man used wooden trackways to get from ridge to ridge. Its islands are now hill villages, one being Glastonbury, whose monks drained the land and irrigated it with dykes, sluices and wide channels called rhynes ('reens'). Willow grows here and is still used for artists' charcoal and wicker hampers, fuzzing the landscape with red and gold every spring. In evening light the whole thing gleams with trapped water. What possible appeal this landscape can have for the peony, which evolved on highland trees and bushes in China and Japan, is a mystery.

Perhaps just as puzzling is what triggered a peony obsession in a young Somerset gardener called James Kelway. He began planting them in 1851 at his smart new premises in Langport, which calls itself 'the smallest town in England'. Certainly the peony flower was fashionable in the nineteenth century; it was seen as a symbol of Oriental exoticism and was popular in nosegays because it was said to signify bashfulness in the language of flowers. This codification of floral symbolism had become hugely popular in England from the 1830s onwards, when the first books on the subject appeared in France. By the middle of the century, authors such as Thomas Miller were doing their bit for English flora by synthesising these ideas into pocket-sized books like *The Poetical Language of Flowers, or The Pilgrimage of Love*[1], which combined botanical illustrations with symbolic attributes.

In an age when a great deal could not be said, flowers had a subtle and sometimes erotic role in conveying messages. Ivy, for instance, with its tenacious character, meant reliability – which could be decoded to indicate wifely, rather than mistressly, potential – while white lilies signified purity. From wedding bouquets to gravestone design, the Victorians were attuned to these visual clues, though why anyone would choose the voluptuous peony to suggest reticence is beyond me: it is busting out all over, like an anti-corsetry demonstration, and just look at the names – Pillow Talk, Raspberry Sundae, Fairy's Petticoat, Angel Cheeks. I later found it identified with shame ('they are not the blushes of modesty which suffuse it with its rosy hues …'[2]), which seemed nearer the mark. Whatever the reasons, Kelway planted and bred and cross-bred and planted until his patch of land grew tenfold and his peony plantation – cunningly marketed even then as Peony Valley – was so famous that every June the London to Penzance train apparently stopped at a temporary Peony Valley Halt for its passengers to descend. He had his own peony scent and talcum powder.

Thanks to James, Kelways grows over four hundred varieties of peony today and is one of the oldest exhibitors at Chelsea, winning a silver-gilt medal for herbaceous flowers at the very first show. His diaries – dating back to 1835 – and, a 'Peony Bible' filled with copperplate observations still exists and today's owner, Dave Root, spends long summer hours checking them against the current collection, occasionally discovering an historic or misidentified cultivar. Right now I was waiting in his office at the top of a barn, guiltily aware that I could not have chosen a worse time to visit.

The first truck, he had told me tiredly on the phone, had left for Chelsea the day before, and there were several more to go. The conditions were appalling either way if you were a peony, hot and windy outside, or hot and confined in a truck. Things could not have been any grimmer, really, short of an outbreak of wilt, ring spot virus or blotch. Strange how even peony diseases sounded faintly sexual, I mused, as my eye roamed the room, alighting occasionally on a Chelsea certificate stuck casually on a shelf. Every so often a shaft of sunlight would bounce off one of the medal logos and hit you in the eye, as if to say, 'Match that'. On the wall a framed certificate in magisterial nineteenth-century typefaces announced '*Une médaille d'argent*' awarded at the Exposition Universelle de 1878. Is this what it was all about, I wondered, the prizes? The glory? Or was it the plants?

'It's the prestige,' said Dave, slumping into the nearest chair. 'Nothing compares to it. Hampton Court is the biggest show in the world and it has a huge amount of space, but Chelsea has the cachet. The gold medal at Chelsea, basically, is like the Best Actor Oscar.' He was wearing jeans, a white T-shirt, a tattoo and an ear-ring in one ear. I had been expecting something earthier, more root-like; not this cheery, switched-on creature with a big, dirty laugh. 'God!' he said, 'what a week! It's our biggest display ever because it's our 160th anniversary. The warmth – well, I'd prefer the snow we had in December, to be honest. In all the years I've been doing it I've never known it this bad.'

They always say that. It's a Chelsea tradition. He explained the nursery was famous for its tree and herbaceous peonies, but was big on irises, too. As well as having their own display in the Great Pavilion, they supplied show gardens, the press-stealing plots designed by big-name gardeners for banks, or tourist boards, or newspapers. This year they were working with Australia, among others. Linda in irises was tearing her hair out: of a thousand plants she would be lucky to have a couple of hundred good enough for the Chelsea truck. The cold store was full of flowers flowering too quickly. And some irreplaceable seeds for the Australian plants – which could not be shipped full-grown for bio-security reasons, so had to be nurtured in secure conditions in the UK – had been eaten by Dave's cat. 'She ate two species,' he said admiringly. 'The papers loved that, I can tell you.' He gave me a sideways glance. The source of the leak was not difficult to guess.

Outside, tree ferns bounced past in pots to be loaded onto the truck, and under a huge open-sided tent fans suspended from the ceiling whirred helplessly as the sun blazed through the clear plastic roof. The giant New Zealand tree ferns, arthritic limbs draped in moss like refugees from the set of *Lord of the Rings*, were happy in the heat. Not so the irises. We found Linda in a shady corner at the bottom of the nursery, bending anxiously over her charges. She looked tense and exhausted. So did they: their petals had a lifeless, translucent look, as if they were fading to transparency in the heat. 'All my friends are on Facebook going, "What a great summer!" and I'm thinking, "What a nightmare!"' she said with a wry smile. 'In the end, all we can do is our best. We have our hair done before we go and on Press Day when the Queen comes round I wear a dress and hat. That's the lovely bit. You've got there, you've put them all out, you hope they'll behave – then you have a glass of bubbly and that's it, relax.'

We went to see the tree peonies being retarded in the cold store. They looked miserable, shoulder to glossy green shoulder in the dark. I was beginning to feel quite stressed myself. Linda put out a hand and cupped a fat bloom, hefting it gently. 'Each of these will be wrapped in wadding,' she said. 'It doesn't stop them but it does slow them down.' They use furniture wadding and binder twine, because cotton wool sticks to the leaves, but the prima donna irises wouldn't even put up with that. They hated being stored, Linda explained indulgently. The only solution was to keep the dead blooms on the stem, to try and slow down the ones on the way. A team of five or six people armed with nail scissors would neatly trim any marks off the leaves and tidy everything up. Every half-open bud would be wrapped in kitchen roll. Linda's partner would take a day off, as he always did, to help out on the big day. The whole saga made me think of a dog show.

This scene was, presumably, being replicated right across the country: hyacinths being coaxed to exactly the same height like regiments of floral soldiers, reeds and grasses being readied to dance in the Chelsea breeze, waxy hothouse orchids and swirling water plants, chubby cacti and priapic vegetables, all racing for the same finish line. Growers would be forcing or retarding, applying ice packs or hairdryers, all so they could converge on twenty-five acres of prime London real estate for one brief week in May.

One thing was really puzzling me about Kelways. The money. Thousands of wasted irises, costly cold storage, refrigerated trucks and an individual stand in the Great Pavilion – could it really be worth it for a certificate? You're not even allowed to sell plants at Chelsea – this is an old rule, strictly adhered to until the last day, when a bell rings for the famous 4 p.m. sell-off and everyone stampedes to carry away the watering cans, cuttings, cut flowers and saplings they have spied during the week – so did Dave really make enough contacts with customers to make it worth his while?

'You know about the gala?' he asked, leaning against the truck. Sure did. I'd been trying to get a ticket. The Charity Gala Preview takes place on the evening of the Monday Press Day, after the President's Luncheon and the Queen's departure following her private view. It's so popular the ballot opens the year before and people lurk by their computers, waiting to apply. 'It's one of the top three events in the summer season, along with Wimbledon and Royal Ascot,' he explained, 'because apparently corporate hospitality is all about wives and what they want to do. They don't want golf or football. That's one of the reasons Chelsea is so, so sought after. One of the reasons we all get sponsors is because they get more gala tickets.' I took that in for a minute. That year, their sponsor was Nomura, the Japanese bank. It was a good fit because tree peonies, which arrived in Japan from China in the eighth century, loom large in Japanese culture, depicted in art, calligraphy and design. But clearly as important as the Kelways peonies was their allocation of gala tickets. This year they had seventy and the phone kept ringing with people desperate to get hold of any spares.

I gave him a cheesy grin and he started laughing, promising that if there was a last-minute cancellation he would ring. I was quite relieved when he didn't: it's around £300 for drinks and canapés, £500 if you have dinner as well. So popular is the event – it is frequently said to attract more FTSE 100 chief executives than any other corporate occasion, though who said that and how they found out I have never managed to discover – that exhibitors hold a next-best version on the Tuesday night and business break-fasts from 6.30 a.m. daily, when besuited guests can eat and look around. Taking the President's Marquee for a day will set you back about £40,000, including catering and an evening private view of the show.

The point Dave was making, I decided, was that without the corporate wives and their distaste for blokey sports, the Chelsea Flower Show would be nothing like the size or standard it is today. This keeps dozens, possibly hundreds, of plant nurseries, growers and suppliers afloat. It burnishes the profiles of sponsors and garden designers. It creates celebrities and keeps the BBC busy for a week, broadcasting worldwide. It also keeps the Royal Hospital Chelsea – a charitable institution dating back to 1682 and home to the veteran soldiers known as Chelsea Pensioners – in the public eye.

As I left Somerset I had the feeling I had been rather missing the point, not just at Chelsea, but at the other events I'd been to over the years. What I had mistaken for jolly old traditional English occasions, so long established they virtually organised themselves, were in fact baroque masterpieces of complexity, of joys and sorrows, tensions and triumphs, rivalries and rage. The *raison d'être* of such occasions – flowers, say – was merely a smokescreen, an excuse to get everyone together in the same place. And now the Chelsea Flower Show was just days away from opening, it was time for the whole bizarre summer cycle to commence.

4

A GARDEN GROWS BY THE RIVER

On 5 June 1861 Prince Albert, Queen Victoria's energetic consort, made his last appearance in public. There was no clue he would be dead in six months; on the contrary, he had every reason to feel optimistic. Over the preceding decade he had finally begun to make headway with his adopted countrymen, particularly following the success of his pet project, the Great Exhibition. It was still benefiting London: the glittering Crystal Palace had long since moved from Hyde Park to the southern suburbs but the profits it had generated were funding a whole new cultural quarter in Kensington, later to be sardonically nicknamed 'Albertopolis'. He was here to open its latest addition: a grand new garden for the London Horticultural Society.

Grand is not the word, really. Extravagant might be better. The Exhibition Commissioners donated £50,000 (roughly £2m today) and the Society raised the same – we'd say match funding – plus an extra £23,000 for planting.[1] The injection of capital seems to have gone to everyone's head. The new garden lay below what is now the Royal Albert Hall, then yet to be built, so it had an unimpeded view north to the fashionable hinterland of Hyde Park. It was Italianate in style, enclosed by raised arcades under which visitors could shelter. It contained an orchid house, two French fountains, a Minton fountain, a 100ft-long conservatory, a holly maze, two bandstands, two pavilions, a 'bouquet' of flowerbeds, coloured gravel walks and a soaring column commemorating Albert's Great Exhibition.

It was studded with classical urns and niches in which marble statues represented the seasons. Spring stood '[with] his foot on a bag of wind blowing away primroses' according to the handbook published for the first of the great floral shows,[2] while Autumn dandled ripe fruits in his hands. The tessellated floor was designed to resemble the famed thirteenth-century Cosmati Pavement in Westminster Abbey. Water plummeted forty feet from the top of a central cascade 'with a dash of a Highland stream' into a basin below, which was stocked with goldfish and forty carp – some of them a hundred years old and weighing up to ten pounds – donated by Her Majesty the Queen.

Albert described it in his speech as '... a valuable attempt, at least, to reunite the science and art of Gardening to the sister arts of Architecture, Sculpture and Painting'. No doubt it was: such sentiments were exactly what had led seven practical and well-connected gentlemen to found the London Horticultural Society in a room at Hatchard's, the Piccadilly booksellers, almost sixty years before. One of them was John Wedgwood of the ceramics dynasty. Another was Sir Joseph Banks, the colossus of Kew, president of the Royal Society and right at the top of the gardening tree at the turn of the nineteenth century. If you look very closely you can see a plaque commemorating this event on the outside of the building above the door.

The Age of Enlightenment had caused an explosion of learned societies in London. Wedgwood, admiring the vigorous new groups representing the interests of agriculture, science, manufacture and trade, suggested a version 'for the sole purpose of encouraging Horticulture in its different branches' and 'To form a Repository for all the knowledge, which can be collected on this subject, and to give stimulus to the exertions of individuals for its farther improvement'.[3] The aim was to pool expertise, fund plant hunting and publish papers. A small plot in Kensington was leased for cultivation and research, which later moved to land owned by the Duke of Devonshire at Chiswick, and soon the exhibiting of plants at members' meetings began to evolve into something more entertaining.

Almost from the start the Society was subject to a peculiar tension: the funds it needed came from the upper strata of society and the upper strata of society liked having a jolly time. One anonymous Fellow, in a letter to the *Gardeners' Magazine* about one of the 'public breakfasts', or fêtes, held back in the 1820s, fumed: 'I, for one, most exceedingly regret … that the Society should be made to pander to the sickly appetite for amusement of the fashionable world.'[4] He was in for a miserable decade: carriage jams were reported all the way to Chiswick as the *ton* flocked to its new favourite occasion. *The Times* described it as 'one of the principal attractions of the fashionable season … looked forward to with more anxiety than any other fete, either public or private'. It soon ran into problems, though: one year rain soaked visitors, forcing them to stand on crates in the style of the *acqua alta* in St Mark's Square, there were endless financial tensions and the coming of the railways made accessible rival shows, whose savvy promoters added frivolous extras such as music. Eventually the Society had to sell its plant collection, herbaria and library.

Kensington, therefore, was a new beginning. From the minute it opened the new garden was madly fashionable. Its architects were fashionable – Sydney Smirke had built the Reading Room at the British Museum and Francis Fowke would work on the Royal Albert Hall – and its landscaper, William Andrews Nesfield, was fashionable. Above all, its contents were fashionable: there were new and exotic plants from Japan, the New World and the southern hemisphere and there were new and exotic faces from the world of fashion. The number of Fellows began to rocket and people often joined just to have somewhere pleasant and exclusive in which to stroll – sometimes, it was noted ominously, with children. An event was needed to reflect such enormous popularity and this was to be the earliest true prototype of today's Chelsea Flower Show, the Great Spring Show.

The first of these took place in May 1862, once everyone had recovered from the shock of Albert's death from typhoid fever. Its patron was the Queen, deep in mourning, who supported the venture for Albert's sake and allowed the Society to change its name to Royal, as he had wished. Fellows got in at half-price, 2/6-, and could buy the official handbook for 6d. Among the advertisements nailing the preoccupations of the time – 'Teeth without Springs, Royal Tooth Powder prepared from a recipe AS USED BY HER MAJESTY (1s 6d per box)' and 'Ladies' riding trousers of chamoix leather with black feet, of rib'd cloth or Napoleon Blue' – it contained a history of the Society, illustrations of its fashionable visitors and a description of a 'monster tent', 300 feet by 120 feet, supported by two tall masts, full of floral displays and produce. It was a rip-roaring success.

Twenty-six years later Kensington fell from grace in its turn, a victim of coal pollution, changing fashion and the terms of its lease. It disappeared beneath the new Imperial College and Science Museum. The Great Spring Show, however, clung to life, reviving like a thirsty plant in 1888 in the gardens of Inner Temple – despite the annual grumblings of the barristers – and the first show plots appeared, rock gardens with plants *in situ*, to great acclaim. Then in 1912 the grounds of the Royal Hospital Chelsea were used for a one-off show that was such a success it was decided to use that instead. The Great Spring Show had at last found a home.

A few days after my visit to Kelways, reporters, celebrities and gardening bigwigs were mustering outside the Royal Hospital Chelsea first thing on a windy May morning, waiting for the back gates to open. The Chelsea Pensioners, in ceremonial dress of dazzling scarlet with black shakos and banks of medals on their chests, pottered in and out of the gatehouse as we shifted restlessly, notebooks and iPads at the ready. It was quite like the Disney Rope Drop – when early visitors wait to stampede into Main Street USA – but for the Panama hats and oatmeal linen suits, and a light, admonitory English tenor audible on the speakers inside the grounds. 'Ladies and Gentlemen,' said the voice, 'it is ten minutes to seven. Please refrain from doing more work on your stands before the visitors arrive.'

At seven o'clock on the dot the gates swung open and in we poured. The crowd immediately diverged. Keen plantsmen went to the Great Pavilion to see what the breeders had been up to. The rest of us cantered off to the show gardens, the glamour models of the gardening world, which lay in parallel rows to the east of the Pavilion, basking in the sun while their leafy coiffures were agitated by a 19mph gusting wind. A shameful few made straight for what used to be quaintly called 'Sundries Avenue' to negotiate over rose-printed umbrellas, calendars and raffia sun hats.

The grounds of the Royal Hospital lie at a 45-degree angle to the Thames, in a triangle of land that not only includes the famous hospital – built by Charles II for army veterans and still fulfilling the same role today – but the Chelsea Physic Garden, founded even earlier and one of the oldest apothecaries' gardens in Britain. On the east side of Sundries Avenue lies Ranelagh Gardens, a famously raffish eighteenth-century pleasure ground set up to rival Vauxhall across the river, now home to the show's popular 'small gardens'. It couldn't have a better horticultural and social pedigree, but it's a pig for setting up a modern flower show. It takes twenty-five days to build the site and incredible skill to cram everything into it like an executive puzzle. Whenever the Royal Horticultural Society raises the issue of moving it elsewhere there's uproar, so they stay put.

Every year, Chelsea reveals itself to the public coyly, in stages, like a horticultural dance of the seven veils. Sunday is final setup, when only the exhibitors and people deeply involved in some way can enter. Monday is press day. Tuesday and Wednesday are for the Fellows and Members. Thursday to Saturday is for the general public, but you can't buy tickets on the gate; they are sold in advance and most have gone by early May.

This was Monday. It had the same smell of anxiety and fear you get before a big sporting fixture: the very day was sweating adrenaline. Monday is not only Press Day, it is also the day of the Queen's visit, the day of the President's Luncheon – attended by the gardening aristocracy, including as many of the huge committee as can be fitted in – and the day of the Charity Gala Preview to which I hadn't got an invitation. It is also Judgement Day: the moment when exhibitors find out if a year's worth of work and sponsorship has paid off. I was lucky to be there at all, really: I was hardly a member of the gardening in-crowd and I'd had to work quite hard to get a press pass. But there was a pleasingly secretive sensation to being allowed in when everyone else wasn't. It was, in effect, a super-scale enclosure. My London season had finally begun.

'Today is great because the judges are in and you see all the celebrities,' said Mary-Clare Jerram, a publishing director I found inspecting the show gardens. You could tell she was a regular of twenty years: she was neatly and practically dressed with flat shoes and a jacket over one arm. Anyone in a dress and heels and cer-tainly a hat, she observed dryly, was probably a model or a first-timer. Hats at Chelsea were worn for weather, not for fashion. So far today she had seen Will Young, Gwyneth Paltrow and 'Diarmuid, of course'. As she spoke, there was a clanking sound and Diarmuid Gavin, the television gardener, sailed up in the air on his pink steel conceit, the Irish Sky Garden. It dangled from a crane, trailing greenery, and his friends and sponsors from the tourist board Failte Ireland peered down from on high over glasses of champagne. Reporters waited below like a pack of ravening wolves, hoping the mechanism might jam and provide them with a perfect metaphor for the Irish economy.

For me, the Great Pavilion was the soul of the show. This giant white confection, roofed with pinnacles like icing sugar peaks, has a modular construction that requires few pillars. It is light, bright and airy. Everyone loves it, but it can't claim the charac-ter of its predecessor, which held the Guinness World Record for 'Largest Tent' (covering three and a half acres) and was boiling in hot weather, freezing in cold, dark, stuffy and bad for the plants. The old tent was stored and erected by an Essex firm called Piggott's, which had – still has – a 200-year history of supplying army tents and naval rigging. Photos show the construction team hauling on ropes to raise the canvas, looking as if at any moment they might shin up the masts and perch in formation like naval cadets. On its retirement in 1999 it was cut up and made into souvenirs. Despite its shortcomings, people mourned what it represented: a link with simpler days, with produce piled up on tables, for all the world – bar the scale and quality of the enterprise – like a country show come to town.

There is something chastening about seeing perfection, or perhaps being in the presence of people dedicated to the making of perfection, be it in the form of a sweet pea or an exotic carrot. In the Great Pavilion I gazed upon giant flowers and vegetables of eerie magnificence. They looked weirdly human: the hyacinths were all identical in height, with domes of blue or pink petals like Marge Simpson's hair, the pansies scrunched up alarmingly angry features on velvety faces and the Venus flycatchers drooped like elderly testicles in their damp rainforest setting. I found Dave looking relieved and excited with several hundred peonies on their best behaviour. There was a floral display of jockeys' colours and a huge central stand by Hillier's – a Chelsea superstar at sixty-six gold medals and counting – who would be supplying the trees for the Olympic Park. Almost hidden by foliage was the Chillianwallah Memorial, an obelisk in the hospital grounds commemorating a nineteenth-century battle with the Sikhs.

It was in the Pavilion I met a couple in their seventies, who seemed to me authentically 'Old Chelsea'. He was in an immaculate lightweight grey suit. She was wearing a smart navy-blue skirt and low court shoes. Badges fluttered from their lapels as they politely stopped to talk. They had been coming for – oh! – they looked at each other ... years! 1965, they thought. They had been to Harrogate last year but it didn't compare, it was much more commercial. When I asked their names and where they were from they looked horrified. 'Oh no ... we couldn't ... we'd rather not ... well, *Suffolk*.'

They stood out precisely because they were so well dressed. Most people aren't. Or rather, they are not formally dressed. On public days anything reasonably modest goes. There are more jeans than linen suits or skirts. The only silk dresses or proper hats are worn by the handful of people selected to remain in the grounds when the rest of us get chucked out so preparations can get under way for the Queen's visit. In the early years of the twentieth century women would have worn ankle-length afternoon or tea gowns with showpiece millinery, and men tailcoats with button-holes and top hats, only as the decades went on relaxing into suits and boaters.

I remembered Jekka McVicar, who runs an organic herb garden near Alveston, Gloucestershire, and has a glittering Chelsea track record, telling me on the phone that when she started showing there in the early 1980s she wore a coat and hat. 'Everybody, and I mean everybody, dressed up for the first three days,' she recalled. 'When we first started, an old lady told me that the exhibitors used to wear gloves and a hat on their stands all the time.' She said on the first day the gentry would arrive with their head gardeners and write tremendous lists of plants to order. 'You still get aristocrats coming but the head gardeners now come on their own; they'll say, "Lady so-and-so's just seen your display so I've come to buy the list."'

Even the words 'head gardener' seemed impossibly archaic. I had to pinch myself to believe Jekka was talking not about the 1930s but the 1980s.

So where had Chelsea's dress code gone? 'It never had one,' said Brent Elliott simply, 'there was just a broad understanding then of what was considered appropriate.' Dr Elliott is the RHS's historian, the author of numerous books and a respected lecturer. We had arranged to meet at the show because I wanted to grill him about Chelsea's role as a social, rather than horticultural, event. Perhaps only one class, that knew all the rules, had attended? But no, he assured me, it had always been open to the public. Ticket sales brought in crucial income and 'real' gardeners were welcome right from the beginning, wearing the gardeners' uniform of the time: a flat cap, white shirt, tweed jacket and thick corduroy trousers.

Over his shoulder I could see Helen Mirren arriving, a tiny figure in a bright red coat, pink dress and four-inch heels, with an entourage just like the real Queen. She was swiftly borne away in search of a more receptive public: at this end of things people were more interested in Brent. Also the judges were in. Growers and designers could be seen wandering about with a glazed and restive look. No exhibitor could face staying at his or her stand while judging was under way and nobody else was allowed to remain near. The overall effect was like sticking the wrong end of a magnet into some iron filings: wherever the judges went, with their scrupulously neutral expressions and clipboards, there was a lacuna of awe and dread. Brent and I were forced to move repeatedly to escape horticulture buffs, or judges, or last-minute hammering by workmen. Our restless progress, I reflected, seemed to mirror the surprisingly rackety career of the Royal Horticultural Society on its way to respectability.

The judges were a reminder that underneath the froth and commerce, today's Chelsea Flower Show still has a serious purpose. They are unpaid, experts in a particular field, and they award an array of prizes largely unheard of by the public: Hogg medals for fruit and vegetables, Knightian medals for edible fruit, Lindley medals for educational value, Flora medals for gardens and ornamental plants. Only the golds really get any publicity – Dave's 'Best Actor Oscars' – though there are also silver-gilt, silver and bronze medals. To avoid dangerous stirrings of egotism, medals belong to the garden, not to the individuals involved. Technically, you can't say, 'She/he got a gold at Chelsea', although, of course, everybody does.

Generally, it seemed, the crowd was well informed: many were writing plant names in notebooks or tapping them into mobile phones. First names were bandied about: 'Cleve' (West, who had won gold for the *Telegraph* Garden), 'Tom' (Stewart Smith, a multiple award winner), 'Dan' (Pearson, who had just built a new winter garden in my local park). The fashion was for clean lines and light planting and flowers that looked as though they had grown up dancing in sunlit meadows rather than in heated greenhouses. Timber and slate and straight lines predominated.

The *Telegraph*'s garden was bright, full of yellows and fresh greens and studded with what looked like rolls of carpet standing on their ends. It was knee-deep in people. Nearby, Albert of Monaco was entertaining on the sleek terrace of his entry. This is a familiar Chelsea sight: the chosen few looking slightly self-conscious as they conduct a small-scale drinks party in front of a crowd who, despite being roped off at the end of a fifty-foot garden, are often distressingly audible ('Is that the one from *Hollyoaks*? Or, no, is it *Skins*?' or 'She's got those shoes really wrong. Or they're wrong for her legs, anyway'). The plants undergo a similar scrutiny.

As Monday morning wore on, you began to sense people were leaving. Or at least they knew they ought to be leaving. Just as the President's Lunch comes to an end, officials begin clearing the showground of press and anyone else who hasn't got a '3.30

badge'; who hasn't, in other words, got the nod for the Royal Visit. Those who have are expected to scrub up and wear a jacket or a hat or both. The Queen usually arrives after 5 p.m., usually in a Rolls-Royce, with the lesser royals following in a minibus. They go round in strict order of precedence: if she veers off because something interests her, the other party has to take avoiding action. After she has left, via an anonymous catering gate, leaving dazzled exhibitors in her wake, RHS staff sit down and write out all the medal certificates, which have to be affixed to the stands and exhibits by 7 a.m. on the Tuesday.

Royalty is gold dust, pure and simple, and it was sprinkled over every single event of the season. It usually involves an appearance, or at the very least patronage: George III started the ball rolling for Chelsea by granting the London Horticultural Society a charter in the early nineteenth century; the Prince Regent was a close friend of the Duke of Devonshire, who was the Society's President; Edward VII, somewhat surprisingly, was keen on horticulture and Queen Alexandra was a familiar visitor. The formidable Queen Mary, who loved Chelsea, visited annually for fifty years, sometimes accompanied by an irritable George V, who didn't. There is a photograph of the Princesses Elizabeth and Margaret accompanying their mother in 1947: they look perished with cold and boredom, standing with their sensible shoes clamped dutifully together. Despite the time of year, Elizabeth is wearing a huge fur stole. The value of royal attendance at an event lies not in glamour, even post-Diana, Princess of Wales. What they add is a priceless solidity: copper-bottomed, unchanging and socially reassuring.

One stand I particularly wanted to see was Hardy's. I had dropped in to see Rosy Hardy in her cottage garden nursery in Hampshire on my way back from Kelways and she had given me coffee in her kitchen. Everything about Rosy was unpretentious.

She doesn't draw plans for the plant display she builds at Chelsea every year: she just sketches the hard layout that needs to be built, looks at what the plants are doing, piles them all into a truck and wings it when she gets there. She says all this so casually that you would never know how successful she is. Like everyone else, she found it difficult to explain what made Chelsea quite so special. 'It's just the place you have to be,' she shrugged, 'it's where you want to win. And it's the beginning of the summer, isn't it? The start of the social season.'

When I went back to the show two days later, the Hardy's stand had a gold certificate pinned to the entrance. I'd been worried I wouldn't know if it was good or not, but in the event it wasn't hard: it danced with a light energy, an airy glade teleported from the countryside, spiralling inwards to a stand of slender trees. The plants were conscientiously labelled – *hostas verbascum Gainsborough*, delicate blue *anchusa azurea* or Loddon Royalist – and pale yellow spears of flowers marched across a background of fine, feathery grasses. Rosy's husband Rob was bursting with pride: 'She's so talented,' he said, shaking his head, 'it's just incredible.'

You'd think he would have got used to it by now. Rosy and Jekka McVicar are pretty well neck-and-neck in the medals table, the most successful female exhibitors in Chelsea's history. As plantsmen, they are gardeners' gardeners, as opposed to the gardeners most of us know off the TV, and I asked Brent Elliott if this was the biggest change in the show over the years: the rise of the celebrity horticulturalist. To my surprise, he said it wasn't.

'The Victorians didn't have celebrity gardeners but they did have *celebrated* gardeners,' he explained. 'At the beginning the [RHS] membership was all nobility, aristocrats and landed gentry, but there was always a category for "Practical Gardeners admitted to the privileges of Fellowship for a much smaller sum".' He added that a phenomenon of the nineteenth century was the rise, socially, practically and in terms of prestige, of the head gardener on the private estate. The best example had an indirect connection with Chelsea: Joseph Paxton had started as a trainee at the Society's Chiswick garden and then worked for the Duke of Devonshire at Chatsworth before becoming world famous for designing the Crystal Palace on the back of an envelope. It was a radical piece of engineering that got Prince Albert out of a hole and contributed perhaps more than anything else to the Great Exhibition's success, but while Paxton has earned eternal fame – he even has a Knightsbridge pub named after him – he remained a 'Practical Gardener admitted to the privileges of Fellowship' until the day he died.

Paxton became famous in a country that had been conducting a long love affair with the garden. It probably reached back to the days when just having an unproductive piece of land was a statement. When everyone expected food to come out of the ground, or at least to graze upon it before being eaten, the word 'garden' didn't exist. It appeared in the thirteenth century and may have come from the Frankish for 'enclosure'. The English borrowed both the word and the concept from across the Channel: the Tudors and Stuarts copied formal Continental gardens and William and Mary went for tightly controlled vistas, hedged and walled into living geometry. But in the mid-eighteenth century a new breed of gardener arrived. He was often an architect and almost invariably worked for a rich patron. The patron was generally a member of the landed gentry or the peerage – in fact, just the sort of person to found the London Horticultural Society – and his house would invariably sit in parkland, which could be sculpted and landscaped. The naturalistic 'English garden' had arrived.

I went back to Chelsea several times that week, once in my normal evening slot, another time with a landscape gardener friend, but what I was really looking forward to was another great Chelsea tradition: the grand sell-off on the final day. This is the only RHS show – probably the only show anywhere in the world – that resolutely refuses to allow any sales of plants or paraphernalia during the week. The only retail therapy to be had is on Sundries Avenue, a 'sundry' – that wonderful Chelsea phrase – being something small, portable and probably frivolous that is not (and this is important) directly to do with the practical business of gardening.

It puzzled me, this ban. One plausible theory was the compactness of the twenty-five-acre site: it doesn't allow for storage of goods, or for people to be hauling away saplings and teak furniture. But I was sure there was something else, some moral dimension, perhaps long forgotten, and I found a clue in Judith Flanders' book *Consuming Passions: Leisure & Pleasure in Victorian Britain*,[5] in which she discusses the effect of the Great Exhibition on contemporary shopping habits, and its role in the very first British stirrings of what would become mass consumer culture.

It seemed that while Prince Albert and the other high-minded driving forces behind the Exhibition wished it to operate like a museum – an educational and inspiring display of British manufacturing ingenuity – the public simply wanted to buy it all. Flanders quotes a stern editorial in the *Westminster Review*, published the year before the Crystal Palace opened: 'The object of the Exhibition is the display of articles intended to be exhibited, and not the transaction of commercial business,' it says primly, 'and the Commissioners can therefore give no facilities for the sale of articles, or for the transaction of business connected therewith.'

'Looking back,' she writes, 'it is possible to see, from the beginning, the tendency to understand the Great Exhibition as a collection of so many items for sale was constantly being repressed.' Even today Chelsea somehow manages to convey the sense that buying is just a little bit vulgar, that you are really there to learn. Crystal Palace exhibitors got around it by producing 'information leaflets' with trade cards tucked in the back. Chelsea gets around it by ringing a bell at four o'clock on the last day and letting the public take away whatever they've earmarked earlier in the week. It's a genteel SW3 version of the supermarket trolley dash.

I got the shuttle bus on the last day. These run from Victoria Station and from Battersea Park, like charabancs. There was an air of suppressed anticipation, quietly expressed (this being England), and most people had a receptacle: a backpack, a canvas bag, a wheeled case, a trolley. Couples chatted *sotto voce* or studied the map, making plans of attack. In the ground itself there was a more purposeful atmosphere: exhibitors looked both tired and relieved, less on show, more at home, and I could see little knots of people signing their names on lists at different stands and labels being affixed to the back of pots. That's what happens when you fall for a plant at Chelsea. No pouncing: you merely express a decorous interest.

At a quarter to four a strange pressure began to exert itself. Like a flock of sheep, we made south for the area near the Bull-Ring Gate, where operators mounted on huge TV cameras with Gore-Tex rain covers were doing practice swivels. Photographers were jockeying for position. The focus was the big two-storey stand belonging to M&G Investment, the main sponsor, which has an upper balcony. Men in suits milled around, managing to convey the impression that someone very big was about to appear. Every so often a ripple of excitement would seize the crowd and everyone would lift up their mobiles and drop them again, feeling foolish.

Then there they were, the Royal Couple. Alan Titchmarsh and his wife. The crowd erupted. He held up a hand, like Evita on the balcony of the Casa Rosada, and we all smiled goofily. There was something cosy about it, as if we were all on the same team. In a way we were: the Yorkshireman and gardening celebrity has fronted the BBC's Chelsea Flower Show coverage for almost thirty years. As the clock crept on he was handed a school bell, which he handed to Mrs Titchmarsh. At four o'clock on the dot, she rang it. Laughter and pandemonium broke out. Some people surged forward for autographs and others settled on the stands like locusts, claiming the plants and props they had booked earlier.

I watched it all disappear up the road to Sloane Square tube station, a sight barely registered by the locals, who see it every year. The stands began to look balder and more bedraggled. Away went all the sleepless nights and agonising hours of work as people set off with lemon trees and acanthus flowers, with begonias and geraniums and tubs of hyacinths, with tree ferns and fat cacti, with garden chairs and shooting sticks and silver poles with ends coiled like pigs' tails. Groups stood around cars, trying to stuff foliage in. A mini drove off with an apple tree sticking out of the sunroof. The rest of it got sucked underground, like the passengers in those old Tube posters from the 1930s. It was as though the show had sprouted out of the once rural soil of Chelsea and was going back there. In a week or so the whole thing would seem an elaborate dream.

5

NOT A THING TO WEAR

A large seagull, balanced on a blue and white striped awning at the west end of Church Street, NW8, was watching as deliveries of snapper, skate and mullet arrived in white polystyrene boxes at the fish stall below. Peaches and plums in plastic bowls were on sale for £1 and striped nylon bags bulged with maxi dresses and denim jackets. A group of elderly Muslim men, tweed-jacketed despite the sunshine, stood around a bin, lobbing their cigarette ends into it as they chatted. Car engines revved. A radio leaked cheery music. Church Street is a mildly lost part of London: not quite Maida Vale, not quite Marylebone, not quite St John's Wood. At its east end is Alfie's Antique Market and a handful of gentrified clothes and interior design shops. At its west end are fruit, veg and council flats.

Behind the market stalls is a long shop front, its several windows draped with swoops of fabric. Step inside and you are faced by a bank of buttons – grosgrain, or wool, or brass, or plastic – and cards of lace and ribbon in every colour. On either side, stretching to infinity, are rolls of material wrapped around thick cardboard tubes, stacked torpedo-style, each dangling a white tag. Some stand upright with a bolt end draped over them, like very slender veiled women. Others lie prone, fabric odalisques trailing finery. Under a swathe of such material by the door is a wooden plaque: '*Dieu et Mon Droit*', it says, and '*Honi Soi Qui Mal Y Pense*' and then 'By appointment to Her Majesty the Queen, Purveyor of Fabrics' with the royal coat of arms. This is a regal kite mark, the sign of a royal warrant holder; it signifies a retailer has supplied goods to the Queen, the Duke of Edinburgh or the Prince of Wales for at least five years with an unsullied track record. The system became truly entrenched under Queen Victoria, who was a tremendous giver of warrants. Today there are around 850 warrant holders. Very few of them would have heard of Church Street.

Joel & Son has been here for thirty years. Everybody except me knows about it: fashion students and tailors, seamstresses and home-sewing enthusiasts. It is famous not only for its fabrics – a close look at the price tags reveals hand-loomed Italian tweeds and textured Indian silks for hundreds of pounds per metre next to bouncy rolls of cheap and cheerful nylon net or polyesters – but also for its staff. The assistants know where everything is. They can remember the material you loved but failed to buy two years ago. They make suggestions based on the vaguest of creative mur-murings or designs scribbled on the backs of envelopes. They fling rainbows of glorious stuffs onto the white melamine counters and take to them with big silver shears; first a snip through the selvedge and then a whooshing, cavalier swoop through to the other side.

'When I think of you, I think of straight lines and squares,' Alice

Prier was saying, looking at me with her head on one side. 'Some people are circles and curves, you know, like Marilyn Monroe, but on you a dress will hang straight from the shoulders.' Alice is tiny and vivid, with a gamine haircut and a bright slash of lipstick. She is married to a friend of mine and has been designing clothes for women for years. She always wears her own creations, usually in colours straight out of a child's paint box. She rarely wears black and never anything shapeless. She lives in north London. She is rather cool. We could not, if we tried for a million years, be more different. I asked her if she would make me something for Royal Ascot.

Watching Alice in Joel's was like watching a fish in the sea. She flickered from one roll to the next, occasionally yanking out a few inches of fabric and scrunching it up in one hand. Every so often she flung a length over one of my shoulders like a toga and stood back critically. The choice was overwhelming. Did I want print or pattern, crisp linen or coolly whispering silk? Did I want to look sharply tailored or softly feminine? I had no idea. All I could think of were the lovely words – slub, jacquard, chiffon, twill – and the odd linguistic quirks of professions: why an item of clothing only became a 'piece', for example, when it had fashion pretensions, and why men's tailors always said 'cloth' and women's dressmakers 'fabric'. Alice interrupted this unproductive train of thought by wrapping me in a piece of electric-green silk with a printed *kente* pattern, like a TV on the blink. I found it weirdly exciting, as if it wasn't me at all. The possibility began to bubble up in my mind that I didn't have to be me. I was going to be alone at Royal Ascot; I could choose to be someone entirely different.

This idea did not fill me with unalloyed pleasure. In fact the thought of the fashion side of the season was intimidating. In my worst moments I had visions of arriving alone in the Royal

44

Enclosure and a great gasp of horror going up from the assembled regulars. My ideal would have been to stand in a booth made of one-way mirrors, staring at everyone while they couldn't see me. Instead I envisaged a dress that would be boring but not dowdy, acceptable but not loud. Then there were the shoes. I had bought a pair of Roberto Cavalli nude wedges in soft leather and cork. I wouldn't have to wear them in, they wouldn't get stuck in lawns and they would go with everything. But I hate Roberto Cavalli, I hate nude and I hate wedge heels. Those shoes depressed the hell out of me.

'What about a butterfly pattern?' Alice suggested. We had joked about the social butterfly idea. Now she had revived it, butterflies seemed to be hatching out all over the shop. They fluttered across pretty cottons and gauzy nylons. They flapped over childish prints. Even the Brunei princess at the counter, bargaining ferociously over thousands of pounds' worth of slithery pastels to take home for *sarong kebayas*, was wearing a butterfly headscarf. Alice thought they were all too twee, though. She wanted something 'more grown-up'. Me too, I thought, and had plumped for some soft red linen when there was a shriek from the other end of the shop.

Alice was standing by a metal clothes rail hung with soft rectangular folds of material, each one tacked into a piece of white printed card. She was holding one out. It had Charles Jourdan printed on it. 'It's a silk scarf,' she explained. 'Gary, the guy who owns this place, bought them in Paris. A shop went under and he bought the whole lot. They're vintage 70s and 80s.'

'You want me to go to Ascot in a scarf?' I said, appalled.

'They're huge,' she replied, as if it made a difference, 'one hundred and twenty centimetres square. If we only do one seam there's enough. And look at the pattern!'

The pattern was of gigantic, forensically detailed butterfly parts. Fuzzy black circles the size of tennis balls splodged across huge tangerine wings. Big black veins crazy-paved over pure white. It had panels of red, orange, white and, alarmingly, milk-chocolate brown. 'Oh my God,' I said lamely, 'I think that's a fritillary.' But Alice and one of the assistants were undoing one and wrapping it around me. 'Single seam ... leave the fringe for the hem ...' they murmured to each other. 'No room for error ... tall ... we could always come back for another ... how much?' It was oddly relaxing. My body. My dress. My Ascot. And nothing to do with me. In fact, it was so nothing to do with me that I felt quite excited again, as if I was about to emerge from a chrysalis into a more dazzling world. At that point Gary walked past with a papillon dog on a lead. An omen. So I said yes.

Had I been a man, of course, everything would have been much simpler, because men wear a uniform to Royal Ascot. When I rented the DVD of *My Fair Lady*, to revisit the famous fashion scene known as the Ascot Gavotte ('Every duke and earl and peer is here/Everyone who should be here is here ...'), I was startled to see that while everybody was dressed to the nines, standing on a wobbly trellis set with binoculars clamped to their eyes, Rex Harrison as Professor Higgins was wearing a tweed suit and a trilby. He would never have made it into the Royal Enclosure. It's a neat device: it distances him from the action, emphasising his role as arch-manipulator, but it also made the other men look absurdly formal in their stiff collars and top hats. It made me wonder what set of sartorial rules they were following. Why do men dress as they do at Royal Ascot?

To see what bespoke tailoring can do for a chap, have a look at

James Sherwood's *Fashion at Royal Ascot: Three Centuries of Thoroughbred Style*,[1] which had just been published for the tercentenary. Next to the foreword is a photograph of Peregrine 'Stoker' Cavendish, 12th Duke of Devonshire, who was about to complete his final year as Her Majesty's Representative. I've gone off Stoker, ever since I wrote a letter asking him for an interview and he never replied, but his clothes are bang on. He is wearing an immaculately cut tailcoat with a dark red carnation and his race badge in the left buttonhole, an Oxford collar (not too wide, not sticking up), a pale tie (not a cravat) and an Edwardian line cream waistcoat (straight-edged, rather than points). His top hat gleams like an oiled seal and his charcoal trousers are high-waisted, probably cashmere, with a faint pinstripe. He looks very expensive – which of course he is – and he is surrounded by a group of beaming gentlemen known as the Greencoats, clad in unseasonal green velvet and black toppers.

These men, who are mainly former racecourse staff, act as a ceremonial guard to the Queen and generally provide a twinkly, reassuring presence to race-goers. You will see something similar at most events of the season: the Bowler Hat Attendants at Henley, Chelsea Pensioners at the Chelsea Flower Show, Red Collars at the Royal Academy and so on. It's all part of the general colour. In this case, the colour is bottle green, a legacy from the Yeomen Prickers, officers of the royal hunt, who went out with the buckhounds early in the eighteenth century when Queen Anne used to heave her bulk into a carriage to hunt across Ascot Heath. Their job in those days was to keep the deer on track until the hounds caught up.

The intriguing thing about the Greencoats is that they are dressed fairly similarly to the duke. They, too, wear black trousers and shoes, white shirts with soft collars, waistcoats, narrow ties, formal coats and top hats. Their coats are not tailcoats but a looser style, almost a frock coat, their ties are uniform black and their buttons, collar edges and hat brims are gold. While Stoker is effectively dressed to go riding – the cutaway front of his coat and its single button would leave him the freedom to move in the saddle – they look ready to follow on foot; hunt servants, rather than horsemen. The style for both comes directly from English country sports, as seen in paintings and prints on the walls of country houses and pubs.

The difference between similarly structured outfits worn by different social or economic classes lay – still does lie – in the cut and the cloth. Then, far more than now, people would have registered these differences instantly. Before the Second World War, the concept of mass-produced ready-to-wear clothing for men barely existed. Most working-class men had their clothes made at home or they bought them second-hand. Those who could afford a tailor could choose between bespoke garments – made from scratch and fitted to the body – or made-to-measure, when an existing pattern was altered to fit, and some ready-made clothes. All the clues to status were there, for anyone who cared, just as they were with women.

Men's fashion is also as firmly wedded as women's to the cycles of politics and economics. When King Charles II returned in triumph from European exile in 1660, he brought with him French style and a mode of dress just about recognisable as an elaborate and bulky version of the three-piece suit. Gone were the tight doublets and ruffs his late father would have worn – and even more the dreary styling of the Commonwealth – for Charles affected slim knee breeches, stockings, a sumptuous surcoat, a full-bottom wig so like spaniels' ears that someone bred a minia-ture spaniel and called it a King Charles, and immense, richly patterned brocade waistcoats. The message was simple: it was time to have fun.

The court – then at Whitehall – followed suit and when Henry Jermyn, the first Earl of St Albans, began developing land north of St James's many of the new occupants were shops supplying the needs of ambitious young men in the royal retinue. Leather goods were needed – boots, whips, saddlebags – and so were elaborate uniforms. A young man about town needed hatting and shoeing for his outdoor life as well as his indoor life of intrigue, levées and gatherings at court. He would probably have lived alone in a set of rooms, instead of in a family home, so he needed food to be delivered from a cookshop and a good wine supplier. He also needed a coffee house to keep abreast with politics, news and gossip.

Many of the shops in St James's today began in this manner. Berry Bros & Rudd, the wine merchants, started as Widow Bourne's Coffee Mill, a late-seventeenth-century grocery shop. Much later, frivolous young men began weighing themselves on its huge scales, designed for sacks of coffee beans, and their weights were noted in ledgers. Gradually the scales became an attraction; the ledgers still exist and contain hundreds of illustrious names. In 1705, William Fortnum – a footman at the court of Queen Anne – took lodgings with a local man named Hugh Mason. They teamed up to sell the used wax candles he received as a perk of the job. Fortnum & Mason went on to establish the concept of the wicker picnic hamper supplied fully stocked by the store, and is still on Piccadilly today.

Likewise with fashion: over the next century and a half familiar names such as John Lobb the bootmaker and James Lock the hatter appeared on St James's. They are still serving a social elite, now global, and many of them are royal warrant holders. By the early 1800s, tailors were beginning to spread across from Jermyn

Street into new territory on the Burlington Estate, north of Piccadilly, and particularly into a street hitherto occupied by surgeons, who immediately began to move out. The street, Savile Row, rapidly became synonymous with tailoring and men's fashion.

At roughly the same time, the young man who would move English gentlemen's style into something we would recognise today made his appearance in Regency Society. George Brummell was the grandson of a St James's valet and lodging-house keeper but he went to Eton and Oxford and became a widely copied Regency buck. He is often described as a dandy – hence his nickname, 'Beau' – but while the word has come to mean foppish and ludicrously dressed, at the time it meant a man who not only cared about his clothes but cultivated an acerbic wit. Brummell seems to have been much admired by other men and he changed the male silhouette. It was all about fit. And right on cue the tape measure made its first appearance.

Brummel wore a novel form of lower body wear – cooked up with his tailor at Meyer & Mortimer, which is still on Sackville Street – called trousers. The trouser covered the whole leg, rather than ending at the knee, had a single outer seam, and its smooth line was ensured over a boot or shoe by a strap that fitted under the foot. Over this was worn a double waistcoat, a cutaway coat and an elaborate stock (a wide band of material tied at the neck) normally worn on the hunting field. He wore his hair shortish, tied back and usually under a 'high hat', an early form of topper. Wigs had been subjected to a powder tax and were therefore jettisoned. He looked light, young and elegant – instead of comically decadent and bewigged – and everybody wanted to be him.

Everybody included the corpulent Prince Regent. At the age of sixteen Brummell had joined the Prince's regiment, the fast-living 10th Royal Hussars, and caught the royal eye with his style and confidence. This turned him from a dapper young man into a legend: he spent a fortune on clothes and took hours dressing and shopping in the mornings. He neatly inverted the royal levée – a custom throughout the Georgian era, when courtiers attended the King as he dressed – by inviting the Prince to attend *his* daily rising at his house on Chesterfield Street in Mayfair, when his chosen circle would watch as he put together his look for another day.

Portraits and caricatures of the time show the striking difference in pre- and post-Brummellian men's clothes is not just shape but colour. Before 1800, the Prince – 'Prinny' to his friends – wore bright, loose-fitting frock coats or flamboyant military uniforms. He even managed to make the robes of the Garter, the highest chivalric order in the land, look louche. After 1800, he adopted slimming cutaway coats in mole browns, midnight blues and forest greens. A portrait in Buckingham Palace shows him in precisely this get-up, complete with a bow and quiver of arrows, as if he has just taken time out from the archery competition behind him.

It was Brummell who suggested that suitable attire for Ascot should be a fitted black coat, white cravat and pantaloons – the early form of trousers. He was probably more influenced than he realised by the events around him: the French Revolution had dribbled to an end by the late 1790s but it exerted a subliminal influence on clothes; there was a mood of sobriety, of the upper classes being called to account for their extravagance. The other revolutionaries, the new industrialists, also eschewed flamboyance. Gradually, the male sartorial palette contracted into blacks, greys and whites in town, and browns and tweeds in the country. The former can be seen in the suit worn for work today; the latter, as worn by the insouciant Higgins in *My Fair Lady*, in country sports and leisure pursuits: the 'good tweeds' referred to by Edward Gillespie at Cheltenham Racecourse.

Upper-class men, like their women, changed frequently during the day and were expected to dress appropriately for different events of the season. A valet was necessary – look at Jeeves and Bertie Wooster – simply to keep up with it all, let alone maintain the clothes. It put tailors under pressure, too; the historian Richard Walker writes that Savile Row's workload doubled from April to June.[2] As the permanent workforce was small, extra tailors were recruited in strict order of precedence (based on experience) from local pubs – the Scotch Arms on St Martin's Lane, or the Blue Posts on Golden Square, for instance – known as 'houses of call'.

Beau Brummell fled to Paris to escape his creditors in 1816, having flown too close to the sun. Four years later Prinny, having flown too close to good taste, bought himself robes for the most expensive coronation Britain had ever seen, for which he designed a crown set with 12,000 diamonds and wore a cloak of deep crimson velvet sprinkled with golden stars and trimmed with ermine over ballooning silver satin breeches. He wore a jewelled garter and diamond-buckled shoes. He had his estranged Queen turned away at the door of Westminster Abbey. Few mourned his death a decade later.

The Beau silhouette, on the other hand, flattering and sporty, has stayed with us. He deserves his bronze statue on Jermyn Street, where it stands staring disapprovingly at the Wooster-ish candy-striped boating blazers in New & Lingwood's window in the Piccadilly Arcade. For the purposes of Royal Ascot and the Derby, his look is known as 'morning dress' – a nod to its active origins – as opposed to 'evening dress' of white tie and tails. If you beamed in some gentleman from the late eighteenth century for a day's racing, he wouldn't look absurd in today's Royal Enclosure.

6

THE UPS AND DOWNS OF EPSOM

There is a sound when the Derby starts. It's like nothing else I've ever heard. It's 130,000 people begging, praying, willing their horses to win, and it soars up and above the booming fairground rides and the amplified commentary and the rainbow of hats jammed brim to brim in the Queen's Stand and the people waving pint glasses on open-topped buses. It hangs in the air above the scrubby open tops of the Epsom Downs. I wouldn't be surprised if they could hear it fifteen miles away in London. 'When the stalls open, the roar across the Downs is phenomenal,' one man told me. 'There are more important things in life, I know, but just at that moment it seems like it's the centre of the world.'

In many ways it is, because in flat racing terms, even today, the Derby is the race that every owner, trainer and sweepstake holder wants to win. It takes place in early June on the well-drained, chalky uplands of the North Downs. It is just over a mile and a half long, run by three-year-old colts (young males, uncastrated, or 'entire' as it is delicately called in racing), and sometimes fillies, at the peak of their abilities. The winner wakes up in his or her loose-box the next morning an equine superstar, worth many millions of pounds more than the day before. Everybody wants to breed from a Derby winner. It is the blue riband of the Turf, flat racing's answer to the Olympic men's 100 metres and far and away our most lucrative single horse race, with prize money of well over a million pounds. Most owners and trainers will admit they have dreamed of winning the Derby.

The reason for all this hyperbole is partly the course. It is fantastically demanding. From the top of my 1950s open-topped bus – a sage-and-cream exercise in nostalgia, complete with period advertising and an evocative smell of leather seats – I could see almost all of it through my binoculars. It is a horseshoe shape with the open end facing northwest, and it undulates, following the natural contours of the land. That's what makes it hard: the first half-mile of the Derby is a gruelling uphill slog. The horses gallop at top speed almost to the height of Nelson's Column – around 150 feet – and turn left on an adverse camber. The track not only slopes inwards, it goes downhill, demanding perfect pace and balance; in the infamous race of 1962 seven horses fell on this stretch, landing six jockeys in hospital. Then comes Tattenham Corner, where horses can be boxed in on the rails or fail to change legs efficiently enough. After that they round the curve of the horseshoe and go uphill again to the finish line.

Derby time was 4 p.m. Fifteen minutes beforehand the horses emerged from the paddock onto the wide green band of turf, pouring out from the gap between the Queen's and the Prince Regent's stands one by one, like bees coming out of a hive. The jockeys, dazzling dots on top, reminded me of the floral display at Chelsea. To partisan cheers, they cantered off to the start, so far away that I had to switch to the big screen to see it all. There they were, frisking about by the stalls, some hopping, others calm.

The crowd was much the same. There was a hum of nervous anticipation. The hen party on the next-door bus had stopped trading catcalls with a group of nearby stags. The royal box suddenly filled with a line of familiar faces, including the Duchess of Cambridge in a taupe hat like an acorn cup and Princes William and Harry, sleekly clad in toppers and tails with buff waistcoats. People were studying their racecards to check the jockeys' colours and match them with the horses on the huge screens. Most of us were looking for an opulent combination of deep purple satin with gold frogging and scarlet sleeves, topped by a black velvet cap with a gold tassel: the Queen's colours. For the first time in years she had a horse that might do it, Carlton House, and most of the crowd apart from the bookies wanted him to win. The Derby is the only English Classic to elude her.

The roar, when it came, sounded as if a gigantic orchestra warming up on stage had gone straight into fortissimo. I could see the tiny line of horses explode out of the stalls, bunch together momentarily and begin to climb.

In the middle of the course, meanwhile, a massive party was under way. Unlike the occupants of the stands, the corporate pavilions or the open-air enclosures for cars and buses lining the track, the cheery crowds in the centre of the course, 'The Hill', pay nothing if they turn up on foot and around £30 if they bring a car. The racecourse might expect up to 50,000 paying punters for the Derby, but there will be at least twice that out on The Hill. It's a freedom enshrined in law: in 1936 Parliament passed the Epsom & Walton Downs Regulation Act giving statutory recognition to 'the rights of the public to air and exercise over the Downs', while at the same time allowing the racing industry to run its yards and gallops. As a result, anyone can walk a dog, fly a kite, or strip down to their bikini, break out the beers and lie back in the sun to watch the greatest race on earth, slap bang in the eye-line of the immaculately dressed occupants of the royal box.

'Is she here, the Queen?' said Claire Woodlock, dropping her sun cream onto the rug and sitting up. On the other side of the track, about 200 yards away, a stolid figure in a fuchsia and white striped hat could be seen reading her racecard. 'Oh my God! We'll have to get our binoculars out!' Claire and her sister Emma were both at school in Epsom. Their school houses were named after Derby winners ('Mine was Nijinksy!' 'And mine was Minstrel!') and they come every year, with or without their families. They had Union flags but they weren't betting on Carlton House. They were betting, along with a sizeable chunk of the female race-going population, on Frankie Dettori, who could have been riding a donkey. I wondered if they envied the 'hat stands'.

'God, no! I mean, the men look gorgeous but they must be so hot by the end of it. Sweaty Betty or what!' said Claire.

'We're in the commoners' bit here,' added Emma, and they both cackled and raised their drinks. 'No minding our Ps and Qs down here – it's perfect!' They were right: they had the best place on the course.

The second-best place on the course was my open-topped bus. I managed to get a last-minute ticket from Norman Hodkinson, who runs a company supplying period action vehicles for the film industry, anything from Chitty Chitty Bang Bang to the Batmobile. As a sideline, he takes fifteen buses to Epsom every year. He sounded elderly on the phone so it was a shock when he turned out to be in his mid-thirties and dressed like an extra from

Brighton Rock. 'Prince of Wales check,' he said, lifting a natty lapel. 'A pink and blue striped shirt, a *boutonnière* – it should be heather but it's not out yet, so it's lavender – an Edwardian serviette holder that clips onto your shirt so your spaghetti Bolognese doesn't ruin it, snakeskin shoes and a black straw trilby from Primark.' He pulled his pocket handkerchief up a millimetre and added, unnecessarily, 'I'm a bit of a dandy.'

The tradition of open-topped buses at the Derby dates back to the days of the horse-drawn charabanc. 'People used to come from the East End in horses and carts, originally, and they were open on top,' said Norman, 'so now it's buses instead and on Derby Day they have to be open-topped to be in the Lonsdale Enclosure. You can't have an ordinary coach in here.' Because the buses have to be in place by 11 a.m., when all the pedestrians arrive, the drinking day starts early. Just along from us was a group of forty-seven men from a pub in Essex, their numbers sorely depleted because of the recession, who had come every year for eleven years. When I asked why there weren't any women, they said, 'Why bring a packed lunch when you can eat out?' and fell about laughing. They were betting around £50 on each race, maybe a lot more, and they had been drinking since six. They waved at the girls on the bridal bus, causing screams of delight and a Mexican wave of pink feather boas, deely boppers and pints of Pimm's.

'Jesus,' said the Canadian photographer I had asked to come and take some pictures for me, 'it's like your class system right in front of me. We don't have anything like this at home. We just sort of do things together.'

I could see what he meant. The geography of the course meant that the people in the grandstands were physically higher than everyone else. On Derby Day the dress code in the Queen's Stand is as formal as it would be in Ascot's Royal Enclosure, so it was a sea of grey and black top hats and expensive feathers. The 'smart casuals' in the buses – us, office and pub outings, stag, hen, birthday and anniversary parties – were suspended in the middle, facing the course with a steep grassy drop behind us. At the bottom of that was The Hill, sloping up to the centre in a great mass of humanity. A funfair – run for years by the same showman dynasty, Roses Pleasure Parks, with rides like Sizzler Twist, Freak and Oxygen flashing lights and belting out big bass as they twirled – occupied one corner. Next to it was the popular market, selling jewellery, novelties and clothes.

It's this social jumble that has given the Derby its populist reputation. The race has always been nicknamed 'The Londoners' Day Out' because it's so near the big city. Race day moved frequently over the years, but by far the most popular choice was Wednesday, a half-day holiday, which gave it an intoxicating atmosphere. Parliament shamelessly passed the 'Derby Adjournment', awarding itself a half-day off every year. The Stock Exchange shut like a clam. All the trains were packed and London cabs could not be had for love or money. There's an Anna Neagle film called *Derby Day*, shot in 1952, that captures that sense of collective intent, of London emptying for the afternoon. For many people it was the event of the year. When it moved to a Saturday in 1995 – in an attempt to stop the decline in attendance – it lost much of its fizz and pizzazz. Or so they say. To me, as a newcomer, there seemed be an awful lot of it left.

One of the guys on my bus was local. 'It's a very different feel now,' he assured me. 'As soon as you saw the gypsies coming up on the Downs you knew it was about to begin. It was such a great atmosphere. I'd say there were 250,000 people or so back then. It was very rough and ready; you took your life in your hands venturing into the funfair, especially on Derby Day. There was loads of argy-bargy because of too much to drink.' Local boys would fight with the Travellers – always called 'gypsies' then – and the road across the Downs was jammed solid from dawn onwards. He also told me the traffic lights in Epsom had special sensors for detecting jockeys on horseback, so they turned red for longer, and there were horse road signs. It seems to have bred loyalty in the locals: I met many who came every year. 'Ascot doesn't compare to the Derby,' he said firmly, 'I'm sure people there say the same about us, but nowhere else does.'

His estimate of a quarter of a million race-goers was way under, it turned out. 'The crowds built up from around a few thousand in the early days to 10,000,' said Michael Church, the official Derby historian, who has published two mighty tomes on the subject.[1] 'By 1830 you're talking upwards of 25,000. And by Coronation Year, 1953, there were 500,000 people on the Downs for Derby Day. I was there!' I went to see Michael before the race and found him in his study overlooking a lovely garden in Woking, perfectly positioned for Epsom, Ascot and Sandown. He was walled in by books: the form books of racing results ('flat and jumps') from the eighteenth century to the present; stud books detailing the foalings of all thoroughbreds in England and Ireland for almost the same period; Timeform manuals, which contain a biography of each horse and its rating; plus biographies, racing books and pictures, from the 1940s onwards.

The Derby Stakes really started as an afterthought. In the late eighteenth century, Epsom was famous for its springs and was a popular Society haunt. The 12th Earl of Derby, a racing fanatic and huge gambler, had a country house there called 'The Oaks', where he entertained his high-rolling friends. It was not unusual to gamble the equivalent of £100,000 in today's money on a single race. The Duchess of Devonshire, a contemporary, ran up debts of well over two million pounds just on cards during her lifetime. In 1779 the gentlemen decided to race three-year-old fillies over a mile and a half. They called the new race the Oaks Stakes and it was such a success they came up with another wheeze the following year, this time for three-year-old colts, geldings and fillies over a mile (it later became a mile and a half). They tossed for a name and the earl won. Just as well for a race that has lent its name to sporting events the world over: the loser was a well-known Jockey Club figure called Charles Bunbury.

'Back then races were run in heats,' explained Michael. 'There might only be six or seven horses and they would run two at a time, one against another. They would hold a series of races over two or four miles in an afternoon, until a horse won two heats. So they thought, "Let's have a one-off." It was thought of as a novelty event. And it was very successful.' Part of the novelty was its brevity: the earliest horse races were known as 'matches' and involved two horses running over anything from three to eight miles. Heats were just several matches run in a single afternoon. It was impossible to follow on foot and difficult on horseback, so spectators must have seen tantalising glimpses of the action, belting out from behind the tree cover only to disappear again.

Shorter races turned racing into a spectator sport and as people turned up to watch along came food sellers and tipsters and basic facilities. From its earliest days it attracted a raffish crowd. One horrified nineteenth-century writer described '... the temptations of blacklegs, thimble-riggers etc. upon a racecourse, the arena of the out-casts and disorderlies of the country, the demoralisers of the peace, the respectability, and the virtue of our country, the very sink of demoralization ...'[2] This made it wildly attractive to all levels of society. The Derby was said to be the only place a duke and a dustman would rub shoulders. No wonder Queen Victoria disapproved.

On Michael's study wall was a print of *The Derby Day*, a famous painting by the Victorian artist William Powell Frith. When it went on show in the Royal Academy in 1858 they had to put up protective barriers because so many people were desperate to see it. There were queues all the way up Piccadilly. Frith, who had found success four years earlier with a similar genre painting by the seaside at Ramsgate, was on a roll and knew it. It is a huge panorama – on a canvas over six feet long and three feet high – bursting with life and vulgarity. It has a wonderful freedom and charm. Frith went to Epsom in 1856 to do the initial sketches and then used models for the dozens of figures that conformed so reassuringly to every Victorian stereotype of class. You can see a single grandstand in the background, towering over the action, but the painting is set on The Hill.

'It's showing a rich family very nonchalantly having a picnic in their carriage,' said Michael, getting up to point. 'They've got a hamper with all the Fortnum & Mason's stuff, you know. And there's so much going on to entertain them: jugglers, conjurors, a three-card-trick man, a few tipsters, gypsies selling heather. There's an escapologist and a pickpocket. There are people scrounging around, hoping for a bit of pork pie or a lobster claw. There are beer tents and roulette tents. And all these people see very little of the race. They won't know who's won until the news filters down the course perhaps an hour afterwards. It's a little less raucous now, but it's still the same atmosphere.' The grandstand, he added, was used not by the aristocracy, who would have brought carriages, but by tradesmen taking their wives and children. The open-top carriages lined the course six or seven deep near the winning post. When the excitement got too much in the last few furlongs, everyone would leap to their feet.

At one point – I think my question was 'What's a second favourite?' – he looked at me with kindly blue eyes and said simply: 'You really don't know anything, do you?' I didn't dare tell him that until a few weeks before not only did I not know there were different horses for jumping and flat, I also thought all race courses were continuous, straight-sided, flat ovals like my brother's Scalextric track and honestly believed that maiden races were for fillies. I also had no idea that the start was in a different place to the finish. Of all the people you wouldn't expect to catch the racing bug, it was me – who would have thought I'd be entranced by the Derby?

It was something to do with the remark Edward Gillespie made at Cheltenham about racing and theatre. Racing did have all the elements of a stage performance, albeit in the open air: the audience, the cast, the nerves, that absolute focus on a single arena. When the victorious animal was led into the winners' enclosure and fans scrambled to try and pat him they were like autograph hunters at the stage door, just wanting a little piece of history. I loved the sight of the owners, so excited they barely knew what to do with themselves, ineptly throwing buckets of water onto the winning horse while trying not to spoil their clothes. I was intrigued by the jockeys, so oddly compact, with their tough, white, sardonic faces.

Kate Fox, the anthropologist and author, wrote a very funny book called *The Racing Tribe*[3] in which she, also an outsider, applies the methodology she would use in the field – a village in Africa, or an Inuit settlement, say – to the world of the turf. She identifies the trainers as shamans – always credited when things go well, but miraculously never blamed when they don't – and notes the warrior-jockeys' steady rise in status over the past twenty-five years from a superior sort of outdoor servant to big stars in their own right. I found it very useful in making sense of the whole thing. The only thing it didn't mention was a genuine tribe found at the Derby, uniquely in top-class racing, and often, even now, referred to as the gypsies.

'My dad was a travelling man from the New Forest, my mum was more of a showman family,' explained Charlie Cooper, a stocky, powerfully built man in his early sixties, sitting in his spacious family caravan at the far end of The Hill, out of earshot of the funfair. 'Her father used to work on the Downs. They used to put up the latrines. They'd put up a tent and dig a trench and everyone used that. Now it's different, of course, but I'm still working on the Downs. So it hasn't changed that much.' Charlie liaises between the Travellers, the local council and the racecourse authorities, which is how I got his mobile phone number. He's also in charge of the campsite. It's £80 for ten days and you don't have to be in the travelling community to stay there, though most people are. He comes with his extended family, a clan really, and has been doing so for twenty-five years. Home is in Dorset, where he runs a boxing school, among other things. He said to come and find him at the caravan on Derby Day itself: Oaks Day, the day before, would be too busy for chatting.

The main reasons the travelling community was drawn to the races, apart from temporary jobs and giving their families a summer holiday, were running the funfair and horse dealing. The women told fortunes and sold lucky heather. Modern bio-security issues have put paid to the horse trading: you can't have animals informally changing hands with tens of millions of pounds' worth of thoroughbreds lodging in racecourse stables and training yards nearby. The nearest thing you could see to it today would be the annual horse fair at Appleby in Westmorland, 240 miles to the northwest. But Epsom was also a chance for extended clans to meet up, for young people to be introduced and for old scores to be settled. It was, in fact, a season within the season. There was business to be done.

'If anybody had a dispute within the travelling community they would always want to meet up on Epsom Downs,' explained Charlie. 'They would get someone with a good reputation and ask him to see fair play. It's happened to me a couple of times. They agree the rules, they shake hands, then they fight until one man gives in. Years ago lots of fighting men used to come to the fair and say: "I'm the best man at the fair" as a challenge. Some people love it. The old bare knuckle ... we know it's illegal and it shouldn't happen, but it's better doing that than these young lads you see getting shot and stabbed. Ours is all Queensbury Rules stuff.'

He wouldn't be drawn on whether it still happens: it would be surprising if not – a recent documentary showed bare-knuckle fights going on in both Ireland and England, often as a result of bad blood between clans – but then his job is to keep the peace on the campsite. What he did talk about was Spin the Penny, or Two-Up, the heads and tails game played for hours by the men in a makeshift arena for huge wagers in cash. He showed me two George VI large pennies, scoured with Daddies Sauce to a roseate copper glow. With an effortless flick of the fingers, he sent them flying up above his head, spinning as they fell. He summoned a young man called Mark to take us to the game.

Among the parked cars a tarpaulin had been spread on the ground and surrounded with a rectangle of scaffolding poles. It looked like a boxing ring, but you could lean on the sides. Lots of people were, all male, and they watched intently as the man in the middle, the thrower, spun his coins high in the air. Everyone craned to see them land. Then a flurry of cash changed hands and another man began to call in bets for the next throw. In between his fingers was a fan of bank notes, neatly ordered into wads of fives, tens, twenties and fifties. 'The casters run the ring,' said Mark, who had taken the photographer and me under his wing. 'The thrower gives them fifty pounds and they lay that off around the ring. Forty pounds minimum bet but it can be anything up to a thousand. You can win £10,000 in a day. It's quiet now, but after the race later you'll get all the boys coming over. It'll be ten deep. There could be two hundred people.' Sometimes they are so intent on winning or getting their money back they play into the night, the ring lit by car headlights, until no one wants to go on.

The betting ring was a stark contrast to the caravans, where the women and children were: the division of the sexes was striking, the women were friendly but shy, far more reticent than the men. Charlie's ten-year-old granddaughter was persuaded to sing for us, belting out a song in a voice of startling maturity: they had sent her tape to one of the TV talent shows and were waiting to hear if she'd been selected. About a hundred yards away sat a brand new Roma caravan, fitted with pile carpets, swish upholstery and the latest kitchen with all the gadgets. You could add accessories such as LED grab handles, wine racks and an Aga, and a saleswoman had leaflets to hand out, hoping to sell to one of the families. It was worth around £100,000, apparently, even before adding any bits and pieces.

What Charlie couldn't explain was the mysterious appearance of the predicted Derby winner's name, chalked up on an old well outside a pub called the Amato – a Derby winner, of course – just north of the course every year. It is said to be the work of one of the Travellers, using their famous hereditary affinity with horses, and people take it seriously enough to ring the pub from all over the world before placing their bets. It features in the racing press every year. It used to materialise the night before but now appears, more conveniently in terms of media coverage, on the previous Monday. The pub landlord swore blind he didn't know who did it and had never sat up to watch. I eyed him narrowly, remembering my parents lying through their teeth about Father Christmas. The name was chalked on a board propped up next to the well. It was all very neat and suburban, not quite what we were expecting. It has predicted four out of the past ten winners.

Back on Norman's bus, we were all jammed at the front on the top deck, screaming hysterically. The Beau Brummel of the open-top bus world was waving his Primark trilby. Carlton House was dashing along to the finish and while the Queen wasn't quite shouting, ''Ome you go, my cocker!' she looked pleased. As they made the final push, three horses, going hell for leather, bunched together at the front. Then an amazing thing happened: a young Frenchman riding his first Derby on Pour Moi, a bay with a white blaze, stood bolt upright in his irons as they went over the line. It was a photo finish, but he knew he'd won. He didn't quite do a pelvic thrust with an arm sweep, but it wasn't far off: it was a pure warrior moment, an expression of such joyous nineteen-year-old confidence that it made you want to throw your hat in the air. (Many people did.) It was also risky: had he lost it might have ruined his career. Instead the racing hacks leaped to write 'trumped by the tricoleur' and 'French resistance' headlines. Another Derby was over. It had taken just over two and a half minutes.

7

AND ALL FOR A BUNCH
OF STUDENTS

Three days after the Derby, barely enough time for Pour Moi's winning cheque to clear, the Royal Academy Summer Exhibition opened. Life was speeding up: events were coming one after the other, nose to tail, and everything seemed heightened, full of bright colours, big personalities and dizzying levels of expertise. My day-to-day shopping at Tesco on Battersea Park Road began to seem oddly alien ('What do you mean, you don't have celery salt?'), as did going to pubs, say, or paying household bills. My forty-ninth birthday party was thrown together by friends: I was incapable of sorting anything out for myself, partly because I was in shock from the Summer Exhibition Preview Party, which took place before the show itself.

Medieval doom paintings always follow a prescribed format. At the centre is Christ, usually seated on a rainbow, flanked by the

Virgin Mary and St John the Apostle. To his right the virtuous make their way up to heaven while to his left the damned are pitchforked by demons into the fires of hell. A similar concept exists in Ancient Egyptian tomb decoration. It can also be seen on Piccadilly in early June, as guests arrive for the Preview Party and are sorted, with deadly efficiency, into those deemed worthy of a red-carpet entrance and those who are to be banished into normality.

The former have to run the gauntlet of paparazzi lined up along the west side of the Academy courtyard. Most photographers stand at ground level, but a back row perches behind on stools and ladders, hoping for a better view. They look like a dishevelled end of term school photo and are just as cheeky. 'Left leg, darling!' they yell, as yet another etiolated model sways past and pauses to jut a bony hip. 'Smile, Tracey!' they carol as Tracey Emin, former *enfant terrible* of the art world and soon to be the Royal Academy's Professor of Drawing, stops obligingly and gives her familiar lopsided grin.

The scene was so riveting I nearly missed the party. The Christ figure, it soon became clear, was a PR clad in a dress like a white cotton pillowcase. She was flanked by more PRs, all consulting clipboards. 'How do they know who everyone is?' I whispered to the person next to me. She looked amused. 'They know,' she said drily. And they did. The people whose star was in the ascendant were kettled behind a table and then given a gentle shove to set them off along the carpet, which was not in fact red but a discreet pale grey. People who thought their star was in the ascendant but now found it wasn't had the news kindly but firmly broken to them and were escorted to the other end of the table, to make the long, carpetless trudge in along the east side of the courtyard.

After half an hour of this casual brutality I lost my own nerve, even for crossing the courtyard on the distaff side. The steps into the Academy seemed miles away. I had to scuttle in behind a group of people in suits and long dresses who just looked rich, rather than famous. It is for these people that the Preview Party exists. The celebrities are there for press coverage and to banish any atavistic memories of the Royal Academy being a dry and fusty institution. The paying guests are there not just to enjoy the cracking party but because they get first dibs on the art.

The Royal Academy Summer Exhibition, at almost 250 years old, is the largest open-submission art show in the world. It began in the early years of King George III's reign, when nobody but private collectors and their acquaintances had access to works of art in Britain. There were no public galleries and the nation did not yet possess an art collection. But in the fashionable residential area of Bloomsbury something was afoot. Thirty years or so before a philanthropist named Thomas Coram, shocked by the abandoned children he saw on London's streets, set up a home for the offspring of fallen women. It had a central building and two huge wings enclosing an open space (when the children moved to the country in 1937 these wings were demolished, the house became the Foundling Museum and the grounds a park known today as Coram's Fields, into which adults may not go 'unless accompanied by a child'). It was quickly adopted as a cause by the Society women of the time. It was also loyally supported by two famous friends of Coram's, both childless: George Frideric Handel, the great composer, and William Hogarth, the English artist and social satirist.

In 1740 Hogarth painted Captain Coram and gave the portrait to the hospital. He then persuaded other artists, from John Michael Rysbrack and Francis Hayman to Joshua Reynolds and Thomas Gainsborough, to donate works to the hospital collection.

It wasn't purely charitable: without public galleries it was difficult for contemporary artists to get their work seen; here was a chance to tap into the lucrative world of private commissions. Hogarth had an axe to grind, too: British artists were constantly being side-lined not only by the Grand Tourists' obsession with shopping for Old Masters, but by the greater perceived prestige of European painters and sculptors.

Hogarth hit on the ingenious idea of holding a lottery for his painting *The March of the Guards to Finchley*: anyone who bought the engraving could pay extra for a lottery ticket to win the canvas itself. He gave the unsold tickets to the Foundling Hospital, which promptly won. The painting still hangs in the grand Committee Room. The hospital's art collection began to attract interest from society patrons and its historians later wrote: '[The paintings] being exhibited to the public, drew a daily crowd of spectators in their splendid equipages; and a visit to the Foundling became the most fashionable morning lounge of the reign of George II.'[1]

The artists, sensing a market, began to group into loose con-federacies, and one of these, the Society of Artists, held a hugely successful summer exhibition. Everyone in London Society went and many of them bought paintings. Its success moved the archi-tect Sir William Chambers, who was about to be appointed Comptroller of the King's Works, to ask King George III if a group of established artists could found an academy, not only to exhibit their own work and that of 'outsiders', but as a means of educat-ing students.

In 1768 the Royal Academy opened its doors on Pall Mall, then the centre of London's private art world. It housed the Royal Academy Schools – Britain's first art college, modelled on the much older Académie Royale de Peinture et de Sculpture in Paris – and exhibition spaces for contemporary artists. It was to move as frequently as the Chelsea Flower Show: first from Pall Mall to Somerset House, then a royal palace; next to a wing of the new National Gallery on Trafalgar Square; and finally to a ten-gallery extension to Lord Burlington's former town house on the north side of Piccadilly in the late 1860s. This has been the setting for the Summer Exhibition ever since.

The exhibition started the year after the Academy was founded and was held at the start of the season in early May. Indeed it was the opening event until trumped by Chelsea in the twentieth century. A proportion of admission and sales fees went to fund the schools – it still does – and right from the start the public could submit work and visit the exhibition; all they needed was the leisure to paint or the money for the one-shilling entry fee. This excluded most of the population, of course, but it was a start, especially so for the time. Today around 12,000 works are submitted by anyone who wishes – Sunday painters, hopeful students, professional artists, you or I – in the hope of seeing them hang alongside paintings and sculptures by some of the biggest names of the day. It is just as eclectic as the Derby, really. And the logistics are mind-boggling.

Every year in March, anyone walking along Burlington Gardens in Mayfair passes a straggling queue of people stretching along the street and up the ramp into the back of the Royal Academy. As teenagers flit in and out of the black maw of Abercrombie & Fitch over the road, artists of all types carry their hopes and dreams wrapped in brown paper and bubble wrap and tied up with parcel tape and string. To get this far, they have filled in a form and sent in £25 for each work submitted. It's easy to send in your painting, or take it to a collection point in larger regional cities, but most people prefer to deliver in person. It's all part of the ritual. I met artists in the queue from Bow in East London, Loch Ness in

Scotland, Shropshire, Newcastle and the Home Counties. Some were foreigners living in England who had dreamed of submitting for years. Works are sent in from twenty or more countries around the world. Friends and partners come to give moral support and help heft bulky canvases on and off public transport.

'The basement of the RA is literally a rabbit warren. It goes down three floors below the ground,' explained a friend, a portrait painter and former student at the schools who was a Summer Show art handler all the way through his studies. 'You could get lost in there. They're called the Vaults and they've already got dusty casts from the schools and old works in them. Then you've got thousands of show submissions to fit in there as well.' The whole process is overseen by the team of permanent art handlers who are shifting priceless works in and out of the gallery all the time. Even so the sheer volume of art being moved is unprecedented.

As works are dropped off at Burlington Gardens they are unwrapped, barcoded and taken down to the Vaults to be stored for a few weeks. Then in mid-May they come back up, one by one, to be placed in front of the selection committee. 'It's like a chain gang of students,' said my friend. 'You pass each work from one to another and then it's placed briefly on a rickety old leather-bound stool. That's said to go right back to Joshua Reynolds himself, it's one of those Academy myths. It's padded, with a swivelly top, so you put the painting on it and swivel it so the committee can see. There are about ten of them sitting in a horse-shoe shape. If it's a small work they sometimes like to hand it along amongst themselves.'

I had tried hard to see the selection committee (which at a later stage becomes the hanging committee) in action, but it was made clear that this was like asking to see the Queen putting her robes on for the State Opening of Parliament. It was completely off-limits. A BBC film made on the subject had, I was told, been shot at a specially setup re-creation. I got fifteen minutes with the senior curator who was running the Summer Show that year, but five minutes in her mobile rang and the room filled with a booming Yorkshire accent. Even from where I was sitting I could tell it was David Hockney, ringing to discuss his own approaching blockbuster. She mouthed 'Sorry' and 'Off the record'. He took up most of my interview while I stared out of the window into the courtyard.

The judging process takes five days, exhausting for judges and handlers alike. Every morning at around 11 a.m. they stop for tea: not normal tea, but beef tea, mixed with a pint of sherry and made in an ancient jug that is also enshrined in Academy folklore. It's served by the senior Red Collar – a uniformed official who looks after security, liaises with the public and probably evolved from the liveried footmen employed when the gallery was an eighteenth-century town house – to a mixed reception. It's salty and old-fashioned, and nobody has researched whether judging patterns change after drinking it. 'The fact there's a pint of sherry in there suggests the tradition goes back a long way,' observed my mole. 'You can imagine, pre-central heating in April or earlier, those rooms would have been cold. You needed something to warm you up. It's alcoholic Bovril, really, served with Bath Oliver biscuits. Though you can have normal tea and biscuits instead.'

Sherry, Bath Olivers, leather swivel stools: I tried to banish the image of the Sorting Hat in *Harry Potter*, but failed when I found that instead of saying 'Yes' or 'No', the President of the Academy holds up one of two sticks, one with an X ('Reject') and the other with a D ('Doubtful'). The Rejects have an X chalked on them and are returned to the Vaults to await collection. The Doubtfuls ascend to the galleries, ready for the hang. It was remarkably similar to the selection process for the Preview Party and is enshrined in a piece of doggerel writted by an anonymous artist:

> It's left their view almost as soon as in it –
> They damn them at the rate of three a minute –
> Scarce time for even faults to be detected,
> The cross is chalked: – 'tis flung aside 'REJECTED'.[2]

The party I attended that night would have amazed Georgian or Victorian London. A Jeff Koons sculpture dominated the courtyard, shimmering as though it had been doused in petrol and refracting coloured images of the facades around. It dwarfed the familiar statue of Sir Joshua Reynolds, frozen in mid-brushstroke with a palette in his left hand and draped – as he always is during the Summer Exhibition – with a garland of cheery fake spring flowers. The Academy's first president was, I noted with interest, wearing a fine example of a pre-Brummellian three-piece suit, with a frock coat, long waistcoat and knee breeches. Inside there was a buzz of conversation and a rustle of dresses ascending the carpeted stairs. At the top, lines of Royal Academy staff were dealing with queues of party-goers paying for works they had already bought. Had I wanted to buy something I would have missed the chance due to my fascination with trivial celebrity culture: a rash of red dots had swept the galleries, mainly infecting the work of established Academicians and invited big-name artists, but also the popular prints and the smaller, more affordable works.

The Summer Exhibition is frequently mocked by the art world – uneasy, perhaps, at such proximity to reality – but I found the sheer jumble of work a delight. There were showstoppers like the Central Hall, hung entirely with photographs, which contained images by the Cambridge photographer Michael Vogt, blending industrial and ancient interiors – the new and the old, all impermanent – and cavernous Gallery III had been curated by the Academicians Tony Bevan and Christopher Le Brun as a traditional 'salon hang' with pictures packed onto walls of basalt grey. All around the big names was a vast flotilla of works by the unfamous and the unacknowledged: some were extraordinary, some quite awful, some were wacky, some predictable. When you found something amazing it felt truly special, a personal triumph. It was like shopping at TK Maxx.

Lots of us wanted to see a work by Cornelia Parker – the English sculptor famous for blowing up her garden shed – who had squashed flat thirty silver sugar basins and hung them from wires in a gleaming, levitating line, so you wondered what memories of vicarage tea parties, summit meetings and flirtations they held. But getting just as much attention was an open coffin made of animal bones, decorated with symbols made of found objects – old batteries, buttons – by Olu Shobowale, a Nigerian north Londoner who was not known at all. I imagined him queueing with his coffin on Burlington Gardens. The architecture section had a model of an exquisite Art Nouveau staircase designed and built for a private house using computers. You could have stayed a week and not seen it all. Also, right now there was a pulsating, A-listers' cocktail party in the way.

A focal point of the Preview Party is food and drink, which was themed in different galleries – Mediterranean, Asian, Middle Eastern – and served from island bars. One of the Jagger girls, tall and toothy, was assiduously grazing for canapés with a friend. Down long arched vistas, oddly familiar figures – Judi Dench, Salman Rushdie, Jaime Winstone – could be seen drifting past with glasses. Nibbling yakitori on bamboo skewers, I eavesdropped on conversations about parking, school fees, builders and occasionally art. On my second circuit I found Eileen Cooper sitting on a viewing seat chatting to her son and his girlfriend. She was an artist herself, she explained, and had often submitted work to the Exhibition.

'She's being modest,' said a blonde woman, leaning over, 'I'm her agent and she's the Keeper here. The first woman ever.' The Keeper may sound like a defensive position in quidditch but it's one of four officers of the Academy – in this case, the person who liaises between the council and the schools, like an artist crossed with a school principal – and this year Eileen had been on the selection committee for the Summer Exhibition for the first time. I asked her to tell me what it was like and she said I could come in for an interview one day and see her studio in the schools.

For now what interested me was the hang – the arrangement of paintings on the walls. The first-floor galleries of the Royal Academy are classical in style, intimidating in scale and usually painted in a Georgian palette of sages, doves and clarets. Sydney Smirke – architect of the British Museum and the RHS garden at Kensington – added them to Burlington House specifically with the Summer Exhibition in mind. I had been told that as show time approached, the floor of each room was taped out to the same proportions as the walls and works laid out in a horizontal facsimile of the hang. The Academician in charge of the room could climb up one of the art handlers' wheeled ladders to peer down and rearrange works as he or she saw fit. The handlers moved pieces as directed, then hung them on the walls. It's then that the arguments begin, when two Academicians covet the same work for their space, for instance, or feel that their own work has been slighted. Heated words may be exchanged. And everything is D for Doubtful until final approval by the committee on Sanctioning Day.

'Ah yes, there have always been fights,' said Mark Pomeroy, the Royal Academy's archivist. 'It's always been fraught with rivalry, mainly because of wall space. There have been some wonderful arguments.' It was the morning of the Preview Party and Mark was in the soothing, clublike surroundings of the RA Library, protected by oak panelling and oversized eighteenth-century books from the bang and crash of party preparations outside. I wanted to know how the status of the annual exhibition had changed.

'When the Summer Exhibition started, Britain had just won the Seven Years' War,' he said. 'There was huge economic growth just before the Industrial Revolution so there was enough demand to sustain an artistic community in Britain – the first time that had happened. The Summer Exhibition had a monopoly for a long time; until 1805/6 it was the only major exhibition of contemporary art in Britain, so a public developed around it.' When the exhibition first opened it attracted 14,000 people. At its peak, in the 1850s, 350,000 people came to see it. There was another attraction besides the art: there was the chance to see the celebrities of the age, in the shape of royalty and people of fashion. The royal family were patrons – the Queen still is – and had their own private view with members of the court, duly mentioned in the court circular and the press.

'The thing is, that's all it was,' said Mark, 'nothing much happened. So all the energy became focused on the Annual Dinner, a sumptuous banquet to which all the (male) Academicians were invited. It gave them a chance to hobnob with powerful and rich patrons. It grew so much in popularity that in the early nineteenth century it gradually split into two events. You still had the Annual Dinner, which was held in the galleries and was very much an Establishment occasion, with officers of state, the military, the church, royalty and so on. But then you had the Private View, when a few "select friends" were allowed to creep in after the royal family had left. This gradually became an annual event, aristocratic women were admitted and the press soon picked up on it. It wasn't so much a shared social experience as a chance for people to bring friends and family and wander about as a group, looking at the paintings. It was more clannish, really.'

The clannish bit sounded familiar: no one – bar me and a few racing buffs – attended season events alone. Normal people came as part of a group, a miniature exclusion zone of its own, which then formed connections with other groups deemed appropriate or desirable to know. But the simple splitting in two of that all-male, closed-shop event was the thin end of the wedge, a weakening of the Academy Establishment. For as all season events would begin to find, open the door an inch and people would take a mile. In other words, there was no stopping the rise of the middle class.

As the ambitious and pugnacious Hogarth knew, in the eighteenth century art buying was the preserve of the aristocracy. Well-born young men did the Grand Tour through Europe's cultural capitals as part of their education, buying, if they could afford it, as they went. They may not have bought wisely, but they bought, partly to fill the public rooms of their increasingly large houses. As time went on, though, a new type of buyer emerged, a patron enriched by the boom in manufacturing and other industries outside London. Increasingly this was where the desire for art was to be found.

While most middle-class people aspired to buy oil paintings, those who couldn't might be able to afford a print. The print market, already well established, boomed. By the late nineteenth century some of the most voracious buyers at the Summer Exhibition were dealers looking for subjects to be steel engraved and sold in their millions across Europe. Magazines such as the *Illustrated London News* and *The Graphic* became famous for publishing engravings of hit paintings within a week of the exhibition's opening – just as we do now, when catwalk looks turn up in Top Shop or on Asos.com – an incredible feat accomplished by a group of men, often with fine-art training, known as the 'Black-and-White' artists. The print market would collapse spectacularly when photography arrived.

Mark led the way downstairs, to the elegant enfilade of eighteenth-century rooms forming part of the original Burlington House, to see a picture on long-term loan. It was another Frith painting, finally completed in 1883, as a follow-up to *The Derby Day*. It was called *A Private View at the Royal Academy, 1881*, and while it had lost the raffish charm of its older sibling it was a fascinating social document: not only were its figures recognisable, and a fine mix of professions – politicians, painters and celebrities – their names were handily noted on the frame, including that of Frith himself.

'It's not an accurate description of the people who were there on that day,' said Mark. 'It's more what *might* have been. This is the throng, the great and good, the *beau monde*.' Dominating the canvas, appositely off-centre, was Oscar Wilde, newly down from Oxford and pontificating on the paintings (actually, he's practically the only person looking at them), with two women hanging on his every word and nearby men looking on sourly. Lily Langtry, the muse of the moment, has eschewed the rich colours of the Aesthetic Movement for a dress of creamy white simplicity. Sir John Everett Millais, the Pre-Raphaelite artist, is discussing a painting with a would-be purchaser. Frederick Leighton, the President of the Academy and the Damien Hirst of his time, is there, as is Angela Burdett-Coutts, the philanthropic heiress, and John Tenniel, the illustrator of Lewis Carroll's *Alice* books. Gladstone is part of the crowd, so is Robert Browning. Even Benjamin Disraeli makes a posthumous appearance – he had just died – as a portrait on the wall.

If you look away from the personalities, the walls hold a prime example of a salon hang. The paintings, all heavily gilt framed, reach from just above the floor to the top of the walls and the highest pictures are tilted forward, in order to be visible from below. To a modern eye, it looks chaotic. To a Victorian eye, it was freighted with significance. It was all to do with 'the line', a visual concept in existence since the Renaissance, which defined the best position for an artwork to be appreciated by the human eye.

When the Summer Exhibition was held at Somerset House, there was a physical line, a dado rail about nine feet off the floor. The perfect place for a large history painting, landscape or full-length portrait was considered to be just above it. Smaller 'cabinet paintings' – half-length portraits or small still lifes – worked best just below the line. It was a hotly contested space. 'We've got diagrams of the hang from the 1850s when famous Pre-Raphaelite paintings were about six inches above the skirting board,' said Mark with a grin. 'You could be "skied" – in this painting there's a tiny floral work about twenty-five feet off the ground – or you could be down at floor level. Even at Burlington House, which had lots of space and no dado rail, it was all about display.' It also gave the Hanging Committee some control: the Pre-Raphaelites and Joshua Reynolds, for example, regarded each other with mutual dislike, thus the group's paintings were hung, but grudgingly.

The last chance an artist had to see their work before the Exhibition began was Varnishing Day, so called because it was often necessary to add a last-minute layer of varnish if the pigment had dulled. This was the moment of reckoning, when you finally judged your work against everyone else's. J.M.W. Turner, who entered the Academy schools at the age of fourteen, was famous for his flamboyant Varnishing Day antics: later in life they became almost performances in themselves, for an audience of admiring artists. He was not above blatant competition, either: in 1832, when his old rival John Constable submitted *The Opening of Waterloo Bridge*, blazing with gold and silver, with flags and bunting picked out in vermilion and lake, entirely outshining the subtle grey Turner seascape hung next to it, the maestro appeared and, according to Mark, 'loaded his brush with pigment and blotted in a little buoy in red on the waves. It was just enough to distract people from Constable's painting. Constable was furious.'

Over the years, as the show opened up to the public, its two semi-private events became bastions of exclusivity. The Annual Dinner was politically significant, used as an opportunity for the government to outline policy, particularly on the arts. In one year alone, five serving or former prime ministers attended and in the early twentieth century the key speech, usually by a minister, used to be broadcast on the radio. Older Academicians still remember Winston Churchill doing it drunk when they were children and Alfred Munnings, the equine artist and a notorious conservative, set the Academy's reputation back for decades when he delivered a broadside against modern art and artists in one of his after-dinner efforts. As for the Private View, it was in the fashion columns long before Frith's painting and was soon a spectacle just as rich as the exhibition itself. The press were invited from the 1850s onwards and milled about in the glamorous crowd, scribbling away.

In many ways almost nothing has changed. Sanctioning Day is still the moment when the President and Committee walk through the exhibition to approve it, after which nothing changes and the catalogue is printed. There is still a very grand Annual

Dinner, attended by the cultural rather than social elite: while you do see the odd politician, it would be rare to see anyone from the military or the church. However, it is still formal – black tie, these days – and takes place in Gallery III, the largest of all the rooms, and the guests sit at tables studded with small bronzes from the Academy's collection and surrounded by paintings, possibly their own.

There are two Varnishing Days, one for members, which includes pickled walnuts and dry sherry before lunch, and one for non-members, which features a jaunty steel band in the courtyard and a grand procession over the road for a service and address at the Academy church of St James's Piccadilly. There are three days of private views, mainly for Academicians and Friends. There is a Buyers' Day, to which some ladies still wear hats. Then the doors open to the public and remain so for the entire three months of the season. The only modern addition is the Preview Party.

I visited Eileen after the Exhibition was over, to see exactly what the admissions income was funding. A Red Collar led the way along echoing arched corridors at the back of the building, dimly lit and lined with drawings chests and paraphernalia. A life class was under way, overlooked by 'Mr Legg', one of the Academy's famous plaster casts. He was a Chelsea Pensioner who murdered a fellow veteran and was hanged in 1801. His body was crucified, cast in plaster and hung on a cross, because Academicians wanted to know if Renaissance depictions of the crucified Christ were accurate in terms of musculature. Another cast (nicknamed Smugglarius because he was thought to have been hanged for smuggling) came from the perfect physique of a criminal taken from Tyburn gallows in the 1770s and arranged in the pose of a famous Roman sculpture. These, and the skulls and other curios in dusty cabinets, were a direct connection from the modern schools to their eighteenth-century roots. Another, of course, was the shuffling line of hopefuls outside every spring.

Eileen smiled. 'For all its faults, and believe me, Academicians are always discussing its strengths and weaknesses, the Summer Exhibition is the moment when the artists take over the Academy, it's when they become most involved. Some people think it's a monster that should be squashed, but it is unique and it is democratic. Where else could you get a Hockney hanging in the same room as something by somebody's grandfather?'

Eileen herself, who had come down from the north as a young student in the 1960s and slowly found success as an artist, debunked any clichés of hidebound Academicians. She was warm and open and one of her roles was to help select seventeen postgraduate students from six hundred annual applicants, to spend three years at the schools without any fees, thanks to the Summer Exhibition. 'The student selection is probably the most important thing we do,' she said, 'but it is honestly an incredible thing, being on the panel for the Summer Show. You sit there and the work comes in. It never stops. It's amazing how you get your eye in. You begin to know really quickly what's going to work and what's not.'

I asked about the beef tea and she started laughing. It was, she said, 'quite addictive or quite awful, depending on which way you look at it'. It seemed a perfect analogy for the Summer Exhibition.

8

THE MERRY MONARCH SHOWS
HIS SERIOUS SIDE

'Keep up, keep up!' said the compact figure in black Levis, a checked shirt and a bran-coloured tweed tie, striding across the tussocky grass of Newmarket Heath. 'Feel how much harder the ground is, there, see?'

It was eight o'clock in the morning and Sir Mark Prescott, who runs the Heath House training yard in Newmarket, was already three hours and two cigars into his working day. He had marked up his copy of the *Racing Post* with a fluorescent pen, listed the day's runners, issued instructions to his jockeys across the country and watched twenty-two of his horses walk and trot around the indoor school in an oddly calming, ferociously focused silence. Now he was up on the gallops, the famous outdoor training grounds spread across 600 acres of heath, to watch them run.

I was in Newmarket for the *Daily Telegraph*, writing about the

Jockey Club Rooms. The Jockey Club – until relatively recently the ruling body of racing – was founded in the Star & Garter on Pall Mall in the eighteenth century. It soon moved seventy miles north to Newmarket, which was already seen as the home of the sport, and when it returned to London in the 1960s it kept its Newmarket base. The Rooms occupy an elegant sprawl of redbrick buildings off the High Street, including the original coffee house built by the founders in 1752. You can't normally get in as a non-member, but racing is seasonal and for parts of the year the nineteen bedrooms were underused. They had decided to try opening them up to paying guests, though only outside what they referred to as the 'sacrosanct periods' of race meetings and blood-stock sales. It was a stroke of luck: the Turf, with its aristocratic roots and obsession with speed, formed the backbone of the season. I was dying to get to Newmarket and pick its racing brains.

The town is remarkably small and remarkably unromantic. It is not geared up for tourists: it feels workmanlike, like the campus of a horse university, and its residents barely notice the strings of leggy thoroughbreds trotting through the streets, or the diminutive jock-eys and stable lads – the term refers to men and women, many of whom will be as young as sixteen and hoping to become top jock-eys – upon them. There are over sixty yards, an equine hospital, a parentage testing lab for horses, Tattersall's sale yards, eighty studs (including the National Stud), the National Horseracing Museum, saddlers, farriers, vets and shops selling equipment from back braces to patent leather racing saddles weighing under ten ounces.

What amazed me about Heath House was its discipline. It was almost military. When I arrived at about six, the stable lads were mucking out and grooming. There was no bantering about the night before, no sharing of hangovers. 'I've never been late for work in my life,' said Sir Mark. 'They get one chance and it has to be a bloody good reason. Then they're out.' As the horses thudded past under the artificial light, the lads called quietly: 'One cough, sir', 'Three coughs, sir', 'No coughs, sir'. Coughing, he explained, not taking his eyes off the passing animals, was one of the first signs of illness. A sick horse was quarantined immediately. It was a reminder that these weren't his horses, they were his charges, valuable investments belonging to owners and syndicates across the country.

Up on the gallops he still watched intently, reciting names and resumés of the animals ('Useful little filly'; 'He won yesterday') as they cantered by. On the way down other strings were returning from different directions.

They have a map of the heath at the Jockey Club. It is as complex as a diagram of Heathrow and as highly organised. There are dozens of gallops on different surfaces – peat moss, grass, a soft grey all-weather substance that looks like the contents of a Hoover bag – and the trainers have to book slots to use them. As we descended the shoulder of the hill, the little town just visible below us, Sir Mark suddenly stopped. 'The grass you're standing on has been here for nearly 350 years,' he said. 'It's the same grass that was planted by King Charles II in the 1670s. Over there is where you see his sedan chair in one of the paintings in the Jockey Club.'

He was right: I found it on the wall of the Morning Room. HRH's sedan was parked like a seventeenth-century Tardis, high on the buff-coloured hill, with horses dashing to and fro, legs splayed fore and aft like rocking horses loose from their runners. The Jockey Club's equine art collection is sensational, containing works by everyone from George Stubbs to Sir Alfred Munnings, but the most charming were these early paintings from the days when perspective had barely taken hold – in Newmarket, at least –

and anatomy was a newish discipline in the horse world. The jockeys were grooms and there were tall 'rubbing houses', almost like sail-less windmills, where the sweating horses could be rubbed down with straw. It seemed incredible to me that these simple contests between horses in a quiet corner of England had become a multibillion-pound industry today.

Newmarket is too far from London and too specialised to be part of the main social season, but it does start off the flat-racing year in late April with the 2,000 Guineas Stakes and 1,000 Guineas Stakes, opening again for the week of the July Cup and again in the autumn. It has two separate courses, both built in the seventeenth century on either side of an ancient and mysterious earthwork – the much-painted Devil's Dyke – and even today the grandstands are relatively modest in scale. If somebody says they are going to Newmarket they are generally from East Anglia, into racing, or both. Its race meetings are dressy occasions, but they are not about high fashion. London and its flashy race-goers seem very distant.

King Charles II's courtiers probably felt the same, but more so, as they packed their things for the long slog to Newmarket. The Stuart monarchs were excellent horsemen and, judging by contemporary accounts, were well aware they looked more impressive on a horse than off. It was Charles's grandfather James I, King of Scots for thirty-six years by the time he came to the English throne, who found Newmarket a handy stop-off on his long journeys between Edinburgh and London. It was no coincidence that it was hard by good hunting country: he first came in February 1604 and went hare coursing on the heath. He took lodgings, later building a large racing palace and establishing spring and autumn meetings. The town was already known for its informal 'matches' – when one horse raced against another – and in 1622 the first recorded horse race was run between animals owned by Lord Salisbury and the Marquis of Buckingham for the colossal wager of a hundred guineas.

Charles I continued the Stuart interest in Newmarket, but it was his son, restored to the throne in 1660, who really loved it. He rode in – and won – the Town Plate, the oldest extant horse race in the world and the first run to written rules. He made the entire court decamp there twice a year, much to their disgust. Even by the late seventeenth century the journey from London was hard. Courtiers were forced to rent rooms and live in some discomfort, or commute up with the King from Audley End in Essex. Charles also built himself a palace: two elegant symmetrical pavilions, one for him and one for Queen Catherine, connected by a range of staterooms. The King's Pavilion still stands. It's called Palace House and is a handsome town house made of tiny, blush-pink bricks, with the earliest example of a counter-balanced sash window in Britain and magnificent stables – the most venerable in the country, though largely rebuilt – lying semi-derelict over the road. Between them they represent the royal touch that turned racing from a rural pastime into a glamorous pursuit for the super-rich.

Chris Garibaldi, the director of the National Horseracing Museum, has an office in Palace House and took me across the road to see the stables. By 2015, if the final 25 per cent of funding comes in, they will house the museum and a charity that retrains racehorses, complete with four-legged residents. Charles's stables now lie beneath an Edwardian rebuild by the Rothschild family – this was their Newmarket base for many years – and some original cornicing, made of a friable chalkstone called Suffolk clunch, has been ingeniously cut up and recycled for the stable stairs. When the Rothschilds sold up it became a trainer's yard and after that increasingly derelict and vandalised. Now it had an air of expectation about it: looseboxes stood as they had been left forty years ago: buckets hung on a rail, numbers were painted beside each saddle rack, iron mangers were intact.

'The whole site was used by the royal family until late in the eighteenth century,' explained Chris, 'then the Prince of Wales, later George IV, was accused by the Jockey Club of instructing one of his jockeys to pull a race. He maintained until the end of his life it was all above board, but they found against him and he left Newmarket in high dudgeon, sold his interests here and moved his whole racing operation to Brighton.' If this was a blow, the town didn't show it. The bi-annual invasions of courtiers may have stopped but the racing went on and at the end of the century the portly figure of another Prince of Wales, later Edward VII, hove into view. It sounded as though royal influence had turned Newmarket into a resort town – Bath, say, but with horses instead of waters – and it did have a mini-season of dances in the Assembly Rooms and racing house parties. But Chris was quick to point out that Charles II, however licentious his manner, was not all about fun: he had made a significant contribution to early English racing.

'The reason it's called the Sport of Kings is not just the Merry Monarch stuff, Charles knocking about with Nell Gwynn in Newmarket,' he said. 'His interest in the selective breeding of race-horses was a lot about his interest in improving the bloodstock to replace cavalry horses lost during the Civil Wars. It was about securing his position as monarch. Over the next 120 years or so the sport of racing hived off as a sort of entertainment, but its origins were grounded in the arts of war. Horses are power. And that theme survives incredibly late: the National Stud, at the other end of Newmarket, was given to the nation for the improvement of cavalry stock prior to the First World War. Once you get that, you realise that racing's not just a sport. It's a sport that is central to our national narrative.'

I thought back to the long races Michael Church had mentioned before the Derby was first run. They were tests of stamina – run for miles with multiple heats – which is exactly what you would need from a cavalry horse. It was the admixture of more delicate foreign blood, the dished-nosed, slender-legged horses of Arabia and North Africa, which turned our native bloodstock into the greyhounds of the horse world. Rather late in the day it occurred to me that until the arrival of the motorcar the horse was the fastest vehicle on earth. The equivalent today is Formula One.

Back in the Jockey Club I picked up what I thought was an onyx and brass ashtray on the mantelpiece, only to find I was holding a horse's hoof. It was the sort of thing I would have expected to find in Catholic Spain, or Malta, like saints' hair or nails sealed into reliquaries. The brass lid was inscribed 'St Simon. Foaled 1881, died 1908. Winner of the Ascot Gold Cup 1884'. One great racing name, the Duke of Portland, had presented it to another, King Edward VII. It was beautifully polished, with a pearly translucence like alabaster. There were three other hooves there as well – enough for a whole horse – with gleaming lids, all inscribed with the sort of pedigree and performance detail that the racing world delights in.

The guide in the National Horseracing Museum next door laughed when I asked her about them. 'Hooves are nothing!' she said, gesturing at the head of Persimmon, one of St Simon's most successful sons, peering over a stable door from a display case. Both door and head were real. 'People are shocked because they think it's a trophy,' she added, 'but it's a sign of devotion, really, from the owners to their animals.' It seemed more than that to me. You wouldn't stuff a dog. It was a marker of success, as if they couldn't quite let their winner go. Even to me hoof ashtrays seemed oddly morbid, like Victorian death masks. And I was brought up Catholic.

Whole libraries of books have been written about thoroughbreds and their bloodlines, but the museum had a simple circular chart. It is said – though not everyone agrees – that all thoroughbreds derive from three Arabian stallions, the Byerley Turk, the Godolphin Arabian and the Darley Arabian. The Byerley Turk was a warhorse imported into late seventeenth-century Ireland. It has never been proved, sadly, that the Godolphin Arabian was found pulling a cart in Paris, but he was certainly imported from France in 1729. The Darley Arabian was bought while his owner was on campaign against the Ottomans in Aleppo. They were small next to native British horses, with powerful hindquarters, long legs, markedly arched necks and small heads. Crossbreeding was by accident, rather than intention. We do know for sure that 80 per cent of today's racehorses come from the Darley Arabian via his great-grandson, Eclipse. Their bloodlines have been recorded in painstaking, if not to say terrifying, detail.

All was quiet in Newmarket that week because there was no racing. I drove out to the racecourse (or racecourses, rather) anyway. Charles II built the first, an inverted boomerang now known as the July Course, before realising the sun was right in the jockeys' eyes in spring and autumn. So he caused an alternative finishing stretch to be built, widening the boomerang's angle. This is the Rowley Mile, named either after the King's favourite hack, or after a stallion at the Royal Stud. The King himself was nicknamed 'Old Rowley', perhaps in sly reference to his hectic love life. And while he never produced a legitimate heir, one of his many natural sons was the first Duke of Richmond, whose descendants would eventually build the magnificent racecourse on the Downs at Goodwood.

I'll never get over the sheer size of racecourses, the wide swathe of tough green grass stretching into the distance, flanked by white post-and-rails and stands of trees, the colony of grandstands and maintenance buildings clustered near the finish and, in Newmarket's case, huge open spaces all round. This is where the first starting stalls were used and the first photo finish took place and the first Tote appeared. It calls itself, unchallenged, 'The Home of Racing'. The older buildings were low with red-brick walls and gabled roofs, which gave them the cosy look of a colonial farm. Again, the whole thing felt like a theatre before a performance, with its thousands of seats and smart parade ring and VIP areas and food stands all empty and silent.

Before leaving I stopped at the National Stud, an estate of deep-roofed white buildings and immaculate emerald paddocks built in the 1930s. It had been started in Ireland between the wars to provide lightweight cavalry horses to the British Government, before moving to its purpose-built Newmarket facility. Mares and foals were stabled far away from the stallions to prevent the spread of disease. Stallions were separated so they wouldn't fight. I was curious about the Covering Room, the combat arena, as it were, where the nation's thoroughbred gene pool was once ensured. It was padded all over, with woodchips on the floor and rubber walls. There was a huge pair of rubber bootees for the mare's back feet, so she wouldn't injure the stallion if she lashed out. On the wall hung twitches – sticks with loops of twine – used from time immemorial to twist the mare's upper lip, releasing endorphins to calm her down. They used to have a film here showing a covering, a sort of equine *Boogie Nights*, but it is now considered 'inappropriate' and has been quietly suppressed.

Edward VII was far less squeamish: he had a staircase built up to his suite of rooms at the Jockey Club so his mistresses could visit –

or so he could slip away to see them, perhaps, gossip being the only thing that travels faster than racehorses in Newmarket. The King's Suite is in a separate wing to the main building and the upper corridor connecting the two is affectionately known as the Rogues' Gallery. It is lined with portraits of members past and present, starting with engravings adorned with a single aristocratic name: Devonshire; Northampton; Portland. Then come photographs signed Pilkington and Rothschild – the industrialists and plutocrats – and finally, by the 1970s, the first sheikhs and women. 'As you progress down the corridor you see a change in where the money is coming from, where the wealth is sitting,' Chris Garibaldi told me. 'It's moving with the agricultural depression of the 1890s from the great aristocratic households to the mercantile trading class, the bankers and industrialists. It's a story of power shifting from land to commerce.' It was a story replicated right across the season, in event after event.

There are many legacies remaining from the reign of King Charles II. Bloodstock was just one: he left a magnificent art collection, founded the Royal Observatory and the Royal Hospital Chelsea, supported the Royal Society, re-established theatre, allowed women to act and, arguably, pioneered the three-piece suit. He bequeathed us a royal family who have often seemed more at home with horses than with humans, so much so that we never think twice about the fact that two of them have Olympic and European eventing medals and the Queen, who reads *Sporting Life* weekly and the *Racing Post* daily, was Trooping the Colour on horseback until she was sixty, something a modern monarch may never do again.

Charles also linked, for the first time, the rhythms of the English sporting year with the perambulations of the court. Winter was a time to stay in the country and hunt. When the roads were dry in the summer, everybody set off to the races at Newmarket, an exercise repeated each autumn. In between his courtiers settled in London, concentrating on the governance of the realm and socialising. Gradually, this period began to be referred to in sporting terms. It was beginning to become 'the season'.

9

THE BUTTERFLIES EMERGE

There is a portrait of Margaret, Duchess of Argyll, hanging in Tate Britain, painted around 1931 by a fashionable society artist called Gerald Leslie Brockhurst. The Duchess, then aged nineteen and still Miss Margaret Whigham, had just finished a triumphant season as Debutante of the Year. Two years later she would marry the dashing American amateur golfer Charles Sweeny in a Brompton wedding that attracted such crowds that central London came to a standstill. The portrait is extraordinarily sophisticated, more suited to a 40-year-old than an ingénue. She stands facing the artist, set against a background of charcoal-grey skies and forbidding hills – probably the landscape of her beloved Scotland – and if you step well back her face, pale and dark-eyed, looks like a skull. Her dark hair is short and fashionably shingled and she is wearing a black velvet jacket embroidered with foliage of old gold. Later in her life she would look like the Wicked Queen from *Snow White*. At this age, she has the same brittle chic as Wallis Simpson – she's just a lot better-looking.

'Until 1930, a débutante had been a person any man over the age of twenty would run a mile from,' she wrote in her autobiography. 'The prevailing image ... was that of a painfully shy mouse, lacking both make-up and conversation. Suddenly and unaccountably, all this changed. The girls of 1930 not only had good looks: they knew how to dress; and they had far more confidence than their predecessors. All at once the well-known married beauties, who held sway in London society, began to feel threatened ...'[1] For 'the girls of 1930' think 'Margaret Whigham': she would go on to have two marriages and numerous liaisons and to provide the second biggest sexual scandal of the 1960s after the Profumo Affair.

When I found her autobiography on a friend's bookshelf, I immediately balanced it on its spine. It fell open three-quarters of the way through, on the well-thumbed pages concerning her divorce from Ian Campbell, the 11th Duke of Argyll. She magisterially omits to mention what really made her notorious: when her husband sued for divorce – a scandal in itself in 1963 – the prosecution produced Polaroid pictures of the duchess fellating an individual who, because his face was out of frame, became known as 'The Headless Man'. The newspapers could hardly believe their luck. All the Duchess was wearing in her Art Deco bathroom at home at 48 Upper Grosvenor Street, it was reported, was a three-strand pearl necklace.

Today it all sounds hilarious, but it ruined her. Her husband had accused her of adultery with numerous men and the judge (male, of course) delivered an excoriating verdict. Like everyone else, I couldn't resist reading about it, mesmerised as much by her towering ego as the racy goings-on of the fast set. Even her book title had a characteristic sting in the tail: it was called *Forget Not*, a direct translation of the Latin Campbell motto *Ne Obliviscaris*. But I genuinely did want to find out about her life as one of the undoubted stars of the last generation to come out – the phrase meant a girl's transition from the schoolroom to Society – in the formal manner, before the Second World War swept all the old rituals away.

The roots of those rituals were very old, although the word 'débutante' – from the French, meaning someone making a first appearance – was not really used until Georgian times. Once it was, the acute accent gradually became optional: it was a thoroughly English tradition. As far back as the reign of Queen Anne, and no doubt long before, this rite of passage for an aristocratic girl reaching adulthood had involved a formal introduction to the monarch. Originally her parents simply brought her to court, richly dressed and clearly virginal, to announce her presence in the marriage market. Once the passage of the court between town and country was established under the Stuarts, it made sense to have these presentations early in the season, in the spring, as everyone arrived back in Town.

The season itself was changing. Under William and Mary – King James II's Protestant daughter and her Dutch prince, brought over at the instigation of Parliament to replace her Catholic father – two significant developments took place. One was Parliament's insistence on fixed sittings. Having risked their necks by inviting the joint monarchs to rule, they were not falling for the old Stuart trick of dissolving Parliament except when in need of funds. The other was the introduction of the first turnpike roads, thus making long-distance travel easier.

Until the late seventeenth century, roads were the responsibility of local parishes, which had little incentive to maintain them.

Travelling by carriage was appallingly uncomfortable: exposed 'high roads' had to be taken in winter, to avoid sinking into mud and ice in the valleys, and it was so cold that coachmen's boots were nailed to the vehicle's roof so they didn't freeze and fall off – the origin, a carriage driver once told me, of the term 'dropping off'. Taking a family to London, or a daughter to court, was simply not feasible for landowners living far from southeast England. Furthermore, the expense of a sojourn in London was ruinous.

As transport improved, however, the aristocratic families of the early eighteenth century could divide their time neatly between their country estates and grand town houses in Mayfair or St James's. Even that was not easy: the historian G. M. Trevelyan wrote of this early period in his *English Social History*[2]: 'The London season was over by the first week in June when people of fashion dispersed to their country homes or adjourned to Bath. A longer residence in town would have ruined many families who had strained a point to bring their daughters to the marriage market.'

Even by the second half of the century the London season was still short and intense. The social whirl was orchestrated, or regulated, by a formidable bunch of women known as the Lady Patronesses – the very ones who dominated the London Horticultural Society's early public breakfasts. Famous hostesses such as Viscountess Castlereagh, the Countess of Jersey, Countess de Lieven and Countess Esterházy – all members of the Prince Regent's 'Carlton House Set' – wielded supreme control over the fashionable midweek balls at Almack's, the assembly rooms on King Street in St James's. Only those of whom they approved – authentic and generally titled members of the *ton* – could purchase annual vouchers for entry. The very word 'voucher' implied personal approval, the fact that your social status had been vouched for by a powerful other. They could be withdrawn from anyone who fell from favour, which meant public humiliation. Here surely were the origins of the enclosure: invisible forces that kept the chosen few in and drove others to try and enter. Even the Duke of Wellington was once turned away for being inappropriately dressed.

It was against this broad background that a couple of charismatic women came out and lived much of their adult lives. One was Georgiana, Duchess of Devonshire, born Georgiana Spencer and part of the Whig aristocracy. The other was the reckless charmer Jane Digby, Lady Ellenborough, who was thought racy for the time – which was really going some – despite being married to the Governor General of India. She married three times before ending up with the love of her life, a dignified Syrian sheikh.

When Georgiana was nine, her family moved into the only example of a private eighteenth-century aristocratic town house – a palace, really – that still exists in London. Spencer House, just off St James's, opens to the public on summer Sundays and was completed in 1766 for her father John, the 1st Earl Spencer. Its elegant Palladian facade overlooks Green Park and it was built to impress, inside and out. Guests arriving for balls and parties entered a hall built to resemble the Temple of Jupiter in Rome, its frieze of ox skulls signifying festivity and death. They swept up stairs under a barrel-vaulted ceiling decorated with charming plasterwork flowers to the *piano nobile*, the suite of staterooms on the first floor.

The staterooms were designed by James 'Athenian' Stuart in the latest neo-classical style. The Great Room had a coffered ceiling in green, gold and white, and Stuart himself decorated the Painted Room, which had an apse and elegant columns, in 'the antique manner'. It is still one of the most celebrated eighteenth-century interiors in England. It conveys, as it was meant to, that the Spencers were both cultivated and spectacularly wealthy. The diamond buckles alone on the shoes John Spencer wore on his honeymoon cost the equivalent of around £30,000 today. The expense of bringing their daughters out would not have been an issue. At Spencer House Georgiana's presentation was planned like a battle campaign, from her colossal wardrobe to rigorous training from various tutors in deportment, manners and other accomplishments. She was an instant success.

Within two years Georgiana was married to one of England's foremost dukes, a triumph for her mother, and by the turn of the century she was anxiously preparing her own seventeen-year-old girl for presentation. Her biographer, Amanda Foreman, describes the process:

> The rituals of a court presentation were extremely demanding: grace and a dignified ease were paramount – the poor execution of a curtsey could ruin a girl's first season … A debutante was required to walk slowly up to the Queen, make a deep curtsey to her knees and, if she was the daughter of a peeress, wait while Her Majesty kissed her forehead, and then rise and make another curtsey to the Queen and a smaller one to each of the royal members present, and then walk backwards out of the room, keeping her eyes on the throne.[3]

All this in a hooped dress with a three-yard long train.

For Lady Jane Digby, preparing to come out a generation later in 1824, the whole thing was agonisingly constricting. 'It would be a solecism if a girl not yet out in Society or even one in her first season went for a gallop in the park,' observes one of her biographers drily,[4] describing Jane's stultifying round of shopping with her mother – silk gloves, dancing slippers, white ostrich feathers, sprigged muslin – and riding out, safely chaperoned, at the fashionable hour of 5 p.m. on Hyde Park's Rotten Row, 'a prime shop window in the marriage market'. The dozens of dresses required – for morning, evening, 'walking out', dancing and riding – and the cloaks and headgear that went with them would, it was hoped, form the basis of a marriage trousseau. Jane made her debut at a Royal Drawing Room in March 1824, curtseying to George IV. She met Lord Ellenborough in April at Almack's and was married within the year.

It is difficult for us today to conceive quite how small, and quite how interconnected, the British aristocracy used to be – and quite how much power it wielded. In terms of the season, it seemed important to know. If the system was so impenetrable, guarded at every point by formidable hostesses, primogeniture and court strictures, it seemed remarkable that it had not only survived into the twenty-first century but had clearly expanded along the way. Finding precise numbers was surprisingly hard, though the historian G. E. Mingay mentions 'some 400 families who could be described as great landlords ... able to meet the expenses of the London season, to act as patrons of the turf and the arts ...'[5] in eighteenth century English and Welsh society, describing the great house and the London season as the two great status symbols of landowners. I thought of Michael Church and his reference books on equine bloodlines. That was the sort of information I needed.

The College of Arms is the official repository of human pedigrees for England, Wales, Northern Ireland and the Commonwealth. It is a large C-shaped building set back behind black and gold wrought-iron gates in the City of London. It sits just at the point where dreary Queen Victoria Street swoops up and away from the River Thames and overlooks St Benet Paul's Wharf, the Heralds' church, which was built by Sir Christopher Wren.

This is where you go to check your quarterings, petition for a coat of arms or have arms designed. When the Duchess of Cambridge, formerly Kate Middleton, married Prince William, the College designed for her family a scalloped lozenge with three acorns to signify the three Middleton siblings: oak leaves for the woods of her Chilterns home, a golden chevron for her mother's maiden name, Goldsmith, and white chevronets to reflect 'the alps and the family's love of skiing'. It dangled from a pretty blue ribbon, showing she was unmarried. It looks remarkably like an enclosure badge.

Since their incorporation in the fifteenth century, Heralds have been the keepers of the records of who is really who in Britain. The system originated in the simple need to identify nobles fighting in battles or competing in tournaments: coats of arms evolved from their helmet crests and shields. There are six Heralds for England, Wales and Northern Ireland, who run their own practices under the umbrella of the College, like barristers. Some indeed are lawyers. They are part of the Royal Household and appear on formal occasions in embroidered tabards and flat velvet hats. Below them are four Pursuivants and above them are three Kings of Arms. At the very top is the Earl Marshal, one of two Great Officers of State, a hereditary position held by the Duke of Norfolk. Much of their work involves the elegant language of heraldry, medieval French.

I had an appointment to see the Lancaster Herald, Robert Noel. The whole class thing was bothering me. However hard I tried to ignore it during the season – the enclosures, after all, represent a fraction of the people who go – it wouldn't go away. It was there in the marketing of the events and in the separation of different ticket holders, in the occasional flashes of furious snobbery you got from 'old hands', and the amused, sometimes bewildered comments of foreign visitors. There was also the depressing fact that many British people I talked to didn't go to things because they thought they might not be welcome, or didn't have a smart enough hat.

Everywhere I've been during my career as a travel journalist, from New York to Yogyakarta, has had a class system. The Thais have a king and the French have nobles. The Japanese Imperial Court occupies a virtual fortress in the middle of Tokyo. Why was ours world famous? Was it an intrinsic part of us, like our ability to eat picnics in the driving rain, or was it just an unusually powerful construct? The royal connection mattered to the events of the season and had probably contributed to their survival, but it was further down the pecking order that interested me: that driving need to exclude. I suppose what I really wanted to know was why people thought they had the right to be snooty. And if anyone would be able to tell me, it would be the Heralds. They're the only ones who have got it down in black and white, or rather, *sable* and *argent*. They deal in facts.

As I walked up the double flight of stone steps and into the College, a receptionist smiled a cheery greeting. Her desk was in the corner of a panelled hall, next to a canopied wooden throne enclosed on three sides by a low balustrade. This was the Earl Marshal's Court. Nearby was a table full of heraldry publications and postcards. 'If you're interested but don't want too much detail,' she said helpfully, putting a call through to say I was there, 'the big red book's rather good. It looks as though it's written for children but all the information is completely accurate.' I was holding *A Humorous Guide to Heraldry! For Little Tykes & Old Folks Alike* (its author was a fourteen-year-old American) when

Robert Noel walked in. 'Ah,' he said, looking at the book rather as a GP might if they caught you reading *The A–Z of Family Ailments* outside their surgery, 'come on through.'

The original building, he explained, burned down in the Great Fire. This one dates from the 1670s, late in the reign of Charles II. 'We're not as old as you might think,' he said with a grin, 'as Fellows from All Souls always like to tell us when they come.' All Souls was founded in Oxford in 1438. The College of Arms was first chartered in London forty-six years later. He said that it was originally involved with town planning, statistics and fringe diplomacy as much as it was with genealogy, but one important source of income for Heralds was registering the gentry, which they did on long tours of the provinces known as 'visitations'. However much the fees were resented, being on a county's Register of Gentlemen gave a man the right to sit on a jury, for instance. 'Gentleman' was broadly synonymous with 'landowner', and until the Reform Acts, only landowners could vote.

We sat in a small square room with a distant view of the river. Outside, the summer sunshine made the three-sided brick courtyard glow. On the walls were parchments dangling crusty-looking seals and floor-to-ceiling bookshelves held runs of the *The Gentleman's Magazine*, *Walford's County Families*, *Crockford's Clerical Directory*, *Kelly's Handbook to the Titled, Landed and Official Classes* and the Army, Navy and Air Force Lists.

I told him what I wanted. 'Well,' he said, 'it's all rather O-level history, but I'll have a go,' and off we went, starting with the swashbuckling Saxon ealdormen (later contracted to 'earls'), adventurers all, competing to gain favour with the squabbling Saxon kings. This was the 'proto-period', which lasted roughly from 600 to 1120. Later that century, Richard the Lionheart – who was always away on Crusades and preferred France anyway – appointed powerful deputies at home and as a result the early peers, then only earls and barons, began to grow in status as regional rulers. The later mediaeval period saw the arrival of dukes, marquesses and viscounts, completing the five ranks of peerage we have today.

At regular intervals a reassuringly solid figure would clunk onto the table, but Robert demurred when I said I wanted to put them in my book. Charles Kidd at Debrett's said the same thing. The subject is so complex, and so rooted in the mists of time, that actual numbers are like unicorns, a lovely concept but highly improbable. So put it this way: after the Norman invasion the 'peerage' probably numbered a few dozen. Wow. That really was tiny. Three hundred years later there were perhaps double that number, but this dropped after the murderous Wars of the Roses. Nothing much happened, aggrandisement-wise, under the Tudor monarchs. It was the Stuarts who shamelessly flogged titles for cash. James I forced landowners to buy baronetcies – around £1,000 each in England, much less in Scotland – and numbers crept up to the very low hundreds. Mingay mentions that before the premiership of Pitt the Younger 'the number of English peers was held fairly steady at 160 or 170...', but by Pitt's death in the early nineteenth century it had risen to nearly 300.

And that, you might think, would be that. A nice, hermetically sealed class of people at the top of the pyramid and everyone else scrabbling around beneath. That's what it was like in France, for instance, where aristocrats were barred from marrying out or working. 'They didn't pay tax, either,' said Robert, 'you were exempt if you had a certificate from the Sun King's [Louis XIV] genealogist. They neglected their estates to be at court because the King wanted them at Versailles. They were unemployed and unemployable. So they became a weight on the system, hence the French Revolution.'

Their British equivalents, however, did pay tax, could work if they really had to and could marry out – especially if pots of money were involved – ensuring a steady influx of vigorous new blood. So they didn't become moribund. In fact, they became more numerous. As public health improved and more children survived, enormous families widened the pool of the well born. Because the elder son inherited the titles, land and most of the wealth under the English system of primogeniture, the younger or less talented children dropped down into the yeoman class or ended up somewhere in between as gentry. Meanwhile, the world's first Industrial Revolution was creating a new breed of rich that was rising like cream.

It was this that was the real battleground: this was what made the Wars of the Roses look like a picnic. The English system, far from being too rigid, was *not rigid enough*, or not for the people already at the top, at least, who had to work to repel the invaders. Instead of boiling oil they used insider knowledge. For the invaders, of course, there was always a chance of infiltrating, but it was competitive, so they skirmished among themselves. Subtle, often ludicrous, distinctions in manners, dress, speech and habits arose between different shades of the middle ground. At least with the Indian caste system, however unfair, you knew where you were: in England, you had to prove it. Hence the dismal etiquette books of the 1890s, the enclosures, the dress codes, the quirks of language and behaviour – from which way you held your knife to the pronunciation of words – all of which so fascinate other nationalities.

Ferreting around in the British Library I found a 1970s PhD thesis by Leonore Davidoff, a sociology professor from the University of Essex. *The Best Circles: Society Etiquette and The Season*[6] was about the enormous social changes of the early nineteenth century and the need of the ruling elite to pull in the wagons, as it were. She described the codification of social and domestic life under the title Society and its 'accompanying calendar of events, the Season', adding that: 'Like all status groups, the traditional aristocratic elite were obsessively concerned with the question of access to their ranks.' She describes a world operating within strict parameters. The leading country families arrived in Town to attend Parliament and debate continued into the night at the mansions of the great hostesses, until they were forced to leave in late summer by the appalling stench of the Thames. By August they had fled to their estates or gone north to shoot on a new sort of playground, the grouse moor. The season had expanded into a length and form that are recognisable today.

The wheels only really began to come off in the agricultural depression of the 1880s. The historian David Cannadine writes of the last quarter of the century: 'At the very top of the pyramid were 250 territorial magnates, each with more than 30,000 acres and £30,000 a year to their name ... At the very pinnacle of this group were ... the twenty-nine prodigiously wealthy super-rich with incomes in excess of £75,000 a year.'[7] When imports from the Americas and Antipodes triggered a massive fall in land values, for the first time in British history land became a liability. The electoral franchise was widening. The public schools were moulding a powerful middle class. Presentations at court 'dramatically increased', he notes, for the Prince of Wales, later Edward VII, loved unsuitable, rich and entertaining people, and a rash of American heiresses nicknamed 'The Buccaneers' stormed the marriage market. 'Within the space of one hundred years,' Cannadine says, '[aristocrats] were to be eclipsed as the economic elite, undermined as the most glamorous social group, and superseded as the governing class.' His concluding chapter is called 'Lions into Unicorns'. Deary me.

Few people thought that deeply about it, of course. That's why novelists like Thackeray and Galsworthy are so important, because they turn an analytical, often unflattering, lens on the accepted behaviour of the day. Most people went through life doing what they, their parents and perhaps their parents' parents had always done, usually in the way they had always done it, because it was 'the thing to do'. Anyone going to a season event today is on some level buying into the whole charade, from wearing a hat to drinking champagne. We may not plan to be posh, we may not even think about it, but we do what is done. It's all part of the fun.

It wasn't fun for families less financially secure than the Spencers, who struggled to bring out their daughters as the eighteenth and nineteenth centuries wore on. The London season ate money. It demanded clothes, ladies' maids and the use of a carriage and a fashionable mount for the girl, not to mention the enormous cost of opening up a London house for a relatively short period and staffing it. No wonder as families got bigger it became acceptable to rent. Tremendous skirmishing went on as to who would get which property – there are still houses all over Mayfair, Fitzrovia and Bloomsbury that were used for the season – and the arrival of their temporary occupiers would be announced respectfully in the daily press.

From the moment a young girl reversed out of the Throne Room, she was an adult. She wore her hair up instead of down and her dresses long instead of short. Her parents would take her, for the first time, to the events of the grown-up season – Ascot, say, or the Summer Exhibition – where she would meet marriageable young men. Her shelf life was short: once 'out', the longer she remained unmarried the lower her stock would fall. There is a painful account of this in Anthony Trollope's 1874 novel *The Way*

We Live Now. Georgiana Longstaffe, out for several seasons but not yet married, is driven to desperation by her father's refusal – for financial reasons – to open their London house for the season. She goes to stay with the fantastically rich but socially dubious Melmotte family, only to be ignored by her friends in Hyde Park and quietly excluded from the best balls. When the Melmottes' star falls, so does hers. She begins the novel aiming for an earl and ends it settling for a Jewish banker twice her age. In the eyes of the world, then broadly anti-Semitic, she is finished.

By this time 'court drawing rooms' were held at St James's Palace and had moved to 10 p.m. in the evening. The *leitmotif* was modesty and innocence. Girls wore short-sleeved dresses – white, cream or palest pink – with veils and trains of a prescribed length, and three ostrich feathers pinned upright in their hair like the Prince of Wales' crest. They wore long white gloves and the simplest jewellery. A footman would call out their names and they would step forward to be presented by their mother, or a relative who had herself been presented. They still had to perform a deep curtsey in front of the throne before backing out of the room. As more people joined in, the introduction of young women to Society became not just an extension of normal adult ritual but took on an identity of its own. It became a feminine monopoly: men had sport and politics and women had daughters to dress, accomplish and marry eligibly. The debutante season in this more refined form would last for roughly a century.

By the 1930s, despite the relative formality of the court of George V, things were beginning to change. 'Evening courts' were held at 8 p.m. in the Buckingham Palace Throne Room, which still forms part of a grand suite of staterooms decorated for George IV. The lists of names in the newspapers gave way to glamorous photographs of debs and chaperones arriving at the palace, generating the sort of attention that housemates got in the early days of *Big Brother*. Their motorcars still clogged London for much of the day, inching along the Mall towards their big moment, as had their grandmothers' carriages. The wait was often so long that the occupants took books and knitting and practised heroic bladder control.

When Margaret Whigham, later Duchess of Argyll, came along – not an aristocrat, but rich upper-middle class – her looks and money swept her straight into the highest levels of British social life. Her father was a wealthy Scottish businessman, she was schooled in America and in Audley Street, and when the family took a house in Mayfair for her debutante year it was duly reported in *The Times*: 'Mr and Mrs George Hay Wigham and Miss Margaret Whigham have arrived at 6, Audley Square which they have rented for the season.'

She had far more say in her season and social life than Georgiana Spencer and Jane Digby would have had over a hundred years earlier. She could go out with men on her own. She could dash about London and stay in the country un-chaperoned. She deliberately planned her coming-out dance for 1 May, the opening day of the London season. It was, she recalled, 'a calculated risk, for once all the other debutantes had been to my dance, it was possible that their mothers would not bother to invite me to theirs'. They did, of course. She writes of her dance partners and her dozen lovely evening dresses and her day outfits for the Derby, Ascot 'and the many lunch parties to which I would be invited'. Independence was on its way, certainly, but her life would still have been familiar in many ways to girls of presentation age in Georgian London. And, like Georgiana and Jane, she was married to a man with money and status within two years.

The girls of the 1930s didn't know it, but the season they inhabited – a set of prescribed rituals leading to the peal of wedding bells, preferably at a Mayfair church – would be fatally damaged by the impending war. It would stutter along for a while longer, in a somewhat diluted form, before settling into a new reality altogether. Presentations, cancelled during the war years, would never quite regain their original élan. Meanwhile, I needed a break: the whole thing was making me claustrophobic. Luckily I had the perfect excuse to abandon the British Library: it was time for a night at the opera.

10

MUSIC ON THE MITTEL DOWNS

T he black-and-white photograph is small, a snap really, taken on the coast of France in 1904. It shows a young man in a cap at the wheel of a two-seater car, with its flap-down windows and comically upright steering. He is driving it straight up a stony beach from the sea. Behind him is the barge he has just hired to cross the English Channel, in the days before Channel ferries existed, by the simple method of attaching it to the back of a packet steamer. There is a set to him – something about the way he is heading so determinedly up the beach – that is striking. I discovered the picture in the tiny archive gallery at Glyndebourne. It went a little way to explaining the puzzling exis-tence of a full-scale opera house in the English countryside.

The Glyndebourne Opera Festival – regulars always refer to it simply as 'Glyndebourne', just as race-goers call Royal Ascot 'Ascot' and rowers call the Royal Regatta 'Henley' – takes place annually from May to August, on land owned by the Christie family near the East Sussex village of Glynde. There has been an opera house here since 1934, but in the mid-90s, sixty years to the day after the original opened, an entirely new structure was unveiled to great acclaim. It now holds over a thousand people in a contemporary horseshoe of handmade brick, concrete and recycled pine and its grey fly tower squats discreetly above the jumble of old mellow brick that is the house. This was probably once a medieval manor but today it sits among a tranquil lake, lawns and a ha-ha. Beyond rolls the gentle countryside of the South Downs, dotted with storybook sheep.

As we strolled about on the lawn before the performance began, elegantly dressed and eyeing up the rest of the audience, we could hear all around us the clink and ting of cutlery and wine glasses and see the sudden billow of gingham or white damask as tablecloths were unfurled. Glyndebourne is famed for the calibre of its music and staging, which can compete with any small opera house in Europe. Being English it is equally famed for its 'Long Interval', the hour and a half break mid-performance that allows the audience to hitch up its skirts, keep a wary eye on its starched shirtfronts and tuck into picnics of every size, shape and provenance imaginable.

Some people bring car rugs. Others roll up with tables and chairs, linen napkins, wine glasses and, occasionally, candelabra. New potatoes in warm butter are decanted from Thermos flasks and asparagus is eaten with care. I found one cheery couple encamped in the vegetable garden, with a home-made picnic on a Formica-topped folding table. He was an opera buff and their early dates had been at Glyndebourne in the 1960s. Over the decades she had learned to combine evening clothes with the sort of four-season warmth and wicking capabilities you'd expect to find in climbing gear. They said they liked a little distance from the melée.

The prestige spots overlooking the lake had long been marked out by wicker baskets and wine coolers. The lightweights – in culinary rather than cultural terms – eat in one of the three restaurants or picnic in a marquee. Holders of the cheaper tickets might have a sandwich while sitting on their jackets. It doesn't matter. The point is Baron Scarpia may scheme to seduce Tosca and Nemorino may wait for the potion he has drunk to win over Adina, but both are on hold until everybody has polished off smoked salmon, asparagus, strawberries and other summer treats served on anything from bone china to ancient Tupperware. The formally clad diners then dutifully carry all the detritus back to their cars.

John Christie, the young man in the photograph, was responsible for all this. He would later inherit Glyndebourne from his father, but in 1904 he was teaching at Eton and was in the grip of two grand passions: Richard Wagner and the petrol engine. 'He was becoming a Wagnerian,' said Julie Aries, Glyndebourne's archivist and curator, 'so he decided to drive with friends to the Wagner festival in Bayreuth. There were four of them in that car, one in a cheese crate strapped to the back, along with the spare petrol, which you bought from the chemist in those days. There were no Tarmac roads, it was appallingly dusty and the engine kept overheating.'

The Bayreuth Festival made a huge impression on Christie. The Bavarian town was home to the simple brick and stone Festspielhaus, or festival theatre, conceived by the towering nineteenth-century composer and part-funded by his patron 'Mad' King Ludwig II. It was designed to stage an annual festival of his own work, which had been running since 1876, featuring the 'Bayreuth Canon', his final ten music dramas, including the four-opera, fourteen-hour tale of Norse gods, *The Ring of the Nibelung*. Even a century ago tickets were hot. Today, people wait years to attend.

Tickets to Glyndebourne are nothing like tickets to Bayreuth, though it does take around ten years to become a full member ('Dead men's shoes,' said one middle-aged man I met who was on the list, 'and it's getting to the point whether they're his or mine'). Nevertheless, to be invited is a huge treat. I had been invited. My mate Philip is a music buff and every so often his wife cracks under the strain and a ticket for the Wigmore Hall, or occasionally Glyndebourne, falls into my lap. My part of the bargain is doing the picnic. I was writing my ingredients list the day before our visit to a production of Donizetti's *L'Elisir d'Amore*, when the phone rang.

'Hi, it's me,' said Philip.

'Hey!' I said, 'How are you?'

'Fine,' he said, evenly, 'but aren't I meant to be giving you a lift?'

There are moments in life when the world stops turning just for a second as you take in some sickening reality – being dumped, defaulting on your mortgage, failing an exam – and while I realise that getting the day wrong for Glyndebourne is a tiny blip in the great scheme of things, it's right up there in the world of social solecisms. It puts a strain on a friendship. Not just because it's expensive, but because there are so many musical people out there who would bite your arm off for the chance of a ticket. Your guilt will therefore be doubled. And you will never, ever be asked again.

How? How? kept running through my mind – the date was everywhere, electronic diary, physical diary, Post-It note on the fridge – but I told Philip very calmly that I would see him there at five o'clock. Then I rang my brother and had hysterics. Then, on his instructions, I rang a minicab, put on a dress, grabbed a selection of picnic bags, plastic plates and ice packs, raced to Victoria Station, bought half the posh food section at M&S, caught the train to Lewes and leaped in another taxi. By five, I was pouring Prosecco in the picnic tent and trying to hide the ready-made food packaging under the table. It had been my most stressful day in years.

That is the miracle of Glyndebourne. Half the audience comprises busy people who have battled to leave the office on time. The other half have left it slightly late and endured a heart-stopping hour of inching through the Sussex lanes with Queen Anne's lace and saxifrage dancing on the verges and their blood pressure going through the roof, before screeching into a parking place and galloping for the auditorium. Yet the orchestra starts and the lights go up and there you are, lost in eighteenth-century Florence or pre-Revolution France or Renaissance Nuremberg. The interval – especially on a warm evening, when shadows slide across the lawns and people picnic in splendour and couples stroll and sheep baa – adds to the utter sense of removal from the everyday. All allied to the sure knowledge that you are seeing and hearing some of the best musicians there are.

We took our seats in the great curve of warm timber, the packed audience rustling with anticipation. A burst of applause for the orchestra. A hush. This time the lights came up in 1930s Italy for *L'Elisir d'Amore*, a frothy tale of love, self-delusion and formidable *bel canto* trills, which had sold out the minute the tickets went on sale. Its star was the almond-eyed Australian-American soprano Danielle de Niese, new wife of the current Glyndebourne owner Gus Christie, who knocked everybody's socks off as Cleopatra at Glyndebourne in 2005. She has incredible stage presence. You couldn't take your eyes off her. I thought she was straining a teeny bit on a trill or two, but what do I know? For the unmusical, one of the great treats of Glyndebourne is overhearing people who do know telling each other what they think, like England fans discussing the 4–4–2 formation. Was her voice more baroque than *bel canto*? Discuss. What did everybody think of the young American tenor? (I thought he was great.) Discuss. Overall, they thought it delightful, a definite success. Me too.

'Glyndebourne is the place you'll see new singers reaching the top of their careers as well as the very great singers,' said Ash Khandekar, the editor of *Opera Now* magazine, when I met him in the coffee queue, 'but I don't think you get the *huge* stars in the way you used to in the early years. At one time it was the sort of place where you would see, say, Kiri Te Kanawa early in her career. They sang here because they liked it. They loved the long rehearsal periods and staying at the house and playing croquet in the interval and mixing with quite a glamorous set of people.'

In the hectic schedules of modern opera stars, he explained, even a two-week rehearsal is a luxury. Glyndebourne insists on a six- to eight-week rehearsal period and is famous for creating its own productions, which are staged in-house or toured, rather than joint funding a touring production with other opera houses. When Fritz Busch first started and demanded twenty-four rehearsals before the first night, the orchestra was thrilled: it was used to two. Today an ensemble creates a new staging each time, with all the accompanying risks but a particular magic when everything goes right. It's just very difficult for any star at the top of their game to spare that much time. It seems remarkable the regime has stuck.

When John Christie finally inherited in 1920 he set about building an Organ Room for recitals and concerts. You can still see it: it is panelled, with stained-glass windows decorated with the family arms, deep-blue walls, a double-height barrel-vaulted ceiling and a specially built organ at one end, only the carapace of which survives. As performances grew in complexity, the villagers of Glynde attended, acted as extras, sewed the costumes and served the refreshments. When Christie met and married Audrey Mildmay, a soprano who first came to Glyndebourne to take part in one of his Christmas performances, they spent their honeymoon touring Germany and Austria, listening to opera. By the time they got back their ambitions had vaulted: they drew up plans for 'a jewel box of a theatre in the vegetable garden' and started a number of businesses – a builder's, a pumping station, a sawmill, an electricity company – to help it along.

Whenever I have been to Glyndebourne, I have always assumed its origins lay in a batty English family's love of opera and am-dram, which had somehow metamorphosed over the years into something professional, almost in spite of itself. Julie Aries was horrified: 'Oh, not at all,' she said, 'they were aiming high right from the beginning. Their inspiration was from Europe, and the European influence was particularly strong because they had Fritz Busch as music director and Carl Ebert as artistic director.'

Busch had been music director of the Dresden State Opera House and Ebert started life as an actor before becoming Intendant at the Städtische Oper in Berlin in 1931: both left Germany to escape the Nazi regime and accepted the invitation to join the Christies (each assuming the venture would collapse after a season or two) on the condition they retained artistic freedom. No friends, no favours: Audrey, they said firmly, would have to audition along with everybody else. She did and Busch thought her voice delightful. He and Ebert were involved for the rest of their careers. They set Glyndebourne firmly on its artistic feet.

It seems quite extraordinary now, but in the 1930s the Royal Opera House at Covent Garden did not have a permanent company. It hosted visiting opera companies or was leased by impresarios who recruited world-class singers and staged productions around them, but the concept of a fully rounded opera, with the music bolstered by properly directed acting and stage sets, barely existed in England. Glyndebourne arrived with a bang, even if it was remote from the largely urban experience of most opera-goers. The early seasons, which rapidly passed into legend, featured the largely neglected operatic works of Mozart. Not just *Le Nozze di Figaro*, which was reasonably well known, but *Così Fan Tutte* – a comic opera involving elaborate identity changes and tests of female fidelity – then rarely performed and considered to be a ridiculous story anyway.

The press cuttings in the Glyndebourne archives capture the sense of astonishment – almost surreality – experienced by the London critics on the first night, as they set off from their customary urban haunts, wearing full evening dress in mid-afternoon, on the train to the back of beyond. Each train was met, as they are today, by special buses that shuttled the audience efficiently to the house. The gardens worked their quiet magic, as they do today, on the strolling groups of visitors. You could even bring your own staff to serve your picnic, something no longer encouraged, though I have heard people swear they have seen butlers serving at picnic tables in the past and Julie, when she first got her job, sat on a rug with a supermarket quiche and a mug of plonk while next door a waitress served a sumptuous picnic with a different wine glass for every course. There was a room for chauffeurs to relax in as they waited during the performance.

The first night at 'Captain Christie's opera house' was a big deal. He was well connected and Society and county figures turned up. Seats started at a pound and ten shillings in the stalls, or twenty guineas for a box: this was, the papers helpfully pointed out, cheaper than travelling to Munich or Salzburg. Indeed, travelling to

Munich or Salzburg or Milan was the only alternative if you were British and opera was your passion. Pictures of the audience were splashed across the covers of the *Illustrated London News* and the *Sketch*. There was admiration for Lady Diana Cooper – a great beauty and a Bright Young Thing – who appeared in a daring day dress and hat, while the terrifying Countess of Snowdon showed how it should be done in full evening *toilette* with opera cloak and tiara. Christie said he wanted the audience formally dressed 'out of respect for the performers' – nothing new for Covent Garden, but radical for the country – which deeply irritated some critics. However, the little opera house in the countryside shimmied effortlessly into the season, becoming as much a part of the calendar as any sporting event, and while the fashionable were welcome the focus never shifted to them. It was always the music that mattered.

I met Peter Greenleaf on one of the terraces. The evening was sunny, with an English chill lurking behind it like a witch at a christening. He was from Stamford, Connecticut, lived in Moscow and had been a Glyndebourne member for thirty years. He was first brought by friends and fell in love with the space, the history, the gardens, the people who had sung here, the setting, the whole Christie family aesthetic. But he still didn't feel it was truly international, like Bayreuth. 'The audience is overwhelmingly English,' he said. 'I don't hear Italian, I don't hear French, there are people you couldn't mistake for being any other race but English. I don't want to say pasty ...' – at this point he started laughing in an international way – '... but it's the shape of the face, the body, the morphology. I don't think it's as upper class as when I first came, though. And to its credit, it's gotten a lot younger – lots of people in their twenties and thirties come.'

Once the opera finishes at Glyndebourne, things unravel at a disquieting speed. It feels as though someone has closed a music box with a snap. Most people have a long drive ahead, or are taking the bus to Lewes Station. The gardens are now dark and starting to smell cool and damp. The colourful scenes of the afternoon seem like a dream. I wondered, as we drove back to London in Philip's car, if the audience was acting a part as much as the people on stage. Both Ash and Peter had said, tactfully, the English were partly identifiable because of their bonkers style: you would never, ever see an Italian woman wearing an ancient wax jacket over her evening dress at La Fenice, say, or a German picnicking in black tie at Bayreuth. Sometimes these things are unconscious, but sometimes I suspect we delight in playing the eccentric English card. We play up to it.

In 1956, the Rank Organisation made a short film on Glyndebourne and later presented it to the Glyndebourne Arts Trust. It's called *On Such a Night* and was directed by Anthony Asquith, the son of the First World War Prime Minister Herbert Asquith. He was a respected filmmaker responsible for such English classics as *Fanny by Gaslight*, *The Browning Version* and *The Yellow Rolls-Royce*. *On Such a Night* is the story of a young American in London, directed by his hotel concierge to the Sussex Downs for a typically English day out. At Victoria Station his attention is caught by a crowd in full evening dress, all talking about 'the new countess': intrigued and wanting to see a real countess, he follows them. It is, of course, the Glyndebourne train and the countess is La Contessa in *Figaro*, sung by a new soprano. It's a love story and it makes Glyndebourne look glorious. It's also an instruction manual about the dotty upper-class English and the way they do things, as explained to the handsome American by an elderly lady and her very pretty niece. But really it's aimed at English people who would get the joke. It is an amused, gently complacent look in the mirror.

I have often wondered what the season would be like if it was somewhere else. I can't imagine the Germans including so many ball games and horses in the mix: their season would surely involve more cerebral pursuits; a Wagnerian Olympiad at one of King Ludwig's fairytale castles, perhaps, or round-the-clock readings of Goethe, or Nietzsche Nights, or a literary symposium involving the works of Thomas Mann, Günter Grass and Hermann Hesse. The Italians would have opera and film and fashion.

There are many theories about the markedly anti-intellectual qualities of our dog-loving, horse-loving, country-loving aristocracy who, as we have seen, started so many of the season events. Thinking was frequently seen as a slightly irritating urban, or foreign, affectation. It got in the way. What mattered was land, because land was power, and if you combined land with leisure you got country sports. As one Edwardian character says in Isabel Colegate's 1980 novel *The Shooting Party*, 'If you take away the proper functions of an aristocracy' (running the estate, looking after the tenants), 'what can it do but play games too seriously?'[1] Glyndebourne has never had a patron and the last member of the royal family to visit was the late Queen Mother, in 1997.

Weeks later I interviewed Ash Khandekar at his home in Somerset. He is Indian, although brought up largely in England: I thought he might have a good take on Glyndebourne and its Englishness – and perhaps on its place as a latecomer, at under a century old, to the season. He went to his first opera here before the 'old house' – by which he meant the opera house – was knocked down. He could remember the distinctively English house party atmosphere and the much smaller audiences, where everyone seemed to know each other. Even now, despite travelling to opera venues and festivals the world over, he has never seen anything quite like it.

'The English country house opera, which Glyndebourne started, is *very* English, it really is,' he said. 'The idea of giving up your summer to full-time entertaining based around a theatrical experience is extraordinary. The only equivalent I can think of is seventeenth-century France, or perhaps the court of the Medicis, putting on an entertainment for a vast array of guests who come and disport themselves around your palace. At Glyndebourne you feel there is this family who have created a sense of court around them. People almost pay homage. In Europe you get the sense of a shrine to a composer – Bayreuth and Wagner, the Rossini Festival at Pesaro, the Puccini Festival at Torre del Lago – but in England there's this peculiar homage to a country house, built around opera.'

Or, as Charles Moore wrote in his *Telegraph* column that summer: 'The Christies at Glyndebourne, and more recent arrivals, such as the Ingramses at Garsington, have been perfectly serious about musical standards, but they must also have wanted, in an admirable way, to show off.'[2]

The country house thing doesn't surprise me at all: the British have always been unusually obsessed with bricks and mortar and houses have always been a short cut to becoming established by rooting yourself firmly in the land. There's a whole canon of literature on the subject, from Ben Johnson's seventeenth-century poem *To Penshurst*, sucking up to the Earl of Leicester and his new house Penshurst Place, to Jane Austen's novels *Northanger Abbey* and *Mansfield Park*, and Evelyn Waugh's elegiac *Brideshead Revisited*. Not to mention film and telly, *Downton Abbey* being the current success story. The whole subject is closely allied to the class issues that are always lurking, pike-like, below the surface of the season.

No, what's surprising is the opera. For an art form that seems utterly un-British – show me a single stiff upper lip or a ball game in Wagner or Verdi – it seems to have colonised the nation with remarkable success, partly due to its appeal to wealthy landowners. Lord Ashburton, of the Baring banking family, owns Grange Park in Hampshire, which has hosted a thriving opera festival since 1998. Garsington, in Oxfordshire, once home to Lady Ottoline Morrell and a motley collection of Bloomsbury freeloaders, had a successful summer opera festival for twenty years and on the death of its founder Leonard Ingrams, also a merchant banker, transferred to the Getty Estate at Wormsley in the Chilterns. Woodhouse in the Surrey Hills, Stanley Hall Opera in Essex, Dorset Opera at Bryanston School, which in the holidays reverts to its country house status, are some of a dozen or so examples. None of them could survive without private land on which to operate and a cushion of money. The fact they came about at all is purely down to Glyndebourne.

Until the Second World War, John Christie ploughed a huge chunk of his personal fortune into his opera house. After the war, the first business sponsorship began to appear and a subscription system evolved so that the audience members themselves absorbed some of the cost. The only problem is the fish tank effect. Buy a goldfish a bigger tank and it grows to fit, so you buy a bigger tank and it grows to fit that. Everything escalates. The same concept operates with cultural or sporting occasions: just as sponsorship allows Royal Ascot to lay on more races and facilities, and leads to more ambitious gardens at the Chelsea Flower Show, it allows Glyndebourne to up its game. The risk is changing the ambience and scale of the occasion, and that's a headache for organisers, who often market these events on their quirky English charm and, yes, exclusivity. Growth and tradition: what a juggling act. So far, Glyndebourne has kept its skittles in the air.

Ash thought the corporate presence was unavoidable. 'It's more visible around first nights,' he said. 'You notice more champagne around then, but that changes as the season goes on. Glyndebourne is essentially still a family firm, but it depends on sponsorship. It's also a major theatre, highly professional, with very good acoustics. There's much more space, so they can subsidise more tickets for young people.' What you don't hear is anyone raging, Ascot-like, at the changes, perhaps because the new house allows for more artistic excellence and a higher international profile. Increasingly you see little groups of foreigners joining in the fun. And the alfresco dining continues unabated: they cunningly built in broad covered terraces so picnickers can set up under cover without conceding defeat: it will still be freezing and they can just pretend they're outside.

From my point of view, culture was over for the summer. The Summer Exhibition and Glyndebourne had been a brief, dangerous swerve into the world of the mind. From here on it was back to sport, sport and more sport, peppered with a little rock music and the odd brass band. My feet, I felt, were back on truly English soil – and the going was good to firm.

11

NOBODY'S LOOKING
AT YOU, DEAR

Sometime between the Derby, the Summer Exhibition and Glyndebourne, I was standing in Alice's flat in Islington, staring into the mirror. Looking back at me was a tall, harassed-looking woman in sick-coloured shoes, wearing a simply cut dress that could have escaped from the Sensational Butterflies exhibition at the Natural History Museum. Alice folded her arms and nodded. 'We'll take it in a bit at the back,' she said, 'but otherwise it fits perfectly.' It did. The silk felt cool and voluptuous, skimming over me with the gentlest of touches. At my request the dress was modestly cut: I reckoned the butterflies could take the limelight. And boy, they did. They were huge. Half of me loved them. The other half felt quite alarmed.

They say there are women who want to be seen and women who just don't want to get it wrong. I fall into the latter category. I have never been confident about clothes. The only reason I mention it is that lack of confidence – sartorial and social – underpins the entire concept of the dress code: confidence is what makes them work. It also helps that you can be turned away if you transgress them, of course. Every year the boutiques in Henley-on-Thames make a fortune when furious Englishwomen and mortified foreigners come galloping in looking for a dress that reaches to their knees, having been turned away from the Stewards' Enclosure for wearing frisky skirts or trousers or, less probably these days, culottes. At Royal Ascot it's not hem length but spaghetti straps or 'insubstantial' hats. Today dress codes are overt, trying to enforce some degree of modesty on a culture that has forgotten the meaning of the word 'demure'. In the past the rules were invisible, so the fear of getting it wrong exerted a powerful force. If you knew, you knew. If you didn't, you didn't. It really mattered.

'Dress codes came in with the new middle class emerging in the early to mid-nineteenth century,' explained Emmanuelle Dirix, a cultural historian who lectures on the subject of fashion in London and Brussels. 'Suddenly all these arrivistes could outspend the upper classes, so the cultural capital, the *knowing*, became much more important. The etiquette books of the time were really all about how to spot the fraud.' I slid back on the huge black leatherette sofa and thought how very tribal it all was, a snarling fight for territory disguised in feathers and furs. I also thought I could hear a scrabbling sound deep in the sofa that was possibly a mouse.

Emmanuelle had agreed to meet me at the London College of Fashion's original campus, off Oxford Circus. The mid-twentieth-century building, six floors of stark concrete modernity, is roughly the same age as Barbara Hepworth's *Winged Figure* on the corner of the John Lewis department store next door. It opened in 1963, but its roots lay in much older technical institutes and trade schools, set further out in Clapham, Marylebone and Shoreditch and aimed at young working-class men and women. They were trained in millinery, dressmaking, hairdressing and tailoring, among other things. Term ended in March so they could apply for jobs in the many industries gearing up for the balls, dinners, parties and events of the season, and similarly the new building's location was no coincidence. It was, as the *Hairdressers' Journal* pointed out at the time, 'a magnificent one ... Mayfair, Savile Row and Bond Street, centres of Haute Coiffure and Haute Couture, are immediately south; Regent Street and Great Portland Street, home of the light clothing industry, immediately east.'[1] It was a fashion factory.

In fact, there is no such thing as English *haute couture*, or at least not according to Emmanuelle. The phrase, she said firmly, refers only to high fashion made in Paris. It has done ever since the 1850s, when demand for luxury goods in the French capital exploded under Napoleon III and his glamorous wife, the Empress Eugénie, leaving us with an irritating legacy of using French terms (often preceded by 'haute') to denote luxury goods, classy food or dead ends on expensive roads. It was Eugénie who set the fashions of the day. She soon began to patronise a talented – and, ironically, English – couturier called Charles Frederick Worth, who had been born in Lincolnshire and had worked his way up as a draper in London and Paris. Worth was not the first couturier, but he was the first to understand the value of what we would now call marketing. He established his *atelier*, first known as Worth et Bobergh and later the House of Worth, at No 7 rue de la Paix in 1858 and set out to get his clothes seen. One arena he chose was the racecourse.

'Racing has always played an important role in fashion,' said Emmanuelle. 'When Eugénie showed up at the races at Longchamp wearing her stole off the shoulder, within days all the ladies in Paris were doing it. So the couturiers started sending their models to the races: they knew the press would be there and the press just loved it. Ideally you wanted a scandal – a scandalous model, say, or scandalous clothes, perhaps just a little bit too tight – and you wanted your models to be seen with the right sort of gentlemen. Couturiers like Worth would have had three or four models parading up and down and that was what was reported, far more than the horses.' It was also often the courtesans or mistresses, less constrained but widely noticed, who took the fashion risks, setting the outré trends that would later be more discreetly interpreted by Eugénie and her set.

Back in Britain – at Newmarket, Epsom and Ascot – a facsimile of this fashionable French racing scene began to emerge. Horses had hogged the limelight for well over a century; it was time for them to share. Aristocratic women wore Paris fashions where possible because it showed not only could they afford them, they had travelled to Paris to get them. Once there, they had to stay for a while because bespoke clothing demanded numerous fittings for the achievement of perfection. A woman wearing *haute couture* had stayed in a fashionable *arrondissement* for some time, probably had Parisian friends and could pepper her conversation with bon mots. She knew the city's covered galleries, its elegant salons and its miraculous, electrically lit streets. She had money and a man, or an inheritance, to provide it. All this was conveyed in the wearing of a single dress.

Failing that you wore couture from an English house, all of which would have been based in London, in Mayfair, around Dover Street, close to the heartlands of gentlemen's tailoring on Savile Row and Jermyn Street. This was also a statement: Paris might be a city of luxury and modernity, but London was a city of power and commerce, centre of a huge empire, and money was pouring in. Hence the new class of wealthy women who literally followed fashion – British fashion, in this case, as was suitably patriotic and confident – and the fashion they followed was aristocratic.

'The middle classes were never seen as style leaders,' said Emmanuelle, crushingly. 'They were looking towards the royals, the aristocrats, the debutantes [for a style to follow]. The aristocracy were fighting to hold on to the political power that was slipping through their fingers, so there was that constant, peculiarly British way of taking outsiders down a few pegs – putting them into a class box, undermining them and making sure they knew it. The papers would run bitchy comments like "the wife of x industrialist was wearing a red dress", the implication being that she didn't know red was last season. It was great for business, though, because when you were insulted, you went out and bought yourself an entire new wardrobe. Then the upper classes would see you had assimilated the look and they would react in horror and promptly move on to something else.'

It seemed like some awful Greek myth: Tantalus yearning to be on trend and never quite getting there. It also triggered the creation of something we take for granted: fashion collections linked to the seasons, another of Worth's innovations. Instead of buying clothes for a specific purpose, or because something had worn out, you needed something because it was new. It was another lucrative form of what sociologists refer to as 'status anxiety', an exhausting state of mind for the sufferer, but of enormous benefit to business. The poor old followers not only had to keep shopping, they had to learn skills – the right way to tie a tie, or take their gloves off – that were absorbed quite naturally by the ruling classes as they grew up. Oh, and one more thing.

Worth was the first designer to put his label in a dress. He couldn't have put women under more pressure if he'd tried.

At this point our interview lurched to a halt. The scrabbling sound had become insultingly loud and industrious. 'It's a rat,' hissed Emmanuelle, leaping to her feet. 'It must be looking for all the food my students drop down the back of the sofa.' There was a sudden, self-conscious silence beneath us. It was clearly a fashion rat, bingeing in secret. We picked up the bin and shook it. We tried to lift the sofa, but to no avail. Eventually a security guard appeared. 'Mice,' he said judiciously, 'Loads of them. Wouldn't worry about it.' I did worry. My recording of the interview is punctuated with long, anxious pauses while Emmanuelle, distracted by rodent action, struggles to recapture her train of thought. I really didn't want her to stop. I wanted to know what she thought about Black Ascot.

Late on 6 May 1910, King Edward VII died. He had been suffering from bronchitis for two weeks and had endured several heart attacks. His last words to his son, soon to be George V, were 'I am glad', not because the succession was secure but because his horse had won at Kempton Park. His death plunged his family and the country into genuine mourning – he was an affable and popular king – and Society into a quandary: Royal Ascot was a month away, everyone's *toilettes* were already made, but the death of a monarch demanded a long period of official mourning – even, if protocol was properly observed, the cancellation of all social events.

In the century before, the Victorians – and particularly the Queen – had turned mourning into a fine art. The death of Albert drained the court of colour overnight: one of Victoria's mourning dresses is displayed in Kensington Palace, along with the diminutive sets of black clothes worn by her children, black jewellery and drearily matching accessories. The best mourning jewellery was made of jet, the fossilised wood of monkey puzzle trees, found in great seams on the North Yorkshire coast near Whitby and elaborately carved and polished. A wife's mourning ensemble, 'widow's weeds', was designed to keep everyone, particularly would-be suitors, at bay until an appropriate period had passed. Even mourning fabric was grim: black crêpe was deliberately lustreless and unflattering. Men got away with slightly darker clothes than usual and crêpe hatbands.

The higher the class, the more people would be involved, from relatives to servants, and the longer the mourning period. Fashionable young women chafed under the social restrictions imposed by the death of a little-known relative, which could ruin their season and their wardrobe and, they must have felt, their life. By the middle of the nineteenth century a widow stayed in full mourning – and largely withdrawn from the world – for a year, after which she could raise her veil and embellish the crêpe for another few months. Then she went into half-mourning, when she could choose to wear grey and/or touches of lilac, and even some jewellery.

Her behaviour was subject to intense scrutiny at all times. In the case of royalty, Society was also expected to make an effort, wearing sombre clothes and not having too much fun. Given her way, Queen Victoria probably would have removed the 'Royal' from Ascot for ever: it was Edward, then Prince of Wales, who pleaded its cause in the years after Albert's death: 'It is an opportunity for the Royal Family to show themselves in public – wh.[sic] I'm sure you much desire,' he wrote to her, adding, perhaps more honestly, '& after all Racing, with all its faults, still remains, I may say, a National Institution of the Country'[2] Victoria herself died in January 1901, five months out from Royal Ascot, which went ahead, albeit in mourning.

Now the new king, George V, saved the day by decreeing that the races would go ahead, given his father's love of the Turf. Tailors, seamstresses and milliners across the land must have fallen on their knees and given thanks. They had been handed a bonanza: in normal life, women would have dyed their dresses, hats, shoes and even parasols black, but this was not normal life, it was Ascot. Style was required. White might even be acceptable, especially for young women. Mayfair and St James's went into overdrive; many rich women had to order a second set of clothing. There are photographs to prove how very fashionable Ascot 1910 was – the camera was rapidly becoming absolutely key in the dissemination of fashion ideas among women – and how resolutely cheery in the face of tragedy. Nobody would have approved more heartily than the late king.

'Black Ascot is important for a variety of reasons,' mused Emmanuelle, the mouse forgotten. 'It's that outing that changes black firmly from a mourning colour to a fashion colour. Everybody shows up in black, yes, but they don't show up in black crêpe, the traditional mourning fabric, they show up in black fabulousness. Liberty even publishes an advert a day or two after the King's death that says, "All mourning fabrics available, no price increase". They realised that if Ascot was going to go ahead, which it would because the King loved racing so much, all these people would have to get new dresses made. They couldn't dye them. If you look at the photos you can see they're wearing fashion dress, not mourning dress; [the outfits] don't cry "My heart is bleeding". The whole narrative of black changes now. And for the first time ordinary people – women, rather than men – could see in the newspapers what would normally have been in fashion magazines, which, until the 1920s, were incredibly expensive.'

The fashion ramifications of Black Ascot are still with us. It led

indirectly to the popularity of an eternal fashion staple, the Little
Black Dress. And the designer and photographer Cecil Beaton was
so impressed by its panache that his fifty race costumes for the
1956 stage musical *My Fair Lady* – and five times that number for
the 1964 film – were made entirely in black, white and grey. The
film was shot not in Berkshire but on the Warner back-lot in
California, with the cast perched on a rickety white trelliswork set
for the race scenes, but the fashion was magic. It made a star of the
doe-eyed, slender Audrey Hepburn, though oddly enough, if you
look at the stills today, her costumes border on the vulgar: they
would not look out of place in the Edwardian music halls.

My own *toilette* was progressing steadily. Alice knew a milliner
called Susie Hopkins, who was making me a hat. She said it would
be a butterfly and in answer to my increasingly panicked queries
assured me it would be a stylish and understated butterfly. She
said all the milliners were praying that Kate Middleton would be
a hat fan because the Queen, who had single-handedly kept them
all in business both by her hat usage and by inspiring everyone else
to wear hats, would not be around for ever. She said that women
stepped up to a hat; it made them move differently. You could tell
a lot about a person by their hat: almost everything, in fact.

I was beginning to feel a bit exposed. Not just psychologically –
though I had never realised that clothes conveyed quite so much
about a person – but from a fashion point of view. Would my butterfly dress and hat make me look a complete idiot? In my
imagination the insects on the scarf silk began to take on absurd
proportions and mad hues. This feeling of mild paranoia was exacerbated by a visit to Vogue House to interview Kate Reardon, the
editor of *Tatler* magazine. Just as Jonathan Aitken is always prefixed by the word 'disgraced', Kate Reardon is always prefixed by
the word 'soignée'. And the only way to reach her, like Rapunzel

in a tower of glossy magazines, is by threading your way through a liftful of models and journalists at No. 1 Hanover Square, the UK headquarters of high fashion.

The walls and corridors of *Tatler* are very, very white and Kate Reardon's office is very, very bright. She wasn't in it. She was in a meeting and was soon to be on her way to another one, so my interview would have to be fitted into the fifteen-minute space in between. Outside her office was a rectangular white room, filled with glossy heads bent over desks. Bar the odd murmur and the dry tap of keyboard keys it was weirdly quiet. This, I imagine, is what the computer room at Roedean or Benenden would look like. There are not many men at *Tatler*: I worked on another floor at Vogue House for two years and the only *Tatler* male I can remember both exasperated and fascinated me. The energy he expended on his look was mesmerising: hair, shoes – including some awful black and white checked Converses – drainpipes today, flares tomorrow, stripes, florals, shorts up to his waist, trousers down to his bum, always surrounded by a cloud of chirruping women. He was, I suppose, a 21st-century Beau Brummel.

Kate walked in, clad in a floaty green dress and heels, clearly busy and, yes, soignée. I liked her. When I asked about *Tatler*'s relationship with the season she rolled her eyes. 'It's like Santa Claus, I don't believe in the social season any more,' she said. 'It used to exist in a highly defined way: everybody knew where they stood, which was lovely if you were on the inside. Now I don't believe it exists as an entity. There are remnants, but nowadays all the grand entertaining is corporate, whereas it used to be for nice English people and a bunch of dogs.' She looked at her watch.

Tatler's role in the season has been crucial. One of the longest-running magazines in existence, it started life as Richard Steele's

Society Journal, which came out on Tuesdays, Thursdays and Saturdays and among other things focused on social events, salons and balls – the stuff of the court circular. Three centuries later it was still keeping tabs on the doings of the upper classes and until the 1980s it was required reading for Sloane Rangers (the countrified town dwellers identified with the Sloane Square area of Chelsea, whose patron saint was Diana, Princess of Wales). Somewhere along the way it lost its definite article, though older readers may still refer to it as *The Tatler*. Tina Brown, a former editor, famously referred to it 'an upper-class comic'. Today's *Tatler* is far more ironic, far more sophisticated and infinitely more cosmopolitan in its outlook. So who, I wanted to know, was documenting the season now?

'We do have these events in the magazine but we're careful,' said Kate. 'None of them is a no-brainer. We will still have a photographer at Ascot but we work very hard to find the images we want: elegant, aspirational, sophisticated and glamorous. Hugo Burnand will be doing it so his taste and experience will inform the pictures he takes. Violet Henderson, who edits our 'Bystander' section, knows that world as well.' Burnand had just shot the official Royal Wedding photographs that April, cycling off with his team through the London streets to document William and Kate's big day. And 'knows that world' sounded like a euphemism for 'in it'. Perhaps *Tatler* wasn't as aloof from its old stamping grounds as it liked to think.

Kate was looking at her watch again and apologised, suggesting I come back at a later date. Yes, please. I wanted to ask about 'Jennifer's Diary', the famous *Tatler* chronicle of social events written by the late Mrs Betty Kenward until she defected to *Queen* magazine – at the time this was like Guy Burgess leaving for Moscow – and I wanted to look at their archive. I also wanted to know why she thought everything had changed so much in thirty years. Instead, I asked her if she ever worried about what to wear.

'Used to more, I think,' she said, laughing. 'But I'm much more nervous about riding in the Celebrity Ladies' Race at Goodwood this year, to be honest, I'm genuinely worried about that. Anyway, as Nanny used to say, that most soothing of aphorisms, "No one's looking at you, dear!"' And she wafted off to her next meeting blithely unaware that I would hug those words to me like a hot-water bottle for the next few weeks.

12

TOPPERS AND TAILS

My brother has a very big head. In the all the forty-nine years I have known him I have never noticed this. In fact, it only transpired on the opening day of Royal Ascot when I dragged him into the hat concession because I wanted to have a look and we asked idly how much it would be to replace his battered silk topper, bought second-hand in the 1980s.

'What size is your head?' said the woman. He held out his hat.

'Wow!' she said, impressed. 'That's huge!'

He looked smug. She didn't fall over backwards, but she did use the sort of admiring tone that would make any chap walk a bit taller, adding: 'Four thousand pounds.'

'WHAT?' we said in unison, like those people on the *Antiques Roadshow* who have just discovered the umbrella stand is a T'ang vase.

'If it was in top condition,' she added hastily, before we could try and sell it to her. 'They don't make the silk plush any more. The factory that made it in France closed down years ago, so the real silk plush ones are almost like limited editions. And the big ones are really hard to get hold of because men's heads were just a lot smaller back then. Most people wear grey felt now, they're easy to buy because they still make them.'

My brother was looking at his hat in amazement. I was looking through the fence at the Royal Enclosure, studded with toppers like chimney pots on a London skyline, trying to work out which ones were silk plush and how much they would all be worth if you held everyone up at gunpoint.

It was Tuesday, the first day of Royal Ascot, and I had come down for a dry run, to walk the course as it were, wearing a smart dress and modest hat in the Grandstand rather than the fully hatched butterfly I was going to wear for Ladies' Day in the Royal Enclosure. That's where my brother and sister-in-law were. They came out to meet me for a cup of tea and collapsed on a bench, exhausted. They were guests in the White's tent. White's is a gentlemen's club in St James's with a spectacular gambling history. Beau Brummell was an enthusiastic member. It has its own tent, a private enclosure within the enclosure as it were, as does the Derby-winning Royal Ascot Racing Club, and several others. There may be a more exclusive section of the White's tent, for all I know, an enclosure within an enclosure within an enclosure, like an upmarket *matrioshka* doll.

Then I saw the hat concession and my brother said he would come too, and here we were, both speechless. 'You ought to talk to my boss about it,' said the girl, giving me a card for Oliver Brown, a tailoring company on Lower Sloane Street. 'He knows a lot about top hats. He buys all these.' I thought I'd wait until after

Ascot. It's a stressy time for hatters, June. But when I rang he said to come in anyway: once race week was actually under way, things calmed down until the linen suit rush for Goodwood.

The owner of Oliver Brown was not Oliver Brown but Kristian Ferner-Robson. He was in a tiny office at the back of the shop, which smelled of new tweed and leather. It was full of country wear – shooting, hunting, fishing – for men and women. Every spring, a sign advertising formal wear for Royal Ascot – sale or rental – goes up in the window; I always see it from the bus. Our chat was interrupted several times by clients popping in to leave pairs of twill trousers and ask about jacket alterations.

Kristian started selling hats at Cirencester – the Royal Agricultural College in Gloucestershire – when his father invited him to the Royal Enclosure one year and he didn't have a top hat. He bought one on the Portobello Road for £25, realised at the racecourse it was worth a lot more, sold it the next day for £250 and began dealing in hats as a sideline. He bought Oliver Brown eleven years ago because it is perfectly placed in southwest London: minutes from the Royal Hospital Chelsea, near the Sloane Club, and clearly visible from passing four-wheel drives doing the school run.

Stories vary about the first top hat. The wearer may have been a London haberdasher called John Hetherington and the year may have been 1797. It may have been a Middlesex hatter called George Dunnage a few years earlier. Lock & Co. on St James's think it was invented in France and adopted by Hetherington. Whoever and whenever, it was clearly a shock to Society. Kristian claimed a passer-by had collapsed, breaking her arm, and Hetherington had been arrested and fined five pounds. Why it appeared is perhaps the more pressing question: men were happily wearing short wigs and tricorn hats. To suddenly place on your head a tall, straight-sided column of beaver fur – they were called 'beaver hats' until the early nineteenth century – was outré, to say the least. It was certainly timely: once Pitt the Younger levied his wig-powder tax in 1795, the hat was back.

There were well-established hatting industries in Stockport and Luton, and in London hatting took place south of the river in Southwark, along with other 'stink industries' such as tanning and dyeing. Mercury was used in the felting process and its fumes were dangerous. Hatters were sited well away from the airy West End squares where their customers lived. In the days before rainproof clothing, hats were essential; all men wore them to protect their hair or elaborate wigs. Their manufacture involved glueing hatting felt onto a head-shaped mould of linen stiffened with shellac and finishing it with braid or other detailing. Felt was made by back-combing wool to mat the fibres, then steaming it into a flat, durable material. The very best felt was made of fur, usually rabbit, but beaver was best of all.

England had been trading beaver pelts with North America's indigenous tribes for a century by this time. The last Scottish populations had long been wiped out and the European beaver, mainly in Russia, was rapidly following suit, so the discovery of North America, with its vast beaver population, had opened up a new trade. The Hudson's Bay Company was established by Prince Rupert, Charles II's cousin, who obtained a Royal Charter in 1670. This magnificent document was kept at Hudson Bay House on Bishopsgate until the 1970s – aside from occasional sabbaticals as debt security – when it went to the Hudson's Bay Company in Toronto. Rupert hired two French adventurers rebuffed by their own country to make an exploratory expedition to northeast Canada. They returned on the *Nonsuch* with £1,380-worth of beaver pelts, which were auctioned at Garraway's Coffee House on Cornhill. The King duly signed the charter.

Pelts were bartered for European goods – knives, pots, blankets and beads – and English hatting thrived. One Native American association claims over 20 million beaver-fur hats were exported from England between 1700 and 1770. Add that to the huge domestic market and it's easy to guess the effect upon the beavers. At the peak of the fur trade, Canada alone was sending 200,000 pelts annually to Britain[1]. As populations began to decline around the Hudson Bay, the Lewis and Clark expeditions into the American West in the early nineteenth century opened up new opportunities: pelts were obtained by hardy white trappers known as 'the mountain men'.

Back in Britain, meanwhile, the beaver hat was some way along the road from high fashion to respectability. By the 1830s the beaver trade was unsustainable and the timely invention of silk plush – a specially loomed silk with a pile as long as 8mm – suited the increasing use of what were now known as 'top hats' in formal circumstances, such as the opera or parliament. By the 1850s, Prince Albert was wearing a top hat. It had become a symbol of propriety, respectability and, if made of silk, status. His eldest son, Bertie, would spend a great deal of time subverting this.

Kristian briefly explained the vagaries of the top hat market. 'The grey ones are made nowadays, they're not antique,' he said. 'It's the black silk ones that are rare. The silk hasn't been made for forty-five years, because the French family that owned the factory near Lyons had a big row and burned the looms. It's silk plush, between five and eight millimetres long, which is how you get that incredible shine. It would take a highly skilled weaver two or three days to make enough silk for one hat and now those skills are gone,

even if you could rebuild the looms, it would be extremely difficult to do.'

In pre-Revolutionary France, the Lyons silk industry was world
famous, employing over 100,000 workers. Later their weavers featured in the catalogue for the 1851 Great Exhibition. By the
1870s one factory, run by the Martin Brothers, had 3,500 workers
making '*velours et peluches*' (plush). Maybe it was their descendants who had so inconveniently fallen out.

The other issue is size. Men's heads have increased by one or
two sizes over the past century or so, so the demand for large hats
is strong and there are fewer of them. 'The age doesn't really
matter,' said Kristian, turning over a hat to show me the mark.
'The price depends on the condition, the shape, the height and
most importantly the size. They go up from 7¼. 7⅝ is incredibly
rare, 7¾ even more so.' My brother's head is 7¾. 'I've probably
had two or three hundred of the small ones over the years, but of
those two, perhaps ten?' he continued. 'Our hats cost from six
hundred to a few thousand pounds, but the racecourse takes a
pretty big mark-up so they're more expensive there.' Men's hats
have swung from black to grey over the years at Ascot, he
explained, adding that if grey you wanted one of the older grey
felts, which went a sort of musty grey, the precious patina of age.

Business at Oliver Brown depends on new blood. 'The Old
School have their kit already,' said Kristian, 'it's their father's or
grandfather's. Our Ascot business has nearly doubled every year
for four years because so many people are going for the first time.
It's all new money. And we love new money.' The people who
haven't been before or don't go regularly – foreign owners bringing horses to Ascot, for example, hoping to be in the winners'
enclosure, prefer to hire once a year – are what keep all these businesses going. And first-timers are anxious to wear the right thing.

Men's fashion at Ascot seems frozen in time, its development arrested somewhere around Series One of *Downton Abbey*. This was, of course, Britain's last gasp of glory before everything unravelled during two World Wars. And men have never really tried to kick over the traces, whereas women have: the Ascot Authority wrestled with miniskirts and hotpants in the 1960s, whereas most men happily went on wearing something their antecedents would have worn. Sometimes they were wearing something their antecedents actually had worn: old was good, worn was fine. Even pretty threadbare was fine. In fact, threadbare was better than new: it subtly proclaimed inheritance.

Before I went, Kristian showed me an amazing topper in a green-lined hatbox, brought in by one of his dealers. With a rustle of tissue he put his hands down the sides to ease it out. It was an unheard-of size 8 and it was in superb condition: the leather inner band had no sweat marks, the plush gleamed like patent leather, the brim was lightly turned, the crown sported a flat bow. Even my brother's head would have disappeared inside that hat. 'It's like seeing a perfect diamond,' murmured Kristian. 'It's the most beautiful hat I've ever seen. I'm very excited about having it here.' There was a slight pause, then he added: 'I just can't wait to sell it.'

left: Tatler & Bystander magazine, 1963: hard at work after 250 years and still covering the London Season as the Sixties were beginning to swing.

© Illustrated London News Ltd/Mary Evans

below: Legendary dancing teacher Madame Vacani puts the finishing touches to a debutante's curtsey at the Cygnet House Finishing School in Staines, 1952. *Getty Images*

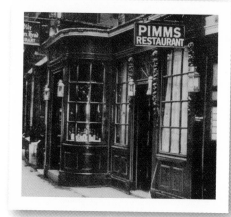

above: A striking portrait of the Duchess of Argyll – then nineteen-year-old Margaret Whigham and one of the year's most glamorous debutantes – painted by Gerald Leslie Brockhurst, c. 1931. © *Richard Woodward*

right: Until the second half of the twentieth century there were five Pimms Restaurants in London. James Pimm created a range of alcoholic fruit cups, originally to go with oysters: No 1 is still a season stalwart. *Image courtesy of DIAGEO*

EXHIBITION EXTRAORDINARY in the HORTICULTURAL ROOM.

left: Oxford and Cambridge eights approach Hammersmith Bridge during the annual Boat Race: a mile further on, protester Trenton Oldfield swam into the race in 2012. *Getty Images*

bottom left: George Cruikshank in characteristically acerbic form in this caricature of a fashionable Horticultural Society meeting of the 1820s: note the reference to the Irish Potato Famine in the top left hand corner. © *Heritage Images/Corbis*

below: A Chelsea Pensioner, one of the army veterans resident at the Royal Hospital Chelsea, in scarlet dress coat and black shako in front of the exhibits at the Chelsea Flower Show. *AFP/Getty Images*

above: Opera-goers accessorise formal evening dress with coats to ward off the country chill at Glyndebourne Opera House in West Sussex.
© *Alpha Press*

right: John Christie, the owner of Glyndebourne, with his wife, the soprano Audrey Mildmay and children Rosamond and George in 1937.
© *National Portrait Gallery, London*

Dinner-jacketed picnics in the beautifully landscaped gardens of Glyndebourne Opera House in the Sussex countryside.

THE START FOR THE MEMORABLE DERBY OF 1844.

The starter drops his flag for the scandalous 1844 Derby: *Running Rein*, the winner, turned out to be a four-year-old called *Maccabeus*. *Private Collection/The Bridgeman Art Library*

Johnny Murtagh and *Motivator* in the tiny winner's enclosure after their 2005 Derby victory, surrounded by the ecstatic owners of the Royal Ascot Racing Club. *Press Association Images*

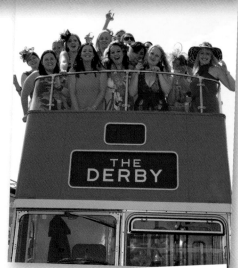

above: William Powell Frith's delightfully rackety painting *The Derby Day*, a smash hit at the Royal Academy in 1858, complete with roulette and beer tents, pickpockets and spectators on top of coaches. *Manchester Art Gallery, UK/The Bridgeman Art Library*

right: A hen party crammed on top of their open top vintage double-decker bus in the Lonsdale Enclosure for the Derby. © *Doug McKinlay*

below: A world away from the Queen's Stand: the sunbathing, picnicking crowd on The Hill watches anxiously as the 2011 Derby thunders towards them on the big screen. © *Doug McKinlay*

Porters balance works for consideration on a stool apparently owned by Joshua Reynolds in Charles West Cope's painting *The Council of the Royal Academy selecting Pictures for the Exhibition, 1875.* © Royal Academy of Arts, London; John Hammond

Carriages and motorcars parked in the quadrangle of Burlington House on Piccadilly for the Royal Academy Summer Exhibition 1910. *Getty Images*

D for Doubtful: The selection committee contemplates thousands of entries for the Royal Academy Summer Exhibition in 1939 – note the D sign in the President's hand (X is on the table). *Getty Images*

'Black fabulousness': Edwardian race-goers make the most of mourning at 'Black Ascot', following the death of King Edward VII in 1910. *Getty Images*

A jockey is dwarfed by fashionable race-goers at Royal Ascot in this illustration from *The Bystander*. In 1927, it seems, grey top hats and even cravats were all the rage.
© *Illustrated London News Ltd/Mary Evans*

Eliza Doolittle dresses up and Professor Higgins dresses down in the Royal Enclosure – actually a Californian movie set – in the 1964 film of *My Fair Lady*.
Moviestore Collection/Rex Features

One of the regular 'hat acts' pirouettes for the cameras on arriving for Gold Cup (Ladies') Day at Royal Ascot 2011.

Race-goers arriving by train protect their outfits from the summer weather with a sea of umbrellas.
© Doug McKinlay

Young Ascot fans choose from hats or 'fascinators' and wear skirts as short as they like en route to the Silver Ring enclosure.
© Doug McKinlay

Race-goers make their way from Ascot railway station across open fields to the racecourse for Royal Ascot in 1930. *Getty Images*

Clapham Junction

above: The author parades in silk butterfly dress, gold butterfly hat and 'those shoes' at less glamorous Clapham Junction. © *Doug McKinlay*

left: Una-Mary Parker says it with flowers as she models a hat en route to Ascot in 1964. *Getty Images*

A quiet day in the Pavilion at Lord's Cricket Ground: note the MCC logos on top of the towers and the players in the Players' Box to the left.

The Eton v. Harrow match, the only remaining schoolboy fixture at Lord's and the oldest continuously played cricket match in the world. The Eton batsman are wearing blue caps, the Harrovian fielders navy and white stripes.

The Queue: tents in orderly rows in the golf club car park opposite the All England Lawn Tennis Club for The Championships at Wimbledon. *Getty Images*

The author and her Millets tent in The Queue.

Blazers and hats at the ready as occupants of the Stewards' Enclosure at the Henley Royal Regatta wait for the races to begin.

Two rowing eights with the Umpire Boat behind power their way up the 1 mile and 550 yard Henley Royal Regatta course against the current.

Open water swimmers complete the same course in the Henley Classic, held in the early morning the week before the regatta begins.
Getty Images

Glamour at Guards Club: the final year of the Cartier International Polo at Smith's Lawn – Audi have now taken over the sponsorship.

More chatting than treading divots: half time at the Coronation Cup at Smith's Lawn, Windsor Great Park, for the Cartier International Polo.

A giant dragonfly squats on the island on the lake at Secret Garden Party, the ever-expanding music festival at Abbots Ripton, Cambridgeshire.

The whimsical charms of Secret Garden Party: the Temple of Wanton Woodland Creatures occupies a copse on the festival site.

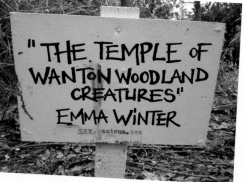

"THE TEMPLE OF WANTON WOODLAND CREATURES" EMMA WINTER

King Edward VII and some of his fellow guests at a house party for 'Glorious Goodwood' in 1904 sport startling white top hats. *The Goodwood Collection*

Two years later the King has replaced his top hat with a white Derby: other guests have followed the more casual line in panamas and boaters. *The Goodwood Collection*

Cardboard horses graze on The Trundle, the Iron Age hillfort above Goodwood Racecourse, on Ladies' Day.

Spectators on The Trundle enjoy a bird's-eye view of the course and have their own loos and bookies provided by Goodwood Racecourse.

Victorious model Edie Campbell (in silks by Jasmine Guinness) celebrates her win in the first celebrity ladies' race, the Magnolia Cup, in 2011. *Getty Images*

above: Players from Island Sailing Club (Cowes) and Royal Southern Yacht Club (Southampton) square up for their annual cricket match on Bramble Bank in the middle of the Solent. *Getty Images*

right: It's Pimms O'Clock even first thing in the morning at the Marina Village in West Cowes, Isle of Wight.

below: Over 100 wooden keelboats, the X One-Designs or XODs, line up for their centenary race at Aberdeen Asset Management Cowes Regatta 2011.

13

THE ROYAL ENCLOSURE AT LAST

It was Ladies' Day. It was mid-June. It was raining. A keen wind whistled through the wings of the gold butterfly on my head, rattling its antennae. I had perched it on my lap on the bus to the station, millinery not really being the thing on the No. 77, but at Waterloo I didn't stand out at all. The monochrome current of morning commuters flowed around bright eddies of jollity, each with a nucleus of picnic baskets or thin plastic bags beaded with moisture and clanking with bottles. A startling amount of flesh was on show: miles of leg and acres of cleavage. Top hats marked the more formal groupings. And on the fifty-minute train journey to Ascot, people going to mid-morning meetings were marooned as corks popped, hats were adjusted and make-up repaired. A few buffs carried the *Racing Post* or hand-written betting calculations. The ticket collector wore an indulgent smile. Despite the unseasonal weather, in the lovely

words of one eighteenth-century race-goer: 'Every person's spir-
its seemed to be on the wing.'

As London suburbs gave way to open fields grazed by ponies
and cows, my nerves subsided. I had been dreading going to the
Royal Enclosure on my own as you dread going to a new school –
I know, pathetic – but in this happy, variegated crowd it was hard
to feel uneasy for long. 'Ascot's just a chance to dress up for the
day,' said one guy, strap-hanging with one hand and holding a plastic glass of fizz in the other, 'and everyone, fellas and ladies, loves
a chance to dress up.' Three women told me they liked my hat.
My dress felt amazing: I couldn't stop running my hand over the
silk, wondering at the quirk of fate that had taken all those butterfly parts from the life they might have expected, around
someone's neck on the Champs Élysées, to the show-off day of the
social year in Berkshire.

On arrival, the crowd surged out of the station and funnelled
into a wide path that switch-backed straight up towards the
course. It ran between dripping fields doubling as car parks and
trees pattering with raindrops. The horizon of hats rose and fell
with the landscape and then began a strange vertical ascent as
everyone scaled the steps of the steel bridge carrying the path over
the main road, in the teeth of the wind and rain, clomping gingerly
down the far side and peeling off in three familiar directions: posh,
left (Royal Enclosure); middles, middle (Grandstand); everyone
else, right (Silver Ring). People who couldn't be bothered to dress
up paid eight pounds on the heath.

By the time you get to your bit of Ascot racecourse you have
walked half a mile and, in some cases, drunk at least half the
contents of your picnic basket or clanking supermarket bag. But
already the atmosphere is glossy. It's utterly different to Derby
Day.

I was myself becoming seasoned. I felt quite sentimental when I caught sight of the paps, hard at it in front of the Grandstand where the Tarmac doubled as a catwalk. Big screens ran interviews with fashion gurus and footage of women's outfits. Girls in coordinated colours or matching hats linked arms – an old photographic trope at Ascot, if you look through the archives – and lenses bristled as an elderly woman wearing a vast cone of yellow and white flowers on her head nodded and pivoted graciously.

Susie the milliner had told me Royal Ascot triggered in some women a driving need to be noticed. The quickest route was to wear a novelty hat in the Shilling tradition: Gertrude Shilling being the mother of designer David Shilling, who made her outrageous hats – an open picnic hamper, a mighty sunflower, a Mexican sombrero the size of the parade ring – from the 1960s onwards, amusing and appalling other race-goers in equal measure. The other approach was to wear not much at all, a uniquely British style of dress the uncharitable might describe as 'hooker chic'. Every year the papers pounced on the most egregious examples with joy and delight. So did some Brazilians I met, who enthusiastically showed me the pictures on their cameras: not of horses, but of hefty, half-naked girls.

You can see how irritating this is for people who love racing. They could be seen threading their way through the melée, looking as if they were chewing wasps. Press coverage focuses largely on the Royal Enclosure and Ladies' Day and however hard the racecourse tries to call the latter by its correct title of Gold Cup Day – after the longest race of the meeting, a two-mile-four-furlong battle for four-year-olds and older, for enormous prize money – the nickname won't budge. The newspapers coined it in the nineteenth century when they noticed Society women turning up in larger numbers, thanks to better transport and course facilities. Simultaneous competitions were soon under way: racing on the course, fashion off it. There was the added interest, in those pre-celebrity days, of seeing Society beauties. Almost as soon as cameras were invented they were banned in the Royal Enclosure.

The road to Nirvana ran across the back elevation of Ascot's enormous new Grandstand, past a bronze statue of Frankie Dettori doing his famous 'flying dismount' – in honour of seven consecutive wins one unforgettable September afternoon in 1996 – under a concrete bridge, past the huge parade ring with its oval lawn and waist-high hedging, where horses and jockeys could be seen before and after each race, and under a faux-classical cream-painted gateway marked 'Royal Enclosure'. The gateman looked at my fluttering badge – maroon for Thursday – and nodded me in.

My first impression was of a slight muting, as though someone had turned the volume down. My second was of a minuscule slowing in pace, as if life had returned to its soothing pre-motor car, pre-television, pre-internet rhythms. My third was that aside from this retro quality – exacerbated, obviously, by the forest of gleaming top hats – and an increased sense of decorum, the Royal Enclosure didn't feel that different from the rest of the racecourse. Unwittingly, I had put my finger on the great Ascot paradox.

Nobody knows what made Queen Anne decide that Ascot Heath would make a magnificent setting for racing. In 1711, when St Paul's Cathedral was barely a year old, she was hunting with the Ascot Buckhounds – in her own chaise, being too hefty for a horse – and commanded that a suitable racing ground be made. It was laid out in the shape of a rough isosceles triangle, with its base slightly extended into a straight sprint.

Right from the word go, Ascot was different from other race meetings. The historian Sean Magee writes: 'These horses were owned by courtiers or by those closely connected with the court or the hunt, and the sport was essentially entertainment for the court and its adherents, rather than a public spectacle. (This was not the case with other race meetings at the time, many of which were closely linked to local social events.)'[1] The essayist Jonathan Swift, then editor of Tory journal 'The Examiner', attended an early meeting and reported that one of the Queen's ladies was strikingly, even stridently, dressed in male riding clothes. This was an English trend noted by foreign observers. Ascot was already on the fashion map.

Over the decades, the course developed gradually. The first four-day meeting was held in 1768 and the first stand was built twenty-six years after that. In the early nineteenth century Parliament passed an Act of Enclosure that earmarked the land as a racecourse. And as the area of the course used by the Sovereign evolved into a formal Royal Enclosure, it dominated the southwest corner near the finish. The parade ring was in a nearby paddock. While Grandstand race-goers could trek across to see it, later via a concrete tunnel, the occupants of the Five Shilling Stand – now the Silver Ring – just had to imagine it, as they couldn't. In the enclosure itself refreshment tents were close at hand and, most importantly, you got wonderful views of the racecourse: an elegant lawn, stands and shallow 'steppings' clustered around the Royal Box and the finishing post.

Carriages could be parked by the course just nearby – owners stood on them to watch the fun – and this evolved into Number One Car Park, for much of the twentieth century the season's most sought-after chunk of grass. 'When you got to the top of the list you were offered a space,' one regular told me. 'You had it every year and paid for the whole week. It wasn't transferable, but we always passed it on to friends, you just swapped the sticker. It's the convenience: you walk straight into the paddock

or the enclosure and it has – or had – a lovely view of the course.'
Like the best holiday cottages, she added, once you gave up your
slot, you lost it for ever. If you had a space near the rails, you held
on to it like grim death. In fact, families held on to them despite
grim death: while not precisely inherited, the same spaces were
used by the same names for decades.

The old Ascot, in other words, was unapologetically designed
for the ease of Royal Enclosure members. The enclosure was
meant to be different from the rest of the course. This was what
lent it the social cachet that somehow rubbed off on Royal Ascot
as a whole. People poured in to less exalted parts of the grounds,
dressed in their best but minus the stringent rules, and felt they
were attending a race meeting that was a cut above the rest.
All the different race-goers coexisted happily, like fish in a
tank. For social observers, it was a perfect analogy for the class
system.

Here's the paradox. Ascot racecourse sits on some of the most
valuable real estate in Britain, technically owned by the Sovereign
but part of the £8.1bn landholding known as the Crown Estate.
Since the reign of George III, all income from the Crown Estate has
gone to the Exchequer (now the Treasury) and since 1961 it has
been managed for the Queen by a Trust with a duty 'to maintain
and enhance the value' of its holdings. This leases the racecourse to
the Ascot Authority. In the past, as virtually a royal fiefdom, the
course had no need to justify its existence. There was one race
meeting a year until 1939. Today, like all racecourses, it needs
income. As well as twenty-six race days annually, including the
winter jump season, it competes with every other conference venue
near London. Royal Ascot, its flagship meeting, treads a fine line
between keeping its aura of exclusivity and not seeming anachronistic and snobbish. The existence of the racecourse depends on

bringing people in. The status of the Royal Enclosure depends on keeping people out.

The Grandstand at Ascot was five years old but everyone referred to it as the 'new stand'. Except for people in the Royal Enclosure, who called it 'T5' after the newest and glitziest terminal at Heathrow Airport. It was a huge airy, tapered structure replacing an angular stand built in the early 1960s. For Royal Ascot it was shared between the Royal Enclosure (on Level 4 and beside the winning post) and Grandstand Admission, with a number of elite floors and private boxes. To get to the upper Royal Enclosure area you sailed up an enormous escalator. It provided more space and more cover. Three times as many people could access the parade ring. The course itself had been moved and improved, losing quirks such as two sections of road crossing the straight mile and covered, on race days, by coconut matting. Put it this way: you wouldn't see that in Dubai or Doha.

In any other arena, it would have been hailed as a triumph. The £220m project opened on time, working to an almost impossibly tight schedule. The building could compete with new rivals popping up in Asia and the Middle East. And the logistics had been nightmarish. The course closed for almost eighteen months, the Royal Meeting decamped to York racecourse, then everyone had to be persuaded to come back again and once they did they were all furious. Royal Enclosure members found the new layout confusing and commercial. Grandstand race-goers felt they had lost out. Everyone except the Silver Ring seemed to think their section was too small, their view worse. A *Guardian* blogger called it 'a shabby way to treat ordinary folk', though ordinary folk seemed to be the only ones not complaining.

Enclosure members get misty-eyed as they remember the days before the temporary restaurant pavilion went up, blocking the sacred sightline from Number One Car Park to the turf. They look back to the times before you had to walk – in the words of one top-hatted chap – '... past eighteen pairs of size triple-D boobs and short skirts and all the things they shouldn't be wearing at Ascot to get to what you really love, the actual racing'. They hanker for the days before there were so many *people*. There is a note of bitter irony in their voices, almost as if they have been jilted by a lover or sacked from a wonderful job. 'Oh, I don't go to Ascot any more,' people assured me. 'It's just not the same as it was. I go to Goodwood instead.'

In Godfrey Smith's 1987 book on the season[2] he quoted an article from *The Times*: '[Ascot] has long lost all claims to exclusiveness,' it stated, regretfully but firmly, 'And with them have gone much that no doubt rendered [it] the pleasantest of race meetings ...' It was written in 1868. People have been moaning about Ascot losing its mojo for ever. It's like moaning about the weather at the Chelsea Flower Show or our World Cup football record. It takes the interlopers about five years before they start moaning about it, too. In four years I will have moaning rights of my own.

The fact is the Royal Enclosure has always been more elastic than its occupants like to admit. It's a bellwether for the real world. When the first stand was built in 1794 Britain's population was six to seven million. As we know, aristocratic families were in the low hundreds; the royal party probably comprised a few dozen courtiers. Soon a lawn had to be roped off to keep out the Prince Regent's raffish friends and by the time a Royal Enclosure proper appeared in 1845 the population was 27 million and it held several hundred people. Under Edward VII it swelled to over a thousand, though you had to be eligible to appear at court (not criminal, divorced or bankrupt). By the 1960s it had jumped to seven and a half thousand. Now, on Ladies' Day, up to 80,000 people roll up to the Royal Meeting and the enclosure accounts for around 10 per cent of them.

It seemed to me, as an outsider, that the Royal Enclosure was completing a transition from exclusion zone to something more egalitarian: a sought-after area that you needed some sort of contact – racing friends, partying friends, a horse – to enter. The world was changing and Ascot had clearly made a decision to step out of the traditional English arena and into the glitzier world of international racing. The Royal Enclosure was no longer a semi-private party and soon there would be a generation that did not remember it as such. And how Royal would it remain? The Princess Royal and her daughter are the only members of the royal family with the horsey credentials to step into the Queen's shoes, and showjumping is their schtick. The new stand looked like a big, shrewd gamble and from my point of view it had paid off: brash, perhaps, huge, certainly, but it had a wonderful swagger about it, an unassailable air of confidence.

Meanwhile, here it was again, that magical racing atmosphere: green turf, white railings (shatterproof plastic, rather to my surprise, to avoid injuries), bookies' stands unfurled like one-man bands, champagne, picnics, *fun*. In the parade ring the horses circled like beautiful, glossy machines, with patterns – checks, triangles, stars – shaved onto their backsides by their grooms, and rugs in their owners' colours. Around them racing types sauntered with varying degrees of insouciance. I could have sat there watching it all day. Instead I set off to Number One Car Park. Friends of friends were hosting a picnic there and had said I could drop in.

I found Jennifer and Geoffrey halfway through a spectacular feast by their car boot. Guests had brought food or alcohol. The picnic table was piled high. Everyone was sitting in folding chairs wearing fabulous hats. Some of the men kept their top hats on, others parked them as far from the mayonnaise and strawberries as possible. 'I first came to Ascot in the early 70s,' explained Jennifer, offering me a laden plate, 'and if you were in Number One Car Park you could just walk up to the end of the course, before that horrible building they've put up blocking the view. As the race finished you could see the horses galloping past. It was just wonderful.'

They all remembered the Royal Enclosure being far bigger, paradoxically, in that there was more space. 'The first year after [the new stand] went up it was absolutely tiny, like a sort of corridor,' she said. 'There hardly seemed to be any space at all. They've sorted that out now – there were so many complaints.' There were, and Ascot racecourse moved fast to make the required changes so that now, six years on, things have calmed down again. Geoffrey chimed in: 'There used to be a nice little old-fashioned stand,' he said. 'The Royal Box stood out proud and it had windows, so you felt you could almost touch the Queen. She used to go walkabout, go off to the paddock. It was so much simpler in those days. No, they've buggered it up totally. But the racing's still very good.'

The great set piece of Royal Ascot takes place daily at two o'clock. This is the Royal Procession, when the Queen and her 'dine and sleep' guests staying at Windsor Castle appear at the Golden Gates, at the end of the straight mile, and trundle the length of the course in horse-drawn landaus controlled by liveried postilions. They turn under T5, make a circuit of the parade ring and transfer to the Royal Box. It's pure pageantry, started by the flamboyant King George IV when he was Prince Regent, and as the carriages pass you can see a great ripple of hats being doffed and people glaring at anyone who has failed to do so. Everybody claps madly, not just because it's the Queen but because the day's racing is about to begin.

A mate of mine, who was brought up in Windsor and who has waitressed but not raced at Royal Ascot, takes her children to watch the Queen and the 'dine and sleeps' trans-ship from limo to laundau in Windsor Great Park every year. It's a tradition for several local primary schools, each of which has its own patch on Duke's Lane, where they wave flags and cheer. After school she drives her children back past the racecourse so they can watch, mesmerised, as the worse-for-wear race-goers stagger back to the station at the end of the day. 'Oh my god, they *love* it,' she said, 'especially when they're sick or falling over. And all the girls are carrying their shoes because they can't walk on those heels any more.'

Trust children to have the clearest view. The trollied inhabitants of the Silver Ring – and even the Grandstand, which had a huge, well-publicised fight just after I left that day – are just as much part of the spectacle as the royal procession. And while the convent half of me disapproved of the sight of Anglo-Saxons on the rampage – women with bulging cleavages, tiny skirts, mottled-ham legs and skyscraper heels ('Miss Piggys!' said the Brazilians), and men with skewwhiff ties and unbuttoned waistcoats – the other half loved it. It was untrammelled, riotous, Bacchanalian partying, probably the best fun of the lot. They were after what all the under-forties in the Royal Enclosure were after – sex, alcohol, a bit of racing – but without the tiresome restrictions of good taste. In fact, the Silver Ring worked in precisely the opposite way to the Royal Enclosure, keeping everyone in, rather than out. The media loved it, of course. Misbehaviour was reported, inevitably, in terms of class, as if Royal Ascot occupied a peculiar moral high ground of its own that was now assailed by the lower orders. 'Royal Bashcot!' was my favourite online headline after the fight.

At the parade ring I met a woman who came every year. We watched the horses make their leggy progress in companionable silence. They swung past, led by smart grooms, some eyeing the crowd, others tossing their heads or doing little sideways skitters, and you could see people checking their racecards and peeling off to place bets. I asked the woman if she thought the Royal Enclosure anachronistic. 'No,' she said, 'I've never been but I really like it being there. I like seeing them all dressed up and going in and out. It's so completely different to any other race meeting. We go racing in France quite a bit and we love it, but you don't get any of this pageantry. It's just racing over there, like anywhere else in the world.'

I spent the first race by the railings, trying to work out what makes such a short burst of activity so entertaining. Royal Ascot has seven of the Group One races – the equivalent of Premier League football – in the European system known as pattern racing, and still, despite being outgunned in the prize-money stakes by courses in Qatar or Hong Kong, it attracts some of the greatest horses in the world. There was the same long canter to the start that I remembered from the Derby, the same fiddling around at the stalls, then a slam and a 'They're off!' from the commentator and that intoxicating sound of hooves as they streamed past at top speed.

The sky darkened again and the course was bathed in a yellow light. The great wall of hats swivelled like sunflowers with the progress of each race.

The walk from the station, it turned out, had been a mere warm-up. I walked for miles, starting at Jennifer's picnic, going to the parade ring, strolling to the bookies to place a bet, going to watch the race, going to retrieve winnings (once) and going to see the winner surrounded by owners and the jockey and trainer and sometimes a cheering ringful of people. Kate Fox refers to this as 'The Circuit' in *The Racing Tribe*. I could indeed see hundreds of other people doing the same thing, stopping on the way to talk to friends or have something to eat or sit down at a bar.

There was one more thing to see: the Owners & Trainers' car park, on the far side of the A329 from the racecourse. Back at Epsom I had bumped into a girl I'd been at school with in my early teens. She overheard me talking and introduced herself. It was a stroke of luck: she and her husband had a few jump horses and raced all year. She said they'd be in the Os & Ts all Ascot Week. I didn't need encouraging. I texted her to see if I could join them. 'Gr8, come now' she texted back, 'We r under the big trees.'

There were big trees everywhere. I was jumping over puddles in my winter coat, holding my butterfly hat on with one hand, getting colder and crosser. Then I saw Annabel waving and followed her to the gazebo next to their car. For the next few hours, people turned up wearing their heels and hats, rushing out of the rain carrying food or drink. There were tipsters, a bookie, trainers, a young female flat jockey, friends of Annabel and her husband Tim who came every year. As night fell, racing chat and raucous gossip and shrieks of laughter flew up above the dripping trees.

'Car Park One used to be the life and soul of Royal Ascot,' explained Tim, 'but in the past few years, Os & Ts is where you want to be. This is the piece of real estate you can't pay for. The racing finishes at about five-thirty and this is where the parties happen. All the big names in racing turn up here; Princess Anne was just over there yesterday – she just arrived, no fuss. The reason [Royal] Ascot is so good is the combination of racing and socialising: if you have a good day's racing and you have a really good party, that's what it's all about. We own four racehorses and my trainer is a friend so we're very fortunate – we invite about twenty people every year.'

I felt completely at home that evening, despite knowing nothing about horses. The Os & Ts existed metaphorically and literally on the edge of Royal Ascot. There was nothing la-di-da about the occasion: it was a works do, in a way, the racing world partying while the big event itself went on in the stands and enclosures over the road. As the night wore on, people switched on their headlights so booze-fuelled antics could be seen silhouetted against the walls of tents and gazebos. It made me think of the Travellers playing 'Spin the Penny' into the small hours at Epsom.

The next morning my butterfly dress lay on the bedroom floor, rippled from the rain. Beside it was a pair of ruined shoes. The butterfly hat lay on its side, as if it had a broken wing. I'd had such a good time I'd lost an antenna. On the radio they announced that for the first time ever, due to the rain, wellies were to be allowed in the Royal Enclosure for the last two days of the Royal Meeting. Things might never be the same again.

14

THE PERFECTLY
PACKED BASKET

It was halfway through the season and I was picnicked out. Even someone who considers the Scotch egg and the gala pie the *ne plus ultra* of English cuisine can have enough of pork products. And eating picnics while dressed in your best clothes is uniquely demanding. How, I wondered, on finding a crushed melon ball in one of my Roberto Cavallis, had the formal picnic become as integral to the season as strawberries and champagne?

The dismal phrase 'cold collation' means a light meal of cold meats and salad of some sort. It is the only mention of food by Jane Austen in a famous scene in her novel *Emma*, when a party sets off in carriages from the fictional Surrey village of Highbury to visit the beauty spot of Box Hill. The servants leave them, with the collation, to disport themselves. The word 'picnic' is never used, though the concept had existed for a long time and was evolving from an indoor feast when the guests contributed a dish to the outdoor repast we love so much today. Jennifer and Geoffrey's guests in Number One Car Park were continuing a long and heroic native tradition in believing that food is more special when it's eaten outside.

The essence of the picnic has always seemed so very English. It has a particular combination of rural beauty and physical discomfort ('Sand in the sandwiches, wasps in the tea,' wrote Betjeman, describing a seaside effort) and, in the case of social occasions, a carefully choreographed informality. It demands fortitude in the face of uncertain weather, balancing plates and trying to sit comfortably on a rug without kicking things over, all of which we suspect other nationalities couldn't or wouldn't do. Like many things in life, there must be some suffering before happiness can be achieved. Once it is, the picnic is a joyous thing, the sunniest of traditions: the very word sounds upbeat, its crisply balanced syllables like two Tupperware lids snapping shut. It brings to mind English summer foods: raised pies and Scotch eggs, asparagus and cold ham, cucumber sandwiches and potted shrimps and mayonnaise. Or, in the words of Ratty to a salivating Mole in *The Wind in the Willows*: '... coldtonguecoldhamcold beefpickledgherkinssaladfrenchrollscresssandwichespottedmeat gingerbeerlemonadesodawater ...'

Of course the idea is not exclusively English. Everyone else in Britain does it. There is a great picnicking tradition in the Arab world. Russians have always loved setting off to the woods armed with samovars, food and containers for the mushrooms and berries they will pick. In Isfahan, in what was once Persia, the great rectangle that used to be the royal polo field is often dotted with groups of black-clad figures eating alfresco. Picnics are not always happy, either. Emma's Box Hill jaunt is a disaster in every way:

everyone behaves oddly, they all view each other with critical eyes, nobody eats and Emma is cruel to another guest and reprimanded by Mr Knightley, the only one to keep his head. It feels untrammelled, like one of those drunken evenings when everything goes off the rails.

Emma was published in 1815 and while the Romantic Movement, which celebrated all things wild and natural, was well under way, it clearly hadn't quite reached Hampshire, where Austen was writing. It had influenced her characters enough that they liked the *idea* of eating in the great outdoors; they just didn't like the reality. Imagine, for a second, wearing your tightest and most formal clothes and trying to eat a picnic in the absence of plastic plates, snap-top boxes, ice packs and Wet Ones. Box Hill was a proto-picnic, really, a brave but unhappy experiment.

It took the energetic Victorians with their rapidly improving technology and increasing amounts of leisure time to embrace the concept fully. Their first action, on escaping the acute formality of the indoor dining room, was to impose order on the world outside. Rugs and blankets were used to denote territory. Zinc-lined hardwood chests, their cavities stuffed with straw or sawdust, could be cooled with new imported ice, rather than the grubby slabs of lake ice kept in eighteenth-century icehouses. There were ice stores under the arches at Waterloo Station and you can still see one of the giant ice wells built by Swiss confectioner Carlo Gatti on London's Regent's Canal: they were completed in 1863 to hold the ice he brought in from the mountains of Norway and Greenland. One of them is part of the Canal Museum: it is thirty-four feet in diameter and over forty feet deep.

A year after that Gadsby & Co. started selling wickerwork in Stratford, East London, eventually moving to the willow-lands of the Somerset Levels, fifteen miles or so from Peony Valley. It was easy to convert baskets for laundry or fruit picking into strong, ventilated hampers for transporting food. They identified a picnic market and made hampers to fit into carriages – or later into the footwells or boots of Rolls-Royces – to wow everyone in Number One Car Park. The former deb Fiona MacCarthy writes of those early days: 'Fabulous cane picnic hampers would have been transported in a shooting brake. For people with no image of these now surely obsolete items ... they were rectangular baskets in red-brown lacquered wicker with buckled leather closures and carrying handles on each side. They contained knives, forks, spoons, Bakelite plates, Thermos flasks and food containers, all with their allotted places, packed in two neat tiers.'[1]

Meanwhile, getting around was easier, due to better roads and the arrival of the railways, so people could do day trips. A jaunt to the races or a regatta was now possible for many more spectators, either by private carriage or in a hired charabanc, and the sheer scale of these excursions is conveyed by a famous picnic plan outlined by Isabella Beeton – whose stepfather was the Clerk of Epsom Racecourse, so she should have known – in her best-selling *Book of Household Management*,[2] published in 1861 and aimed at everyone from the mistress of the house to the laundry maid.

The picnic page was presumably aimed at Cook: for the Bill of Fare for forty people included four roast fowl, two roast duck, six medium lobsters, a calf's head, numerous pies, puddings and joints of cooked meat, buckets of salad, orchard-loads of sweetened stewed fruit, pound cakes, biscuits, milk puddings, cheese, butter and, of course, a large teapot and half a pound of loose tea. Even the redoubtable Isabella was defeated by the thought of making coffee for forty on the hoof, but she suggested endless sauces and seasonings, three dozen bottles of ale, six bottles of sherry, two bottles of brandy, claret, light wine and 'a discretion of champagne'.

Nobody could have embarked upon a venture of this scale without a large number of servants and much of the food could not have been transported without aspic. Aspic was a clear, savoury jelly that had been around since the Middle Ages, or ever since people had been boiling up animal bones to make stock and letting it cool. The natural gelatin in the bones made the liquid set into the perfect medium for entombing food. It not only looked good, if you liked great towers of meat pieces or summer fruit suspended in luminous castles of jelly, but it kept germs away from perishable items (the word probably comes from the Greek *aspis*, or shield) and made food easier to carry. It was very time-consuming, involving boiling, straining and cooling, and it required large cool larders, copper moulds and ice. Food fashions change: the nearest we get to it today is the jelly in a pork pie.

By the end of the century things were loosening up. Picnics started to become lighter and more portable and could be made and carried by the individual. When a Scot called James Dewar invented the vacuum flask – he never patented it and the German company Thermos stepped in a few years later and cornered the mass market – things were set fair for the Edwardians. This is probably the defining era of the truly English picnic.

Despite the great move back to seasonal eating in recent years, we will never be able to recreate the intense anticipation and the fleeting glory of foods that appeared only for a short, blissful month or two each year. It is easier in France, where supermarkets often don't stock fresh food that is *hors de saison*, even if it is available thanks to freeze-drying or chilling. We can only imagine the wait, in pre-refrigerated England, for asparagus beds to send up their slender spears of green, or for plums to sag purple and heavy from the tree, or espaliered nectarines to blaze against a wall.

As the marquees went up for Chelsea Flower Show, orders would go out from cooks and householders planning sumptuous picnics to grocers, fishmongers, butchers and smokeries across southeast England and beyond. Watercress swirled in channels of water near Alresford in Hampshire. Asparagus and soft fruit came by the cartload from the Vale of Evesham and the Welsh border counties. Yorkshire sent young rhubarb forced in darkness in the 'Wakefield triangle', and Jersey Royals, which emerged from soil enriched with 'vraic' – or seaweed fertiliser – caused stampedes in London for the first new potatoes of the year.

Cromer crabs, with their black-tipped claws and pie-crust bodies, would be hoicked from the sea after their long migration to the Yorkshire coast and back, caught in long shanks of pots by the Norfolk crabbers. Boats called 'nobbies' dredged brown and grey shrimp from Morecambe Bay to be potted in butter for later in the season. Wild salmon was smoked or poached. Cornish and Scots lobsters, at their best between June and August, arrived by the thousand, in dripping crates, to be turned into lobster lunches in the Stewards' Enclosure at Henley, as they are today.

Even now, June evenings on Kent strawberry farms see the picked fruit being checked over before going up to Wimbledon – it used to go on the milk train, but now goes by road – to be hulled and sold with cream and caster sugar, a combination (apart from the sugar) said to have been invented by greedy Cardinal Wolsey. Everybody keeps an anxious eye on the weather: too much rain and the fruit will be insipid, not enough and it will be too small. The main suppliers, Hugh Lowe Farms in Mereworth, appear in endless features on TV before the Championships, gamely trying to think of something new to say about the perfect Wimbledon strawberry and the English weather. When the strawberries are on track all's right with the world, as long as you're happy to pay £3 a punnet. And people are: tennis fans get through 23 tonnes of fruit and 7,000 litres of cream annually.

Another feature of the season – and particularly of Wimbledon – is Pimm's, an alcoholic fruit cup, which, like an English watercolour, looks innocuous enough until it smacks you between the eyes. Pimm's is actually an early Georgian, almost a Regency, drink: it's extremely strong, flavoured with herbs and aromatic spices, and was invented by James Pimm to wash down the oysters he sold at his premises near the Bank of England. It was served in a small tankard and as he added new alcoholic bases each was numbered: No. 1 – the most popular today – is gin-based. At one point there were seven flavours – from rum to rye – only three of which survive. Pimm's is always mixed with very clear, very sweet, very fizzy White's lemonade and made even more summery by handfuls of chopped fruit, tinkling ice cubes and torn leaves of mint.

Pimm's was so successful that there were five Pimm's Spirit Restaurants in the City of London until the second half of the twentieth century, catering to the chophouse market and those brought up on hefty English food. Then, in the 1970s, Britain began to change. If the Swinging Sixties had begun to make the traditional season events look comically stuffy, ten years later they made many people angry. It was the decade of inflation, of the Three-Day Week, the ending of grammar schools, pay freezes and the Winter of Discontent. So many people were knocking down their country houses, seeing no way to keep them, that the V&A featured them in an exhibition with a tape intoning the names of the destroyed mansions like a roll of death. Pimm's, like many of the staple social events, went into a steep decline. It survived because it was bought by the drinks giant Diageo.

It is now marketed with a breezy irony, popping up at almost every event of the summer – new, old, traditional, non-traditional, literary, sporting and musical – and its presence is announced by a red and white double-decker bus branded 'It's Pimm's O'Clock!' The whole marketing campaign is based on poking fun at an upper-class twit called Harry Fitzgibbon-Sims – talk about biting the hand that feeds you – and it sells a whole range of frightfully English products: bunting, gazebos, ice buckets and stirrers.

The tastes and smells of all this food and drink must have been forever associated in people's minds with happy summer outings and the events of the season. The upmarket suppliers stepped up to the plate: Fortnum & Mason claims to have invented the Scotch egg, for instance, as far back as 1738, not as a picnic food but as a handy travelling food: a pullet's egg was wrapped in a jacket of gamey minced meat and rolled in breadcrumbs for protection. There are rival claims that it was adapted from an Indian recipe, probably around the same time, but within a century it had got bigger – wrapped around a hen's egg – and switched to minced pork. The store itself became one of the features of Derby Day: Dickens described the queue of liveried coaches on Piccadilly first thing in the morning to collect sumptuous prepared hampers from Fortnum's. It was part of the show: Londoners would hang out of their windows and sit on balconies festooned with bunting and swathes of material to watch the jolly cavalcade pass by.

Today, most of these foods appear in some form or other in the picnics produced for the season. These are often eaten sitting around the open boot of a car – a throwback to the glorious days of the carriage – and with elaborate sets of china and glass. Glyndebourne and Ascot have bowed to the pressure of people's busy lifestyles and now do pre-prepared hampers you can pick up, but to be honest, that's not quite cricket. A true English picnic, whether eaten off plastic or porcelain, is gamely and obviously home-made. Stuff in boxes is a cop-out. Those wedding-present hampers with all the plates and knives in their own little holders are a little *too* perfect. You might look as though you're trying to hard.

When I went back to Glyndebourne later in the summer, I saw an earnest young man arranging a picnic for his partner. He had a perfect position – on the small terrace overlooking the lake – and a white tablecloth, proper plates, a bottle of champagne in a bucket, a single rose in a vase and possibly, for all I know, an engagement ring hidden in his pocket. He looked like a bower bird out to impress its mate. He was observed, with infinite cynicism, by a couple of old hands in black tie, hands in their pockets. They watched as he fussed about with the cutlery. They watched as the vase was knocked over by a gust of wind, drenching the arrangement. 'That'll teach him,' murmured one. 'Quite,' murmured the other. No, in England a collection of ancient old cool bags and battered plastic wine glasses is just the ticket: they will match the inherited top hat and tails.

15

THE LAST OF THE
GILDED YOUTH

'Ooh! Ooh! Ooh! Argh! Argh! Argh!' The simian cry rolled out across the checked green outfield of Lord's Cricket Ground, bounced off the vast expanse of empty seats on the opposite side and rolled back again. It was followed by a thundering sound that vibrated up into your knees: you only had to look across to the next-door stand to realise it was the stamp of many hundreds of pairs of expensively shod adolescent feet. Down on the field itself, the tableau of white-clad young men had suddenly shifted. An Etonian fielder, his baby-blue cricket cap spinning heroically into the air, had dived to stop a ball from reaching the boundary and Harrovians were showing their displeasure. 'H … A … R … O … W!' they boomed, faltering slightly before yelling 'HARROW!' 'Oh God, they've got the letters wrong!' said a voice behind me, and I turned to see a man with his head in his hands.

How I infiltrated the Harrow parents' section at the Eton v. Harrow match, held at Lord's every June since the summer before the Battle of Trafalgar, I'm not quite sure. I paid £17 at a window near the Grace Gate – named after one of England's sporting legends, the alarmingly hirsute W. G. Grace, scourge of amateur county cricket and hero of Victorian schoolboys – and followed a pair of parents who looked as bewildered as me. Their son was batting for Harrow but they were obviously new to the occasion. 'Eton or Harrow?' said a steward wearing a smart green jacket with cream piping. 'Harrow,' they said, and we were ushered into seats up in the Tavern Stand, tucked into the southeastern corner of the famous ground.

Lord's on a sunny summer day is a glorious sight. The grass looks like a gargantuan rectangle of Fuzzy Felt, as flat as a billiard table. This is a visual trick: it is in fact a highly scientific combination of grasses, shaved to within an inch of its life on the playing area known as the square. It is also eight feet lower on one side than the other so has a fearsome roll. The square, to my surprise, held not one but twenty-one adjacent cricket pitches, the use of which was rotated according to grass condition and match status. This one was being played to the far right, near the stands of boys. To our left glowed the brick of the late nineteenth-century pavilion, skirted by a white picket fence. To our right, high on the Mound Stand, the black weathervane figure of Old Father Time with a golden scythe over one shoulder bent down arthritically to replace a bail on a wicket. He is the symbol of Lord's, with his own range in the shop: a fine reminder that of all games none is more prodigal of time than cricket.

On the opposite side of the ground was the J. P. Morgan Media Centre, the stilted, space-age, glass-fronted press and commentary box that opened in 1999, won the Stirling Prize for architecture and was swiftly nicknamed 'Cherie Blair's Mouth' because of its oversized letterbox effect. Through the gap beneath you could see the Nursery Ground, so called because it used to be a plant nursery before the club bought it. All around us was St John's Wood, an expensive residential area filled with blocks of flats that look as though they could be in upmarket Lima or Beirut and amply proportioned brick and stucco town houses, one of which belongs to Sir Paul McCartney. A crow flying northeast over the Mound Stand would soon see the awnings of Church Street market and the roof of Joel and Son's far below.

'Are you a parent?' enquired a friendly woman with a slightly puzzled look. I apologised for gate-crashing and explained I was researching a book. The Harrow parents were delightful: I was offered sandwiches and tea and buns and they pointed out who was in to bat and who had been out for a duck last year and who had been injured. The Etonians, they said, always turned up late-ish. Harrow boys had already done two periods of school before coming but Eton boys had to do an entire morning. 'They're just beginning to trickle in now,' observed a woman who was sitting chatting to one of the boys and knitting, 'then the fun really begins.' Right on cue there was an ominous mooing sound as the Harrovians spotted their rivals filing into the adjacent Mound Stand. This is the only fixture at Lord's where the two sides keep themselves separate. Eton v. Harrow has form.

My new acquaintance was called Sonia Amos and she was the outgoing matron of a house of eighty-five boys called Headmaster's. It was one of twelve houses scattered around what she described as 'a campus in the public domain' in Harrow on the Hill, north London. Match attendance was compulsory only for the two youngest years, who were wearing Harrow's everyday uniform of 'bluers' (dark-blue jackets) 'greyers' (light-grey trousers) and plain black ties, but not, to my disappointment, the famous shallow straw boaters with black bands known as 'Harrow hats'.

The more we spoke the more I thought the two schools well matched, not just on the cricket field: both are ancient – Eton was founded by Henry VI in 1440, Harrow by Elizabeth I in 1572; both are in or near London; both cater for exclusively male boarders; both call masters 'beaks'; both wear bonkers uniforms, though Harrovians wear their tailcoats only on Sundays while Etonians wear them for much of the time; and both have fiendish school argots and complex dress codes involving coloured and patterned ties and waistcoats. These are usually related to sporting prowess or popularity and are therefore symbols of masculine power. Emmanuelle Dirix would have loved it: all that status anxiety at such a young age.

The Eton v. Harrow match is the oldest fixture at Lord's and possibly the longest continuously running cricket fixture anywhere (oddly enough the earliest cricket matches were played between America and Canada, who clearly thought it took up too much time in the busy New World and switched to baseball). The first match in 1805 was probably informal, set up by the boys, but gradually developed into a major event. As the century wore on and the upper classes began sending their sons to public schools, the two schools' long pedigrees and proximity to London increased their prestige.

The match became part of the London season – indeed, an important political occasion – because most of the Cabinet's sons would have been at one or other school. It took place during the summer Long Leave, both teams were presented to the monarch after the match and the prime minister frequently attended. The reason for attending was cricket. The real reason for attending was schmoozing. You went to see and be seen (that essential criterion again) so your *equipage* – your carriage, or later your motor car – would be noticed, so would the modishness of your wife and daughters, and so would the cricketing prowess or otherwise of your son. It was a formal occasion, lasting two days and attended by a far wider circle than just families, friends and Old Boys. At its Edwardian peak some 38,000 people turned up. The stands were packed and the boundary line hemmed in by carriages and spectators. Today, it's one day and the gate is around two and a half thousand, barely filling two of the stands.

Formal or not, it was still a chance for everyone to let their hair down, at least to some degree. Sonia told me that in one of the houses at Harrow there was a painting showing all the carriages pulled up to the boundary at Lord's, with people standing on top of them to watch the match. As at the Derby, the horses were stabled and the carriages pulled into position.

'Oh, there was still one landau here when I first came to Lord's,' said Colin Maynard, MCC Deputy Secretary, who saw me in his office some weeks after the match. 'It used to be wheeled out by the boys and parked by the boundary. I'm not sure which family it belonged to or exactly where it was kept.' Around the Nursery Ground, he explained, there had been twenty 'arbours' – sylvan spaces separated by pillars – where you parked your carriage or motor car and set up a picnic table. Families booked the same spaces every year, strolling to and from the cricket. 'Until 1985 we used to allow thousands of people to sit on the grass to watch, even for Test matches,' he said, 'but people got hit and there were streakers, of course.'

Back in the Tavern Stand, things were hotting up. An Etonian called Ed Abel-Smith had come on to bowl to howls of approval from the Mound Stand and Harrow hero Mikey Cousens was approaching his half-century. All was reported by the neutral voice of the Lord's announcer in the Cherie Box. A row of Eton boys turned to face the stand and point at the boxes above, some of which were occupied by Harrow parents having formal lunches. 'Twenty-one prime ministers!' they bellowed rudely (Harrow has only had four, but they do include Winston Churchill) as the Harrovians put their fingers to their lips and went 'Ssssshhhhh!' When Eton's bowler hurt a finger the Harrovians went 'Ahhhhhh!' and as Harrow's batsmen plodded on an Etonian chorus went up, followed by slightly embarrassed laughter. 'What are they singing?' asked the woman who was knitting. 'I think it was: "Your dad works for my dad!"' I offered. She shot me a look.

Lord's is not the oldest cricket ground in Britain – even in London, Mitcham Cricket Club can claim to be almost twice as old – but it was always elite. It was set up by a late eighteenth-century entrepreneur called Thomas Lord, at the request of a group of aristocratic London players who were irritated at being gawped at, village-style, by non-aristocratic spectators. They used to whack around a much lighter ball than is used today with a much lighter willow bat in what were then the fields of Islington. They gambled for enormous stakes and wished to enjoy their sport in peace.

Lord built his first ground in Dorset Fields (today Square), Marylebone, in 1787, then moved further north, only to be displaced by the new Regent's Canal. He finally settled on the current site, then surrounded by open land. Gambling, as ever, forced the establishment of set proportions for the wicket and a body of ground rules. The oldest rules in existence were written not at Lord's but at Goodwood House in Sussex, where they are still in the safe. However, Lord's was where they were refined. It considers itself – since the year 2000 has branded itself – 'The Home of Cricket'.

The custodians of cricket and the chief tenants of Lord's are

MCC, or the Marylebone Cricket Club, which sports a natty burgundy and gold striped tie known as 'eggs and bacon'. It has a waiting list of twenty-three years for non-playing members, though anyone who has played ten matches over two years for one of its many teams – even women, since 1999 – is fast-tracked. There are 18,000 Full Members and 5,000 Associate Members. The Pavilion is the mother ship, shared, confusingly, with the Middlesex County Cricket Club, the north London county side.

The two clubs never muddle each other up, of course: MCC members can enter the Pavilion for any match and have exclusive access during Tests and One-Day Internationals, while Middlesex members can enter only on Middlesex match days. MCC members' guests sign in on the left as they enter the pavilion, Middlesex members' guests on the right. MCC members can see international players as they walk through the portrait-lined Long Room on their way to bat and clap England cricketers on the back if they return victorious. Middlesex members can't. All have to adhere to a strict dress code of jackets, ties and no jeans and the Pavilion stewards wear cream jackets with green piping on match days to denote their status. The Pavilion smells like an outpost of Empire, as if there should be hot red dust and acacia trees outside.

Early paintings and prints of Lord's in the ground's museum are very like early paintings of racing. Stiff little players disport themselves around the stubbly ground, wearing long-sleeved shirts, uncomfortably tight trousers and jackets and everyday hats. The playing area was not surrounded by stands, as it is today, hence the spectators and carriages hard up to the boundary. Stands evolved gradually, the Pavilion being the first and most prestigious, as did the matches. For many decades there were only three fixtures: Eton v. Harrow, Gentlemen v. Players, which began the following year, and the Varsity Match – Oxford v. Cambridge, obviously –

which started about twenty years later. From 1822 onwards these were annual, interrupted only by the World Wars, when they were played elsewhere.

'We still had Public Schools Week until the 1970s,' said Colin Maynard, 'Rugby v. Marlborough, Clifton v. Tonbridge, Cheltenham v. Haileybury, Beaumont v. The Oratory, probably because Old Boys were MCC members. In the end, the demands on the square just got too much. When you play on a cricket pitch it gets quite roughed up. People are wearing spikes and running up and down, and today's bats and balls and players are heavier; a pitch usually lasts about four days. In 1971 they looked at the schedule of county cricket and international matches and realised the school matches would have to go. Eton v. Harrow survived for historic reasons. To be honest, I don't think the other school matches had the same cachet.'

Right now, you would never have guessed Harrow had won the last seven matches in the series. The parents were supportive but self-deprecating. The tone was one of amused resignation in the very best English tradition. Two beaks behind me provided a hilariously sardonic parallel commentary. 'Invertebrate!' murmured one, when a Harrow batsman failed to capitalise on a weak delivery. 'I can see them being all out by 155,' said the other, suppressing a yawn, 'so at least we'll get back early.' It was like being in *Goodbye, Mr Chips*, but teleported to the twenty-first century. If you looked at the stands, though, you could see staff from both schools patrolling up and down. One of the commentators told me that the chants had got personal the year before and the boys had been told to 'keep it positive'. At least these days it's only verbal. In the past, there have been proper fights.

There are two Eton v. Harrow matches that will be remembered for ever at Lord's. The first took place in 1910, when by the end of play on the first day the game seemed so much in Harrow's favour that spectators started decamping to another match at the Oval. At least half *The Times* match report is taken up with descriptions of aristocrats entertaining each other to luncheon on their coaches. Then on the second day Robert St Leger Fowler, a 19-year-old Anglo-Irishman in his last year at Eton, batted brilliantly, and as Eton caught up and pulled past Harrow, bowled out of his skin to help his side win by nine runs. The excitement was such that a spectator died of a heart attack. The match, as always, was reported in the national newspapers. 'In the whole history of public school cricket,' raved *The Times* on the Monday, 'nothing better can have been seen than Fowler's play on the second day.'[1] Fowler, the Eton captain, was a genuine schoolboy hero. The game has ever since been known as 'Fowler's Match'.

The other marvellous event was nearly thirty years later. War was only two months away, to be fair, and perhaps the Establishment was feeling unusually edgy, but when Eton ended a 31-year unbeaten streak by losing to Harrow, a full-scale brawl broke out. Not between the boys, who then, as now, were well supervised, but between fathers, brothers, uncles and grandfathers. The sudden shift in balance halfway through the game was described thus by the *Eton Chronicle*: 'Old Harrovians from all parts of England began chartering aeroplanes. Spectators who had always regarded Lords (sic) as a clearing house for family gossip even went so far as to face the cricket and enquire earnestly which side was batting; old gentlemen in the Pavilion who generally reckoned on a peaceful two hours' nap between the lunch and tea intervals blew up their air cushions and brought a score card.'[2] *The Cricketer* reported blandly that 'after the match a fight of some proportion took place, presumably between the supporters ... the following year before the match commenced ... the players and supporters [were warned] that if there was a similar occurrence again the match would be taken away from Lord's.' *Wisden's Almanac*, perhaps wisely, declined to mention it at all.

The match hung on at Lord's and is therefore a public event: anyone can go, which is quite odd, like buying a ticket to someone else's school sports day. The Fourth of June, on the other hand, Eton's equivalent of a speech day, once equally well attended by Society, is at the school and therefore remains a private event. I was amazed I enjoyed the cricket so much. It was really exciting, in a Zen-like way. The commentator I spoke to liked it too, partly because of the partisan chanting and partly because the cricket was actually quite good. He was a volunteer, relaying the match to a blind or partially sighted audience, and his full-time job was teaching in a state secondary school. 'The kids are fascinated when I tell them about it,' he said, 'because to them Eton and Harrow are otherworldly, like something out of *Harry Potter*, and the whole idea of cricket at Lord's is surreal.'

As our afternoon wore on, Cousens was out for a respectable sixty-one and Harrow's innings lost momentum. Every run scored set off Mexican waves, ragged choruses of 'Oggie Oggie Oggie! Oi Oi Oi!' and, every so often, snatches of the Harrow school song, 'Forty Years On'. The chorus goes:

> Follow up! Follow up! Follow up! Follow up! Follow up!
> Till the field ring again and again,
> With the tramp of the twenty-two men.
> Follow up! Follow up!

Eton's more cerebral '*Carmen Etonense*', when translated from the Latin, contains similar sentiments, albeit disguised as Roman mythology:

Let play take its fair share with work.
Let a sweet alliance join Mars with Minerva.
Whether the reason for glory is the ball or the oar,
There is one glory in victory ...

Both were written in the second half of the nineteenth century, when sports were important in public schools for maintaining discipline, fostering team spirit and using up 'excess' (a euphemism for sexual) energy. They needed to toughen boys up, like Spartan babies, giving them the fortitude to sit in a Malayan palm oil plantation or Ceylonese tea garden for several years without cracking up. There was an Empire to run.

There was also a self-image to create. On the southeast corner of Lord's outer wall is a 1930s relief of a cricket match inscribed: 'Play up! Play up! And play the game!' The words are actually nothing to do with the Eton–Harrow match, or with Lord's for that matter, but it was clearly felt they belonged in the heartland of cricket. They have been mercilessly parodied over the years, of course, but originally they came from a poem by Henry Newbolt, a master at Clifton College in Bristol. They are right up there with Rudyard Kipling's *If* as an expression of all the things the English believed about themselves – decency, fair play, honour, the importance of taking part rather than winning (crucial, and the one that exasperates other nationalities as it only kicks in when we lose) and selflessness in the face of the greater good – all rolled into one and re-applied to the theatre of war:

The river of death has brimmed his banks,
And England's far, and Honour a name,
But the voice of a schoolboy rallies the ranks:
'Play up! Play up! And play the game!'

I thought back to my lunch with the writer Victoria Mather right at the beginning of my research and her passing mention of Corinthian values. I knew what she meant: she meant honour and pluck, a straight back and a level gaze. She meant Fowler plugging on in the teeth of defeat and being modestly self-effacing in victory. There are whole books on these qualities in sport, but why Corinthian? Why not Athenian or Hellenic? The dictionary definition was oddly confusing: it divided into the licentious behaviour of Corinthian youth and a wildly romantic view of amateur sporting values. Writings on the subject often explained the values but not the etymology.

In the end my cousin PJ, a Greek scholar, came to my rescue. 'In the Hellenic world, Corinth was known for its love of luxury,' she explained. 'That's the connotation it would have had in the classical sense.' Over the centuries, she added, it had evolved into something slightly different in England. Shakespeare uses it in *Henry IV Part 1* when Hal, describing himself as a man about town, says '... I am no proud Jack like Falstaff, but a Corinthian, a lad of mettle, a good boy (by the Lord, so they call me!) ...' and by Regency times it had come to mean libertine values, often linked to the aristocracy. But the real change came as the individual sports of the eighteenth century – cock-fighting, pugilism and so on, with their strong gambling associations – gave way to team sports played by the public schools, which were not only steeped in classical tradition but were strongly Christian. The laundering of Corinthian values was under way.

Within decades the libertine connotations had entirely disappeared, but the phrase retained its association with sport in the amateur sense. It never referred to professional sport. 'Amateur sport was something you had to have leisure for,' said PJ, 'so it became associated with class. These chaps didn't need to be paid, they didn't have the taint of business, they didn't need to win for money, which most people did if they were talented sportsmen. You didn't want to be seen to be trying too hard. That famous scene from *Chariots of Fire*, when the Master of Trinity pulls up Harold Abrahams for hiring a running coach, is a wonderful example, and of course it confirms all their prejudices about the fact he is Jewish.'

Not trying too hard runs through so many aspects of English life, from wearing an old coat over your ball dress to the pathological use of understatement. It appears in *The Shooting Party* when Sir Randolph, the host, is appalled to catch one of his guests practising shooting moves with his loader in the library (nobody knows who is more embarrassed) and is perhaps best summed up by Flanders & Swann in 'The English', or 'A Song of Patriotic Prejudice':

> And all the world over each nation's the same,
> They've simply no notion of playing the game,
> They argue with umpires, they cheer when they've won,
> And they practise beforehand which ruins the fun.

Practising too hard and wanting to win too much were not on. Or, as the old cliché went, 'not cricket'. And in the end, it was cricket that supplied the clearest example of the amateur/professional divide that I still found hard to understand: the fixture founded just after Eton v. Harrow, in 1806, and last played, quite incredibly, in 1962: Gentlemen v. Players.

It's fair to say that every sport of the season, bar tennis, was invented or codified by the aristocracy and as aristocrats rarely worked for a living they could be genuine 'amateurs', or lovers, of the games they played. That didn't stop them from talent-spotting others, though, and when big money was riding on a match – as it often was in the early days of private teams – they wanted the best players they could get. A landowner might well use an estate worker who was already on the pay roll and had natural sporting talent as well, for example. Employers and employees played together – something that still exists in polo today and sometimes in elite sailing – but in a social sense the caste system never went away.

'There absolutely was a class element to Gentlemen and Players,' said Neil in the Lord's library. 'Here at Lord's they dressed in different rooms in the Pavilion and they walked onto the field through different gates, they were physically divided. A professional was employed as a cricketer: it was his job and he was paid a wage, not a salary like footballers today. Amateurs – the Gentlemen – were not remunerated, although they got expenses for attending functions and so on, often more than the professional wages.' Even their names were differently displayed, as the writer D. J. Taylor notes drily in his book about amateur sport, *On the Corinthian Spirit*: 'As late as the 1950s a message could be heard crackling from the Lord's Tannoy to correct the score-sheet error that had let "Titmus, F. J." (professional) into the proceedings masquerading as "F. J. Titmus" (amateur).'[3]

Amateurs had an innate sense of moral superiority. Being working class and paid to do anything had something unpalatable about it. It couldn't be helped, but it was still an instant classifier. Each county had its own set of professionals and amateurs, but the captain would always be an amateur. It was accepted he would have the attributes of a gentleman; a natural ability to lead and an instinctive grasp of the values expressed in Henry Newbolt's poem. Until the 'Bodyline' tour of Australia, that is, when the England team on the 1932–33 Ashes tour bowled fast, short and straight at the Australian batsmen's bodies. When the Australians complained, cabling MCC to accuse the English of unsportsman-like behaviour, it was raised in the Commons and the series nearly came to a premature end. Not because of England's tactics, but because of Australia impugning their sportsmanship. Harold Larwood, the professional Nottinghamshire bowler, lost his place on the England team. Douglas Jardine, the amateur captain, did not.

'English cricket has not always lived up to its own ideals,' said Neil Robinson carefully, 'but to be fair, no one [in England] had any idea what was going on. Later they saw the tactic employed in England, versus the West Indies, and decided they didn't want to see cricket being played in that way. Jardine only lasted another year, but the thing was he was this educated Englishman, schooled at Winchester, playing for Surrey, very much officer class, playing cricket in a way that contradicted the spirit of the game as the upper class wished to portray it. Once the Establishment actually saw [the new bowling], they did take appropriate action.' Or, as Anne Boston once wrote in the *Observer*: 'Cricket represents in its most extreme form the Englishman's capacity for self-delusion and his desire to present himself as he would like to be seen, rather than as he really is.'[4]

Amateurism was a major issue for most season events because they were all based on upper-class sports. As time went on, stewards following the rules to the letter found themselves in absurd situations: a famous case was Grace Kelly's father, Jack – a triple Olympic gold medallist for America – who was refused permission to row in the 1920 Henley Regatta because he had been an apprentice bricklayer as a young man. On the cricket pitch, talented players were banned from tours because they worked for a living, or were businessmen. The system might have ended in the

1960s but the social divisions continued for years, and there is still something in the English/British DNA that clings to the concept of plucky amateurism. We still use the word 'gentleman' to mean someone who is truly decent.

Today, all this seems unintelligible, not just from a sporting but from a social point of view. There is a reason that the Eton v. Harrow match attendance has dropped to a fraction of its former levels. As many have pointed out, the Duchess of Cambridge (middle class) looks and sounds classier than the prime minister's wife, Samantha Cameron (upper class), who studiously eschews cut-glass vowels and strolled hatless into the Royal Wedding. The same thing happens in sport. A public school cricketer good enough to turn professional – and there are several in county sides – will be bending over backwards to play down his accent and background. Anyone remotely upper class in government or business will be pushing his or her football- rather than cricket-loving credentials. It's fine for a footballer to apply to become a member of the Royal Enclosure. It would be political suicide to be seen at the Eton v. Harrow match.

16

THE BUTTERFLIES TAKE OFF

Una-Mary Parker went to Eton v. Harrow the year she came out in 1948. She also went to Ascot, the Fourth of June, the Summer Exhibition and the Chelsea Flower Show, met her husband Archie at a house party for Ascot Week and saw *Così Fan Tutte* at Glyndebourne for their first date. When the door of her Knightsbridge house opened it revealed a woman with a ballet dancer's figure in a fitted purple dress, with full make-up and a wide smile. Her voice was a startling baritone. 'Coming out was the launch, it showed you were a grown-up,' she told me, sitting on the sofa with Toffee the poodle, who was eyeing my furry mic cover with disfavour, 'everything was too exciting for words: we'd been in London all the way through the Blitz, hungry all the time, and there was still rationing and clothes coupons.' On the table were six scrapbooks of bus tickets and ball invitations and racecards and letters asking her to lunches or dances.

The post-war generation of debs occupied a twilight zone between pre-war formality and the great social shake-up of the 1960s. Una-Mary, who is now in her early eighties, never went to school. 'The Queen and I must be the only people living who were educated at home,' she said with a smile. 'Governesses came to the house; one for French, two English ones and a piano teacher. I did no maths, I was educated to write because that is what I wanted to do.' She had dancing lessons with Madame Vacani at the Hyde Park Hotel every Friday afternoon and could curtsey perfectly by the age of twelve. Madame Vacani prepared generations of debs for their big moment, the deep, formal court curtsey to the monarch and consort, watched by their peers and the court. Una-Mary remembered Madame Vacani's diamonds and rouge, her immaculate manners and, even in her seventies, the blonde hair wrapped headphone-style around her ears.

Una-Mary made or altered many of her clothes for the season – a great-aunt left her a Paris trousseau made by Paquin – and shared a dance with a friend. She still has the presentation invitation sent to her mother: 'The Lord Chamberlain is commanded by Their Majesties to summon Mrs Hugh Nepean-Gubbins to an afternoon presentation party at Buckingham Palace on Thursday 13th May 1948 from 4–6 o'clock pm. Day dress with hats. Morning dress, lounge suit or service dress.' She remembers the mirrored double doors of the Throne Room swinging open to reveal the King, Queen and two princesses, who walked down the room greeting the debutantes massed on either side. There were no ostrich feathers, no forehead kisses, no backing out of the room. Madame Vacani's curtsey was now obsolete.

Also obsolete was the studied decadence of the 1920s and 30s. The young people of the late 1940s went to endless cocktail parties, at which they drank fruit punch, and girls hoped to be asked out to supper afterwards by a young man. They prayed for a full dance card at balls, rather than being left to sit with the chaperones – who were still out in force – as a visible failure on a little gilt chair beside the dance floor. For the sociable Una-Marys, it was heaven. For the girls with empty dance cards, it must have been hell. She remembers one girl walking the streets for hours rather than admit to her mother she had no supper partner, and others who spent whole evenings in the Ladies to avoid gilt chair humiliation.

Mothers were still clearly a formidable presence. The deb season had long since spun off into a separate existence of its own, a feminine counterpart to the masculine worlds of politics, war and sport: mothers organised, fathers indulged and girls did what they were told. It was the women who drummed a moral code into their daughters: no going back to a young man's flat, no kissing in taxis, no presents bar books or chocolate (clothes or jewellery being for mistresses) and no getting a reputation as 'fast'. 'To lose your virginity then was the kiss of death,' Una-Mary said bluntly. 'Archie wouldn't have married me had I slept with anyone else first.'

The Queen ended the formal presentation system in 1958. After the war the whole thing was becoming increasingly embarrassing: the image of the debs – the 'girls in pearls' who appeared in the portrait page at the front of *Country Life* each week – causing traffic jams on the Mall would make the monarchy seem anachronistic and out of touch, thought the courtiers. Buckingham Palace garden parties took over from presentations and for a while they tried inviting peers to bring unmarried daughters along, but it didn't really work. At this point, with the 60s on the horizon, you might have thought the entire thing – white dresses, tea parties, dances, lists of eligible young people – would collapse altogether. But for the women who built their lives around it, it was too great a blow. It was like telling butterflies they couldn't pupate. So they just kept going. The fact they managed to do so was almost entirely down to two famous social columnists and the rapidly expanding world of the glossy magazine.

The glossies, aimed exclusively at women, had their roots in far older publications. *Queen* magazine, for example, began a regular etiquette column called 'Au Fait' in 1880 and when *Tatler* had its anniversary party in 2009 the cover line was '300 Years of Mischief'. This was a bit of a stretch – the title has come and gone like a Cheshire Cat over the centuries – but there is no denying the longevity of the formula: fashion, beauty and famous faces, whether wood-block prints or colour photographs, sell magazines to women. And while the driving force is now popular celebrity, many magazines – *OK!* and *Hello!* for example – still love a title or a model with posh antecedents. The columnists of the post-war period bridged these two worlds. They stepped into a vacuum, operating as social arbiters for a system stripped of its figurehead. One newspaper once described 'Jennifer's Diary', the most famous social column of them all, as 'the last bastion of the structured pre-war class system'.

When Una-Mary came out, Betty Kenward, the immaculately coiffed and be-pearled real-life 'Jennifer', wrote about her dance. Mrs Kenward, as she insisted on being known, suffered from a familiar British syndrome: sliding down the minor gentry ladder due to lack of funds, but retaining an acute awareness of her status. 'She ignored other social editors and referred to other journalists as "the Penny Press",' said Celestria Noel, who knew her well. 'She never admitted she was one.' She was a grafter, though: once she landed her famous slot in *The Tatler* in 1945 she attended two or three events a night and wrote her much-parodied copy, which was famed for its eccentric punctuation and pored over mainly by the people who were in it. In her obituary, the *Daily Telegraph* quoted an immortal example:

> 'I stayed on for supper in the Boissier box, where, besides Mr and Mrs Roger Boissier, I met his brother and sister-in-law Mr and Mrs Martin Boissier, and their attractive daughter Miss Susan Boissier; their cousins Mr and Mrs Peter Boissier, and their sons Commander Paul Boissier, who commands a submarine, with his wife Susie; and Mr John Boissier, and his wife Annie ...' and so on, and so on.[1]

She was also strongly territorial, as Una-Mary was soon to find out. 'Betty Kenward knew me before I was married,' she said, laughing ruefully. 'She was nice about my dance and my wedding. Then Jocelyn Stevens asked me to do the social column on *Queen* and she cut me dead – for twenty-five years.' She also swiped her job, despite fervent denials from Una-Mary's editors. It was Archie who heard first and broke the news to her outside a party, advising her to go straight up to Mrs Kenward and offer congratulations. 'I told her how pleased I was, of course, but I was sort of, "Bloody hell!"'

After that, with Mrs Kenward at *Queen*, Una-Mary went to *The Tatler* for some years, and when she left, a Yorkshireman called Peter Townend took over. He had cut his teeth by editing three editions of *Burke's Peerage*, *Debrett's* main rival. He was genuinely interested in genealogy, which is perhaps what drove him to step in where the Lord Chamberlain had left off. He had an encyclopedic memory. He was a professional snob. He wrote to mothers as their daughters reached seventeen to suggest they bring them out. He kept a meticulous log, published in the January issue, of the cocktail parties and coming-out dances, so nobody's dates clashed. He also had – and this was the real source of his power – a 'little black book' of eligible young men. They were not necessarily straight, they were not necessarily interested, but they were eligible, and most hostesses would have given their eye teeth to get hold of it. Mrs Kenward hated him.

This was the world that greeted Celestria – who would later become editor of 'Jennifer's Diary', by then running in *Harpers & Queen* magazine – when she came out in 1971. At this stage the whole thing was unimaginably relaxed. There were a few very glamorous dances – Una-Mary remembers one from her daughter's deb season with a disco decorated as a Formula One racetrack – but generally the mothers were in retreat. Once they'd sorted a dance and a few March tea parties they left 'the young' to get on with it. Girls were now thinking about university, travelling and careers. The deb season had turned into a loose confederation of party-goers, who shared a social background and common values. Occasionally it resulted in marriage.

I was expecting Celestria to be tall and icy, I don't know why. She turned out to be much smaller than me, wearing an old skirt, T-shirt and tennis shoes, with fine, straight hair and the sort of utterly English face that would be right at home under a towering powdered wig. 'The great source of dresses was Valerie Goad's shop in the Fulham Road,' she told me over a Prosecco in a Chelsea bar, 'cotton voile with a silk moiré bodice for eighteen pounds, silk and velvet for twenty-eight pounds. I had one of each and I had a Liberty print dress by Gina Fratini. It was very milk-maidy. There was that awful phase of people throwing food and flicking butter pats at the ceiling, so you needed something that washed well. Most of us had untidy schoolgirl hair and shiny pink faces with clumpy mascara and pearlescent blue eye shadow. It was before conditioner, so we had terrible split ends as well.' For a glorious moment I envisaged someone lobbing a butter pat at Margaret Whigham, chillingly glamorous in her silk-satin Mainbocher sheath. Later I found a 1970s bell-sleeved Gina Fratini long dress in flowered cotton on Rockmyvintage.com. It seemed to come from an age of innocence.

Before the war, Celestria pointed out, an upper-class girl automatically became a debutante at the age of eighteen because her name was on a list at court. 'Then look at Lady Diana Spencer, the most famous Sloane Ranger of them all,' she said. 'She was seven years younger than me and she wouldn't have dreamed of being a deb. By the 1980s, nobody did.' The surprise was not really that the system had run out of steam. The surprise was that it kept going, like the orchestra on the *Titanic*, for so very long.

Celestria loved her season. She was on her way to university at Oxford so she had a spare year. Like Una-Mary she was naturally sociable – 'light a candle and I'm there' – and even more than being in London she loved driving around the country in her Mini, going to parties in country houses. She was perfectly happy sitting next to the old uncles and grandfathers at dinner, hearing about their lives and experiences. 'It was very make do and mend. It just wasn't as expensive in those days: people didn't hire marquees; they opened up their houses. Nobody thought about security. Some people had large houses with ballrooms they could use, some people would do a party in a barn, sometimes parents would club together. The drink was usually terrible white wine or wine cup. The only meal provided was breakfast, the house party system saw to that, and it was usually just scrambled eggs and sausages or something like that.'

The house party system evolved out of the long social visits that people used to make in the country in the days of carriages and early motor cars, when getting around was hard, expensive and took a long time. As trains and cars appeared these could be contracted into what were known as 'Saturday-to-Mondays'. And against the bleak economic backdrop of the 1970s, the system adapted perfectly to help spread the cost of throwing a big party: nearby friends of the hosts would offer to have a number of guests to dinner and to stay the night after the dance. The guest would turn up with a box of After Eights, often having never met their host before, and would leave after breakfast the next day. They would write a 'bread and butter' letter to say thank you, preferably within the week.

Even this casual a version of the deb season had its starting and finishing posts. It began in April with the Berkeley Dress Show, at the Berkeley hotel in Knightsbridge, which was a relatively recent arrival on the scene. The best-looking girls would parade down a catwalk in dresses provided by designers, one high street, one sporty and one couture. Their families would watch and applaud, though not everyone made it to the catwalk: 'The fatter debs, like me,' said Celestria without rancour, 'handed out the programmes.' Her eldest sister was a textbook deb: beautiful and first out on the catwalk, she met her husband during her season and had Juliana's Discotheques – a staple at all the best dances – named after her.

The best-born ones got to push the cake. In May, Queen Charlotte's Ball was held in the Great Room at Grosvenor House, the hotel built in the 1920s on the site of the Grosvenor family's colossal Park Lane town house. The ball had an illustrious history. It began in the late eighteenth century as an annual party thrown for the debutantes by Queen Charlotte, the consort of King George III. It was always on her birthday, so there was always a cake, which she would cut and hand out, and the girls would curtsey in gratitude. When Charlotte died, the ball ended but was revived in the early twentieth century as a charity ball in support of Queen Charlotte's Hospital. Somehow the cake tradition survived as well, with the Chairman of the Ball doing the honours and the girls curtseying to her instead. Inevitably, it became known as curtseying to the cake. And it was an excuse not only to keep curtseying but to wear a long white dress.

'It was a ridiculous cardboard thing on wheels,' remembered Celestria. 'I don't think there was any real cake in it. I was one of six chosen to wheel it the length of the room, like outriders, past all the little tables full of parents and boyfriends, until we got to the end. Then we peeled off and everybody came up and curtsied.' The thriftier aristocratic girls would re-use their white dress, either for one of the Scottish balls or, appropriately accessorised, for their weddings. The ball ran out of steam later in the decade, partly because of the awful behaviour of the guests, who drank too much, gate-crashed and abseiled off the balconies. It got so out of hand that Mrs Kenward formally withdrew her support. And that was that.

People clearly wanted to keep the deb season going, perhaps for reasons of reassurance or perhaps out of nostalgia, so the whole thing continued, bizarrely, against a background of punk rock. Even Queen Charlotte's Ball revived for a while. But life had changed. The grander families had long considered that the 'real' season was over and anyway their daughters were now busy doing exams and applying for universities and jobs. The middle classes with daughters at suitable schools joined in, further devaluing the brand, as it were. By the 1980s the upper-class deb was pretty well extinct. With her went a world of entertainment specific to a certain time of year and many of the suppliers that made it all happen.

'*Mutatis mutandis*,' said Celestria cheerily, 'the upper classes are very good at moving on. One of the things the season has done is fragment: the young girls go to the music festivals, a lot of which take place in the grounds of historic houses, as a rite of passage, just as I would have been to a ball in that house at that age. They're full of public school girls and boys: rather than staying at house parties they take their tents and stay in them instead and they organise it all themselves rather than relying on their parents. They're all at university now, but in many ways they're doing very much as the debs did, there's a circuit. Certain clubs, certain club nights. A generation or two ago, Beatrice and Eugenie would have come out. Now their lives are pretty identical, the labels are just different. The upper-class lifestyle is an ongoing thing, it's just morphed a bit.'

Today, the London Season is a brand, owned by one of Peter Townend's protégées, Jennie Hallam-Peel, and her business partner Patricia Woodall. They run a season of sorts, starting with the Berkeley Dress Show and ending with Queen Charlotte's Ball, and the twenty or so debs they bring out come mainly from one private school in Knightsbridge. The debs see it as a novel – and possibly valuable – addition to their CVs. Thirty-five years on from Celestria's debut, the cycle has turned yet again: these girls wouldn't be seen dead in a barn, they are head-to-toe gloss, designer from shoes to hair, trained in deportment, manners and organisational skills. Though I did wonder what careers they could possibly be planning.

They let me go to the Queen Charlotte's dress rehearsal at the Savoy Ballroom. A long line of pretty girls in jeans, tops and stratospheric nude heels straggled up the stairs outside the door, giggling and awaiting their cues. They were incredibly nice and, to my surprise, nearly all British, the prevailing wisdom among the old school being that modern debs must all be 'Eurotrash' or the daughters of oligarchs. I went to introduce myself to Patricia, who was leaning over a table looking at name cards. She turned on me with a look of such ferocity that I was quite taken aback. 'NOT NOW!' she said, raising both hands and addressing the ballroom wall. 'NOT. NOW.' Blimey. I'd sort my curtsey out for her. That's just what they were doing, too: I kept having to shake my head to check it was the year 2011. It was exactly ten years since Betty Kenward and Peter Townend died.

Afterwards, everyone was tired. I conducted some interviews around a table, including one with a girl of such flawless physical perfection that she practically had 'Deb of the Year' tattooed on her forehead. They were all planning standard gap years – ski seasons, working in Africa and so on – hence the CVs. All, without exception, had loved every minute of their season. They loved Jennie and Patricia. They had learned a lot and made good friends. Jennie explained it lucidly enough: they were teaching the girls life skills that would always be useful. It was the twenty-first century equivalent of Georgiana and Jane's feminine accomplishments. 'Is it going to be a real cake?' was my final, killer question. 'Of course it's a real cake,' said Patricia, crossly, 'it's from Choccywoccydoodah in Brighton.'

Days later I was clumping through Knightsbridge with a terrible hangover, in an anorak and walking boots, researching a new tour. Pottering round Hans Place I caught the eye of the Perfect Deb, coming the other way with a friend. There was a glint of recognition, quickly veiled, and her lovely eyes slid away in embarrassment, as if I was trying to sell her a *Big Issue*. I couldn't blame her, I suppose. But I was quite chuffed when I looked at the London Season website and somebody else had won Deb of the Year.

17

THE TENTED VILLAGE

oug Morihara from Seattle was lying on his back on three flattened pizza boxes. His arms were by his sides and his eyes were shut. He was under a thin blanket. The only evidence he was still alive was a faint hissing sound coming from the iPod plugged into his ears. He was number 871 in The Queue. 'I flew in at seven a.m. yesterday,' he told me earlier as he squashed his boxes. 'This is my fourth time and I stay for the whole five days. I want Centre Court but I'll probably get Court One. For thirty-eight pounds that's fine by me.'

At number 873 were Nell and Pete from Sydney, who had between them one sleeping bag, one warm jacket, a big Brazilian beach towel, a packet of sour cream and onion Pringles and a box of Boursin. 'You never know,' said Pete, 'four hundred people might bail out and then we'll get Centre Court tickets. I've stayed in much worse places than this. And if it rains tonight I'll turf Nell out of her sleeping bag and we'll use it as a poncho.'

Between them was my Millets tent, which now seemed an embarrassing superfluity, especially as I had a sleeping bag and a warm jacket as well.

It was a Sunday night in late June and Wimbledon Fortnight was about to begin. We were in the overnight Queue – which is now so famous that it has capital letters and has spawned an entire sub-culture of its own – and could thus rely on getting last-minute tickets to the world's most famous tennis tournament. Five hundred queuers get a chance to buy Centre Court tickets, five hundred Court One and the rest Courts Two and Three or Ground Entry, which means hovering around the outer courts waiting for people to leave, or joining yet another queue, without capital letters, for returns (a tenner extra for Centre Court, five pounds all others) at 3 p.m. You can't do it online. You have to suffer. Behind us, more tents were going up along the parallel white lines painted on the grass. I was politely asked to repitch my Wimbledon-green two-man tent, as it wasn't precisely aligned.

So sought after are Wimbledon tickets and so hardwired into the British psyche is queueing neurosis – which is indirectly related to the Corinthian concepts of honour and fair play in the sense that if somebody pushes in everybody's notion of justice is upset – The Queue has its own honorary stewards and numbered queueing cards. It has a special glossy booklet explaining Queueing etiquette (no leaving your tent and buzzing off, no live music, no barbecues, bed by 10.30 p.m., reveille at 5 a.m., etc.), ostensibly aimed at foreigners from non-queueing nations, but actually at the many Brits who are beginning to lose the art themselves. Concepts such as shame and collective loathing don't seem to work in the way they used to, but while standards may be slipping, they're jolly well not slipping here.

The Queue deserves its capital letters: it symbolises Wimbledon's unique place in the season. The world's most famous tennis tournament has always been egalitarian. No aristocrats were involved in its genesis: the landed gentry and the military, yes, but no coronets. It is a solidly middle class and mid-Victorian event and as a result has always been more about tennis and the people who love tennis than social kudos. Society went, certainly, and there was royal patronage – the future George VI even played in it in 1926 (men's doubles – he lost) – but there were no formal enclosures in the Ascot or Henley sense and the Royal Box was not about having a giant cocktail party as much as about having the best view of the tennis.

Today dress codes are chiefly for the players, who must wear 'almost all white' – a rule that is dangerously open to interpretation, to the delight of the tennis stars' designers – and the only private areas are for All England Club members, debenture holders, players and people on corporate jollies, who are expected to dress appropriately. Most of these are, arguably, members of the meritocracy, or possibly just plain rich. Few are there by birthright. Ordinary tickets are issued via local tennis clubs or the annual ballot, which anyone efficient enough to plan their life a year ahead may enter. There is now a limited online ticket allocation on the day. For the disorganised or the impatient there is always The Queue and everyone in it is either a tennis fanatic or a tourist eager to see what the fuss is about.

In the morning, bleary-eyed from the shock of waking at dawn to do more queueing – loos, basins, left luggage – I strolled up the line and met Amy Brown. She was miles ahead of me, clasping a giant yellow tennis ball to her chest, and she was buzzing. 'We've just got Boris Becker and I can't stop smiling,' she said, smiling. 'We snuck behind a tent and leaped out and ambushed him and he said, "It'll be my pleasure!" He was so sweet.' On her tennis ball, which is hidden in her house for the rest of the year, were (male) players' signatures: 'Federer, Connors, McEnroe, Roddick ... Tim was the first, though,' she sighed, swivelling the ball to find the former British champ. 'He had to be.' She had been coming for seventeen years and had arrived twelve hours before me. Everyone agreed it was getting more popular, especially with the new roof on Centre Court, which meant rain didn't stop play, so everyone knew it was worth queueing for tickets. The South Africans in pole position had arrived first thing on Saturday, which, although nobody said so, was considered slightly unsporting. The official line said no queueing was allowed until eight o'clock on Sunday morning.

We shuffled past the campsite (which is in Wimbledon Park, over the road from the All England Club), got our wristbands – the colour denoting the court we were eligible for – shuffled through security, shuffled over the road bridge, shuffled through the turnstiles and in at last. Sun poured down on a symphony of dark-green wood, bright-green grass and purple-and-green Wimbledon branding. Narrow alleyways led between the high green walls of the courts. There were banks of dancing flowers and lawns and scoreboards filled with godlike names and pale people strolling in pale sunhats and signs for strawberries and cream and Pimm's and ice lollies.

Nell was surprised at how big it was. Pete was surprised at how small it was. 'In Australia, sports stadiums all have this huge concourse in front,' he said, peering around, 'but this is right next to all the houses. You walk down the hill from the station and da-na! There it is in front of you. It almost looks like it's crammed into one block, whereas on TV the panning shots look like it goes on for miles. They say they're going to Court Nineteen and you assume it must be in the middle of nowhere, but it's just next door.'

In a way they were both right. The All England Club is the Tardis of tennis, comparable to the Chelsea Flower Show in its ingenious use of space. It crams forty-one grass courts (nineteen are used in the Championships), numerous restaurants, a huge media and broadcast centre, players' and members' facilities and the grassy knoll known as 'Henman Hill' or 'Murray Mound' – for fans with ground admission only – into a tapering suburban site of around forty acres. It then absorbs an audience of almost 500,000 spectators over the two-week tournament before reverting to its day-to-day role as a private club. The club has around five hundred members – past Singles winners get honorary membership – and anyone thinking of applying needs an impressive track record in the world of tennis. The quickest way, as someone told me crisply, is to win the Singles Final.

Around me Court One was beginning to fill up. It's circular, like the Roman Colosseum, and the faintly gladiatorial air was enhanced by the fact that young soldiers guarded each tunnel-like entrance. These were Service Stewards, volunteers on unpaid leave, drawn from all units of the armed forces. These particular ones were from REME, the Royal Electrical and Mechanical Engineers. In fact, you've never seen so many uniforms. It's like being in an episode of *Foyle's War*. While some are real – St John's Ambulance, Royal British Legion, Women's Royal Voluntary Service – the ones on court are designed by Polo Ralph Lauren, which is Wimbledon's official outfitter. The American brand specialises in buttoned-up English-style sportswear, bringing it back home as it were. Civilian volunteers, say in the shop, wear Wimbledon-branded polo shirts and buff trousers.

I settled into my seat to enjoy the familiar Championship routines: the ball boys and girls running out in blue shorts, polo shirts and caps; line judges striding on in navy blazers with white edging, white trousers, caps and cricket sweaters and taking up position on splayed legs, like men at urinals; the umpire ascending his ladder like a judging angel; the players, in this case two women, hung about with racket bags and spare bananas; the clouds massing overhead, waiting for play to begin. There was that distinctive pin-drop hush between the warm-up and the first serve of the match, when the umpire intones 'Play' and the performance begins.

It was a really good game. Great atmosphere. Well-matched players. I just kept nodding off. Despite being in my tent at 10.30 p.m. and not even secretly listening to my iPod in my sleeping bag while necking vodka chasers, the five o'clock start had finished me off. The bok-bok of the ball was soporific. The sun was hot. There were no announcers whipping the crowd into a frenzy between points, there was no LCD advertising zipping restlessly around the court and no sponsors' names demanding attention courtside or on the grass. Wimbledon doesn't have sponsors, it has official suppliers: Rolex (official timekeeping), Robinson's (official still soft drink), Slazenger (official ball). The player Billie Jean King described it as 'violent action taking place in an atmosphere of tranquillity'. All is peace. I kept slumping onto the woman next door and then waking with a jerk, terrified of seeing myself fast asleep and dribbling on the big screen.

It's all thanks to the pony roller, really, as our guide Maria told us on a tour of the club before the Championships began. The *alma mater* of tennis started off as the All England Croquet Club, which was founded in the southwest London suburb of Wimbledon in 1868. This was before anyone but the most fashion-forward had heard of lawn tennis, partly because the game originally went under the bizarre name of 'sphairistike'. This Greek word was used by a Major Walter Clopton Wingfield to describe the hearty outdoor game he had invented at his family home in North Wales and to distinguish it from 'tennis', which at that time would have meant a game played inside at royal palaces and the older public schools.

The new game was adopted in a desultory fashion at the club, then off Worple Road, with a handful of courts, but was so popular that within a couple of years they had added 'Lawn Tennis' to the club title. A faded photograph shows a court of the period set up for a match: it looks more like a tilt ground than a tennis court, with two thatched pavilions, a sagging net, coarse-looking grass and a cross-legged ball trough.

The pony roller – pulled by a pony wearing rubber boots to protect the precious grass – couldn't take the pressure of two sports at once. It broke and someone suggested the club raise the repair money by staging a lawn tennis tournament. Twenty-two players entered, about two hundred people watched the final, paying a shilling each, a silver challenge cup was presented by *The Field* magazine and the winner of the first Gentlemen's One Handed Singles Championship in 1877 was a 27-year-old Harrovian rackets player called Spencer Gore. He served underarm. It rained. He thought the game would never catch on.

Tennis caught on beyond anyone's wildest dreams partly because it didn't take up an enormous amount of space, it was considered suitable for both sexes – perfect for discreet flirting – and the technology was improving all the time. Goodyear rubber meant the balls bounced properly on the grass, rackets were strung ever tighter, the casual, sporty *mien* of tennis gear looked good on and off the court. It fitted perfectly with tea on the lawn and English restraint. People were mad for it: croquet and archery lawns were converted, badminton courts enlarged, skating rinks grassed over. The All England Club was right there at the start of this trajectory: there's a tournament poster dating back to 1893, when entry cost a shilling for the first three days and 2/6- for the run-up to the final. In 1922 it had to move to the present ground at Church Road, which had more room. And as tennis took off around the world, Wimbledon managed to hold on to its early advantage – it remains a Grand Slam tournament, the only one still played on grass.

Another boost came from the popularity of the sport with women. The Ladies' Singles began in 1884 and the women's game exploded with the appearance of glamorous players such as the Frenchwoman Suzanne Lenglen, who flew about the court in the 1920s wearing a pleated white dress and a modish bandeau, winning singles, women's doubles and mixed doubles and enjoying the status of a diva or prima ballerina. She often arrived for her matches in furs. Her trend-setting male counterpart was Jean Borotra, the 'bounding Basque', in a long-sleeved shirt and white trousers, the first non-English speaker to win. Demand for Wimbledon was soon so high a railway halt was installed for ticket holders, though if the wind blew the wrong way everyone got smuts on their whites and no one could hear the umpire's decisions, hence the invention of the scoreboard.

Then, as if the popularity of tennis needed any confirmation, in the early 1940s John Betjeman wrote his breathless comic poem *A Subaltern's Love Song*, described by the journalist Simon Jenkins as 'the most famous middlebrow love poem of the twentieth century'. The statuesque, tennis-playing heroine J. Hunter Dunn ('What strenuous singles we played after tea/We in the tournament – you against me!'[1]) was inspired by a young woman seen by Betjeman working in the Ministry of Information during the war. She seemed to him the epitome of healthy Home Counties womanhood.

Never underestimate the suburbs. They have a knack of assimilation. Just as the lovesick subaltern ends his evening with Joan Hunter Dunn a safely engaged man, or disruptive newcomers in

The Archers – the archetypal English radio soap – wind up after six months working happily behind the bar at The Bull, the angry young men of the tennis world – Jimmy Connors, Pat Cash, John McEnroe et al. – are absorbed into the soothing green and purple world of Wimbledon. Women, too: who would have thought it was Tracey Austin – now a commentator, once a precocious fourteen-year-old – who shocked the crowds by storing tennis balls in her frilly knickers? Disarmed by blazers and Pimm's, they are engulfed, amoeba-like, by suburban Englishness, until they give in and become one of us. You would scarcely credit, looking at the coverage of McEnroe during his 'Superbrat' era – superlative tennis, terrible tantrums – that a middle-aged 'Mac' would become a stalwart of the Wimbledon commentary box.

The pony roller is still there. Maria took us to see it. En route she asked us not to photograph anyone in whites, as they would be playing members making the most of being able to use the courts until everything closed down to prepare for the tournament. They couldn't use all of them, though: the five show courts are used only during the Championships and nobody is allowed on Centre Court *ever*, not even the Queen, should she feel like a knock-up. Even at Court Eighteen, right out in the boonies but on the tour because it hosted the longest Wimbledon match ever played in 2010 – eleven hours over three days, and still nobody can remember who won – poor Maria leaped out of her skin when a guy in my group knelt and put his finger on the emerald turf. You. Do. Not. Touch. The. Grass.

What does Wimbledon do to people? Doug, my camping neighbour, had watched it as a child in Seattle. For Nell and Pete it was as much part of their experience of the Old Country as going to Westminster Abbey or the Changing of the Guard. The only true fanatic I know personally, who plays tennis well, worships Roger

Federer and believes that no tournament in the world tops Wimbledon, now works for the *Financial Times* in Hong Kong. Rahul Jacob was brought up in a tennis-mad family in Calcutta and spent his childhood listening to BBC radio coverage and later swiping bits of it for preview pieces as a cub reporter on the local paper. He was over for the tournament, as always, and met me in the press centre, where his case sat beside one of dozens of desks occupied by print journalists.

'I did think it would be elitist before I came here,' he said, 'but I actually think it's the most egalitarian tennis tournament I've ever been to. Not only because of The Queue, but because of the ballot and allocating tickets to tennis clubs. It's like a lottery on several levels, there's a very equal chance of getting in. The fact you can be on Centre Court in the late afternoon for ten pounds, having come with no ticket … it's just amazing, the best feeling in the world after all that queueing. This is pathetic, but the first time I went to the press box and found it was courtside, nearer than the Royal Box or the [players'] Friends' Box, I actually had tears in my eyes.'

I was practically in tears myself as he described squeezing down the green shaded alleyways between the outer courts, sitting so close that players overshooting practically hurdle over you, the proximity of world-class stars, the lack of commercialism, the garden party atmosphere. By garden party atmosphere he meant easygoing, outdoors, summery, not hats. 'The genius of Wimbledon is that it's a championship the whole world is watching, but it feels like a club tournament. It's beautiful, but it doesn't feel social to me. Maybe I'm not picking up on that because I'm not English.' But actually, I thought he was right. It's simply irrelevant.

If there is any old money at Wimbledon it resides in the debenture seats. I had heard people talk about these ('Oh, she's got a debenture') but didn't really understand what they were, so I asked an old friend who used to work in the City. 'Oh yeah, I used to trade those,' he said, 'Wimbledon, racecourse boxes, cemeteries. They're shares issued by an institution to raise money, usually to build something or fund expansion.' Instead of paying interest, he explained, debentures gave the holder the right to buy tickets in the same seats throughout the Championships. They had their own gate into the ground and a restaurant with great views. Debentures lasted for a certain period – five years, say – and if you didn't want to use tickets you could legally sell them on, which was illegal with ballot tickets or tennis club allocations. Wimbledon issued its first debentures in 1920. They had just issued some new Court One debentures this past spring.

A debenture's value lies in the popularity of the event. 'Wimbledon was always the most popular for us,' he added, 'we could always sell them because it was part of the social season and really popular. Back in the 1980s people with debentures were a recognisable type. They were from a certain background, they would all meet up in the same place every year because they always had the same seats; it was a family thing, really. But about twenty years ago corporate entertaining took off and the ticket price on the black market rose exponentially. In 1980 you could probably get a pair of Men's Final tickets for £200. Now it's probably £5,000 to £8,000. That rise in demand is reflected in the price of debentures. A lot of tennis fans and individuals would never be able to afford them now.'

That week I saw Chris Gorringe, the former secretary of the All England Club, talking on TV about Wimbledon's 125th anniversary (the tournament not being held during the war years), and particularly about the turbulent McEnroe 'Superbrat' era. 'Wimbledon has changed partly because professional tennis has changed,' he said. 'There are professional umpires [now]; they're nothing to do with the All England Club. When McEnroe was playing they were retired Wing Commanders and so on – one of his big bust-ups was with one of them. They were stuffy and they were a bit incompetent, they didn't always treat him as subtly as they could ...' In his book on the subject[2], Gorringe says that McEnroe was not invited to become a Member and declined to attend the Champions' Dinner. All champions are invited to become Members. All champions go to the Champions' Dinner. Or so I thought. If true, it was a supremely English spat. But it also showed that Wimbledon shared the chameleon-like ability of season events to change where expedient. They are born survivors, like the upper classes.

Tennis had some of the style of yachting and shared many of the qualities prized in cricket but it was never Corinthian. It wasn't a team sport, it was too domesticated and too easy to poke fun at. It still subscribed fully to the cult of amateurism, though, with its attendant snobberies. Walk into the ground through Gate 4 and one of the first things you see is a statue of the last truly world-dominant British player, Fred Perry. Perry won eight Grand Slams, including the Men's Singles title at Wimbledon three years running in the 1930s, before turning pro and going on to win two more.

Despite his brilliance, he was never part of the tennis Establishment: he was too working class and too hungry for success, which was unpalatable in that genteel world. The late Dan Maskell, the 'voice of Wimbledon', described him waspishly as 'probably the least English tennis player ever to come out of England'. It was the old problem of trying too hard, as summed up by a marvellous throwaway line about Eastbourne, a tennis tournament (once very genteel and ladies only, now men as well) held on the south coast just before Wimbledon fortnight: 'It was thought that practising beforehand spoiled the game.' It could have been written by Flanders and Swann. Perry found the atmosphere so suffocating that he moved to America. That suited English tennis just fine.

You do occasionally hear people complaining that Wimbledon has got too big or too commercial, but generally the quality of the tennis carries it along. It's fashionable to say you prefer Queen's – the men's tournament just before Wimbledon, held at Queen's Club in west London, which is still fairly small, perhaps what Wimbledon was like in the 1970s – or, for true tennis fans, Eastbourne – but few would turn down a chance of Wimbledon tickets. Anyone doubting its success just needs to look at the figures: the All England Club donates 90 per cent of the financial surplus – they avoid the word 'profits' – generated by the tournament to British tennis via the Lawn Tennis Association (LTA). In 1879, the first year for which there are records, the surplus was £116. This year it would be over £35m. Not bad, for a bunch of amateurs.

If spectators from the 1950s, or even the 1920s, were parachuted into the ground today, they would recognise many things: the Royal British Legion band at weekends, the stand selling used match balls, the miraculous engraving of the trophies between victory and the royal presentation – for which, in a bizarre echo of debutante protocol, the women still have to curtsey – the roars from the show courts, the fans taking the weight off their feet with cups of tea, or The Queue, which in the early days was in two parts, north and south, and was occasionally visited by a personage from the All England Club for the purposes of some jolly press coverage.

They would certainly recognise the military lines of ball boys, who used to be picked from orphanages. Before the Second World War they were Shaftesbury Boys, in flannel trousers and long-sleeved shirts, and after the war they were Barnardo's Boys in shorts, who enjoyed fame on the Pathé newsreels but occasionally got sacked for gambling, selling 'lost' tennis balls from the matches ('as used by Rod Laver') or other misdemeanours. Today they are 250 tennis-playing boys and girls – since 1977 – from local schools, who are trained for months and serve for two to three years.

They wouldn't recognise more modern set pieces like the famous aerial cameramen doing panning shots over the courts, or the Hawkeye displays on disputed line calls, or the giant screens on Murray Mound. It's all so familiar and cosy it's easy to forget this is a world-class, deadly serious business, beamed across the world every summer, where the players take away over £16m in prize money between them, with over a million each for the winners of the Men's and Ladies' Singles. Wimbledon, like so much about the season, is all about staggering sleight of hand.

There was an image I couldn't get out of my mind. It was poor Maria's dismay when somebody touched the grass on our tour. Long after the tournament I went to an exhibition of H. M. Bateman cartoons. One was called 'Discovery of a Dandelion on the Centre Court at Wimbledon'. It was a study in horror. The ashen-faced groundsman had fainted. Three mixed-doubles players were kneeling around the offending plant, while an official supported the swooning fourth. The entire crowd – at least half of them, interestingly, dressed all in white – stand open-mouthed in dismay, as do the ball boys, complete with boy scout-style hats and toggles. To make things worse, press photographers were capturing the whole fiasco.

H. M. Bateman was Australian by birth, though he lived in England for most of his life. He went to Westminster Art College and dreamed of becoming a serious artist. He had access to the circles that attended the right schools, the right clubs and the right events, but was always at one remove, the perfect vantage point for the social commentator. In 1921 *The Tatler* published one of his cartoons as a double-page spread. It was called 'The Man Who Dropped It' and showed a Guardsman's rifle clattering to the ground during the Buckingham Palace guard change. Its brilliance lies partly in its deranged style (Bateman himself referred to this manic quality as 'going mad on paper') – a horse is rearing, the sun is frowning, the line of Guardsmen looks appalled, the commanding officer apoplectic and the guilty party is sag-kneed with terror – and partly in its skewering of the English and their notions of propriety, exaggerated to an absurd degree.

A Bateman cartoon captures the moment of solecism, of doing the socially unforgivable, and of course said as much about the tribal response of the majority as it did about the perpetrator. His work was such a hit that he built a career on 'The Man Who ...' 'The Man Who Missed the Ball on the First Tee at St Andrew's', 'The Man Who Crept into the Royal Enclosure in a Bowler', 'The Man Who Bid Half-a-Guinea at Tattersall's'. If you didn't know the rules you didn't get the joke. Those who did usually hung them in the downstairs lavatory – the upper-middle-class humour gallery – where guests had time to chortle at leisure. Bateman died in 1970, having retired to the former English colony of Malta. His work is still funny, even if the world that inspired it has gone. In this particular case, it pointed to a very quaint English, or perhaps British, obsession: with grass.

18

THE CARPET OF GREEN

Budding's Patent Lawnmower is a strangely beautiful thing. It has a swooping frame of cast iron, painted dark green and finished with the sort of smooth wooden handles you find on old gardening tools. It has three separate rollers, one large, two small, and a wide-toothed cogwheel at the side that turns the cutting blades twelve times faster than the central roller. It is halfway between a primitive piece of farm machinery and a modern motor mower. The author Graham Harvey writes that without Budding's big idea, 'the national games of cricket, soccer and rugby might never have achieved their popular appeal nor become the great spectacles of skill and entertainment they are today.'[1] We would also be missing a crucial underfoot component of grand summer gatherings.

I had been struck by the lawn – usually prefaced, with mild irony, by the word 'hallowed' – at the Jockey Club Rooms in

Newmarket: it was a triumph of striped perfection, its two shades of green redolent of spring leaves and garden peas straight from the pod. 'Don't even think about stepping on it,' said the head steward cheerily. 'It's punishable by death – unless you're having a function or getting married.' After that I began to notice lawns: the Lawn Bar on Cartier International Day, the Squadron Lawn at Cowes, the Coronation Lawn at Lord's, the Tea Lawn at Wimbledon. There are famous lawns at Buckingham Palace and the White House. Somehow a lawn always sounds grander than a garden. The word is freighted with the possibility you might not be allowed on it.

Edwin Beard Budding was an engineer from Stroud, in Gloucestershire, and he got his idea from watching the cutting cylinders in cloth mills. His invention was patented in 1830 and his machines can be seen in London's Science Museum and at the Wimbledon Museum – not to mention the British Lawnmower Museum in Southport, whose very existence makes you proud to be British. I saw one on my Wimbledon tour, but failed to appreciate its significance. Budding's idea led indirectly to the 1970s invention of the FlyMo, saving millions of suburban gardeners millions of hours, and to the sit-upon lawnmower, which costs the same as a small car and has allowed sports clubs to maintain more grass with less effort. Having more grass opened up whole new worlds of leisure opportunities.

Nobody knows when lawns first appeared in England but they probably began as glades in the dense woodlands, cleared to admit the sun. The exquisitely fine linen known as 'lawn', used by the rich and fashionable, may have been bleached in such places, separate from the rugged open ground or hillsides used for more common types of cloth. These clearings gradually became much more formal spaces. Jenny Uglow observes in *A Little History of*

British Gardening: 'The first use of our word "lawn" – from the French *launde*, an open space among woods – comes from the thirteenth century, when it was applied to the smooth green of the cloister, a place of peace and contemplation.'[2] Five hundred years later the French Enlightenment philosopher Denis Diderot was writing decisively that '... the English are the kings of the lawn'. What never seems to have been very far away is a sense of enclosure, of containment and of control.

Before the arrival of the mower the only way of maintaining a lawn was by backbreaking hard work. The grass had to be scythed – skilfully, if it was to look good enough – and that meant huge amounts of labour. The lawn became a badge of prestige: a piece of land deliberately uncultivated and unproductive, kept purely for pleasure, and requiring its own staff. It was also peculiarly British. The mild, wet, temperate climate – especially in the southern counties – favoured the growing of lush grass; not the tussocky stalks of the North American plains or the tall, strong grasses of Africa, but a soft, low covering of green with tenacious, spreading roots. This, with application and effort, could become a thing of beauty in itself.

As many of our garden fashions came from the Continent, Henry VIII would have flirted with his various future queens not on a lawn but on an early version of the *parterre*, a geometric pattern of gravel walks and beds edged in box or yew, influenced by the gardens at Fontainebleau in France. The Elizabethans built intricate visual puzzles – knot gardens and mazes – and sowed lawns with chamomile or thyme, sprinkling the green with delicate flowers. The Jacobeans toyed with the close-cut lawn as part of highly structured creations inspired by André Le Nôtre at Versailles. He called it *le tapis vert* – the green carpet – and it would get a grip on the English soul. The naturalistic English gardening style adopted by the early eighteenth-century neoclassical architect William Kent linked lawns with landscape and Lancelot 'Capability' Brown tore out the formal gardens of many great houses and replaced them with sculptural sweeps of grass.

At this point the lawn slowly begins to develop a dual identity. One is all about quiet contemplation and privacy, the other about frenzied activity. Sports had always been played on grass of some sort in Britain, simply because that was the available open space. The village green and the greensward – a word still used by groundsmen at sports venues today – had long been associated with rural pastimes, from maypoles to cricket. It was all pretty rough and ready, though, as befitted games played with pigs' bladders or home-made bats, involving huge numbers of men and frequently turning into running battles between rival teams or villages.

Aristocrats and landowners, on the other hand, played more individual sports on grass, many of which were forbidden to other classes. The joust was an early example, but even during Tudor times this was giving way to less crudely physical activity. Bowls was one. Archery, formerly a battle skill practised by young men, was another, gradually becoming genteel enough for women and requiring a large flat lawn between archers and targets. *Paille maille*, a form of croquet imported by Charles II, required a long, grassy playing area (Pall Mall in London being a former ground).

War was indirectly responsible for nudging team sports up the social scale. The late eighteenth-century wars against France and the growth of the British Empire made the fitness of horses and men important. Cavalry training became more formal. So did the education of young men. The new 'public' schools – so called because before that time upper-class boys would have been educated at home – exploded in the nineteenth century because of this and, as we have heard, valued sport and competition as much as, if not more than, intellectual achievement. Key to this ethos was the codification of competition rules, from pitch size to fouls, so sporting prowess could be measured and honoured. It is no coincidence that this passion for games took off around the time that Edwin Budding came up with his grass-cutting invention. There was no point in having rules if you didn't have a smooth, clearly demarcated surface to obey them on.

Gradually pitches and games fields began to standardise. As the century wore on, perimeters were marked out with white paint, rather than just flags at the corners. Markings inside the field of play became increasingly formal, with goal areas and halfway lines. Only cricket retained its grassy simplicity; the wicket was mown shorter than the surrounding outfield, a rope was used for the boundary line and white paint was used only to mark the creases. Pressure began to mount on groundsmen to maintain the grass perfectly: now they do media interviews before big matches in sports where its condition really matters, such as cricket and tennis.

Today, the sound of a lawnmower is the sound of the summer, as it has been for almost two hundred years. It is the sound of rigid control being reasserted over grass that has lain dormant for the long, wet winter. It is accompanied by the prodigious use of chemicals, much equipment and the deployment of a whole arsenal of weapons against the enemies who might thwart its return to perfection: moles, weeds, moss and next door's cat. It is controversial environmentally because creating and maintaining a perfect lawn demands huge amounts of water, weedkiller and power.

Professionally speaking, it means the head groundsman – he may have a grander title these days, for his rise in status from servant to professional has matched that of the jockey – at every field, course, ground and club involved in the season is beginning a campaign that should reach fruition as the event takes place. Grass with a strong texture and deep roots for racecourses, to bear the drumming of horses' hooves at 35mph; fast-draining fescue-mix on the Lord's outfield with hard-wearing dwarf-rye on the square; 100 per cent rye at Wimbledon, mowed and rolled from its winter length of 10–12mm to a baize-smooth 8mm, tough enough for two weeks of baseline abuse. Grass is protected so rain won't stop play: Wimbledon ground staff, disciplined as a chorus line, can cover a court with breathable fabric in twenty-six seconds and the 'hover cover' at Lord's glides out to squat over the wicket like a giant mother hen.

In between all this arena preparation the enclosures and members' lawns must be readied. Henley is a good example: it takes eleven weeks to raise an entire village of tents and enclosures and car parks, all on grass, and all of which must be removed leaving that grass in healthy condition, or at least on the road to recovery. The Chelsea Flower Show build has to be done in under a month. The worst damage is done by stiletto heels, and despite those old hazards of walking miles and getting pinned to the grass as soon as you stop moving, people still wear them. The Queen's famous block heels are a masterpiece of weight distribution, allowing her to glide across lawns with ease. Wedges and flatforms are the only alternative, but suede will be ruined and rope soles will stain. Men just have no idea.

There's something else about the lawn. It's to do with the curious instinct of the English – or perhaps the British – to fence things off. You see it on beaches from Devon to Dumfriesshire: the little fiefdoms of families and friends, delineated by towels and fortified by windbreaks and deck chairs whose bright colours – always faintly medieval in feel, as are sandcastle flags – belie the underlying message, which is 'Bugger off'. You don't see that in Brazil, say, or on the Amalfi Coast. It seems that our famous island mentality, the desire for strong borders and a large channel – an ocean, preferably – between us and the nearest neighbours, never quite goes away.

Perhaps that is why the lawn spread and prospered and became such a feature of the English season. On the other hand, Budding's lawnmower meant that no longer was pristine turf the preserve of the landowner, so its prestige declined as the century went on. Due to enthusiastic adoption by the middle classes – does this sound familiar? – it ended up as one of suburbia's defining symbols. Children played on lawns. Families had tea on lawns. Lawns rolled out across the Empire, from Naivasha Country Club in Kenya to Hurlingham Polo Club in Buenos Aires. If a lawn wanted to keep its self-respect and remain elite, the fact had to be made clear with 'Keep Off' signs, 'Keep Out' signs, 'Members Only' signs, ropes, railings and the usual set of unwritten rules. This meshed perfectly with the prevailing mood of the season. At the bottom of every English social event, at the bottom of every English sport, perhaps at the bottom of Englishness, there will always be a lawn. But you almost certainly need an invitation.

19

THE LONG STRETCH

There is something primitive about a flaming torch. Particularly when followed by several hundred silent people, sleekly silhouetted against the coming dawn. Or fairly silent, anyway: every so often someone dropped their goggles or stood on a bramble, but the mood was generally one of charged anticipation. 'To be honest I wasn't that up for the torch thing originally,' Tom Kean told me later. 'It was Jeremy's idea. But it works. Somehow it changes the atmosphere on the way to the river. It's magic.'

It was late June, the time when each year the market town of Henley-on-Thames, which sits beside the River Thames at the meeting point of three counties – Oxfordshire, Berkshire and Buckinghamshire – hosts one of the world's most prestigious rowing competitions, the Henley Royal Regatta. In 2004 Tom (who is an investment advisor when he's not swimming) and his old rowing friend Jeremy Laming decided to swim the course the night before Regatta Week. Both had competed at Henley and knew that every year on the long stretch of water between Temple Island – named for its pretty eighteenth-century pavilion – and the town's famous arched bridge, the Regatta Stewards floated parallel lines of white-painted booms to create a perfect rowing course. And, as it happens, a perfect 2.1km swim.

The two crept into Tom's old rowing club in the middle of the night, leaped into the river at first light and swam upstream as the temple floated on a duvet of river mist and the rising sun turned the world a rosy pink. They got caught by security at the Boat Tent – which, to be fair, houses several million pounds' worth of craft in readiness for the competition – and were reported to the Regatta authorities. Still, they couldn't stop talking about it and a friend took some fine pictures. The next year twenty people turned up, the following year almost a hundred. So they decided to turn it into a properly organised swim with a competitive element, a nocturnal echo of the regatta, but with no boats. The Environment Agency, which controls the river, acquiesced and the Henley stewards were supportive as long as the course and oarsmen were not disturbed in any way, which means starting the swim at four-thirty in the morning and ending by six.

So it was that one summer midnight I turned my borrowed car into Remenham Church Lane, which runs north, roughly parallel with the river, thinking I must have got the wrong date. There were no other cars. There were no signs. After two minutes' driving a smiling woman with a Day-Glo wand and her finger on her lips loomed out of the darkness. She pointed silently, wiggling her eyebrows. I turned the radio off and drove gingerly past the dark shadows of Thames Valley mansions, whose expensive bulk I could sense rather than see. At last the headlights picked out shadowy figures laden with kit bags and a field full of cars and tents. The silence was extraordinary: any complaints from well-heeled local residents might threaten the event. The whole thing was conducted practically on tiptoe.

In a logistical operation worthy of the Henley Stewards, who are generally considered to be the most organised people on earth, each entrant was checked on a list and given a numbered orange swimming hat with a numbered wristband and a numbered bag for any gear to be taken to the finish point. I was, I discovered, a 'traditional' swimmer – no wetsuit – but there were triathletes, open-water swimmers, Channel swimmers and club swimmers. There were seniors, couples and regulars from Henley. There was a team from Radley College, the nearby public school, led by a young master who had been a rower. There was a sixteen-year-old accompanied by her mum. There was also Jemma, a colleague of mine from the travel industry, doing her first open-water swim. She said she'd practised a bit in a lake. I made a mental note to keep an eye on her: I swim in cold water all year round. Her husband said he would wait with our stuff at the end.

It was all a bit of a surprise. First Jemma suggested we go in the front group of women, rather than the back, which seemed ambitious for a first-timer. Then the glassy water I had imagined from Tom's lyrical description was shattered by dozens of wet-suited men sliding into it like otters and pounding upstream. There were feet and hats everywhere. The churning water reminded me of a salmon run. Then the women went and all I saw of Jemma was a pair of propeller-like feet kicking water in my face before she disappeared over the horizon. I was left, with the old and the weak, at the back. I remember the sense of panic that I would be left behind, the sweet, almost rotting smell of fresh water, the green swirl of river weed each time I put my face in and, every few minutes, a sickening thud as my head hit a boom. I couldn't steer. In the end I tacked the whole way up the course, crashing from boom to boom as I went. Out of six hundred people I was in the last twenty. And this was my event; the one thing in my entire exploration of the season I thought I knew anything about.

Funnily enough, the experience improved my first day at the Regatta, which had colonised either side of the river with tented roofs and bunting, emerald lawns and white timber, straw hats and blazers of literally every stripe. Standing by the water, peering over shoulders as pairs of sharp-nosed boats streaked by, I was probably the only non-rower in the crowd who really knew what the crews were up against. I could sympathise as they battled the current and each other. I felt an affinity with the single sculls, pairs and coxless fours, who couldn't see where they were going either and also had to do it through a wall of sound on both river banks, something the Henley veteran Sir Steve Redgrave has described as the nearest thing a rower will ever get to competing in a sports stadium.

This was the first waterborne event I had seen during the season and the crews struck me as absurdly big for their boats, just as the jockeys had seemed absurdly small for their horses. It was also the first example of an event that truly embraced the amateur and the professional: its reputation as the Miss Havisham of the sporting summer is rather unfair, for this, of all the events I had seen so far, was the one that offered a chance to every type and age of competitor, from juniors to veterans, from women to foreigners, as long as they were jolly good at rowing, of course. It was a fine opportunity to study 21st-century Corinthian values and I stared hard at each strangely overladen craft, trying to hear the cox's instructions and interpret the answering caveman grunts of the crew.

Every oarsman wants to have rowed at Henley. It doesn't matter if you are a school rower or a five-times Olympic gold medallist, you need to have Henley under your belt. As a result the regatta attracts top-class competitors from abroad, despite the fact that almost nothing about it conforms to the rules, conditions or ethos of the modern sport. 'Henley predates all the modern race rules,' one young rower explained to me outside the Boat Tent, 'so it sort of exists in a little world of its own.' It also exists in a marvellous bubble of nostalgia, if you are in one of the enclosures, and that, as much as its rowing pedigree, charms visitors.

As I walked through the tented entrance to the Stewards' Enclosure, yet another cardboard badge fluttering in the breeze and my dress demurely grazing my knees, I was lucky to find Anthony Herrington sitting on a stool by the river, actually watching the races. Henley, like Ascot, divides neatly into those who genuinely enjoy the sport – they love it, they used to do it or they are supporting someone who does it now – and those for whom the sport is a charming animated backdrop to a summery day out. Tony was one of the former. He was in his seventies and had lived in Henley all his life. He came to the regatta every year with his wife. They were sitting on a run of stools with friends near the finish. They had enamelled metal badges to show that they were members of the Stewards' Enclosure.

As the boats approached, the crowd would suddenly thicken with club or school supporters. If I leaned forward I could see all the way down the riverbank where green canvas chairs with 'HRR' – for 'Henley Royal Regatta' – on the back were occupied by men in blazers or linen suits and women in pretty hats. These were not the eye-catching hats of Ascot. They weren't floppy hats either. They were old-fashioned garden party hats, not too fashionable, not too threatening, probably not new, and very, very English.

There are loads of jokes about the ferocious dress code in the Stewards' Enclosure – I've met several women who have been turned away there – but I was amazed at what a difference it made. Something about having to wear a knee-length skirt inspired people to dress more modestly all round. 'There are no rules about cleavage,' Tony said, amused, 'it's only the legs.' Nevertheless, people covered up. It felt very different from the fleshpots of Ascot and Epsom, its Edwardian decorum reinforced by blue and white striped tents and signs for lobster lunches. It felt gently old-fashioned, less pressurised on the sartorial front, a lot more like these events would have been thirty years ago, before cosmetic surgery and Wonderbras.

Tony pointed out the umpires at the prows of varnished, 55-foot launches with names like *Ulysses*, *Ariadne* and *Argonaut* that followed the boats. Umpires used to follow on horseback up the towpath, but today they float, armed with flags and megaphones to warn crews of potential fouls. The drivers sat amidships, stolid Charons in panama hats or occasionally white cricket hats with green shading beneath the brim, watching the river like hawks. There were usually passengers: a privilege generally accorded to crew supporters. At the finish line, an orange bulb lit up and a tone sounded as the first boat passed. Another tone sounded as the second did so. The puzzling contraption in the middle of the river, with two men peering out of it, was called the Progress Board, a representation of the boats' positions on the course. As progress reports came in, they each moved their model boat to the appropriate point on the 'course'. It was like a home-made version of the flight-tracking screens on an aeroplane.

It took Tony six years to get his badge for the Stewards' Enclosure, which is good going. It takes at least that even if you have a Henley pedigree or some connection with the world of rowing, and over ten if you haven't. 'It's like having your name on a council housing list, isn't it?' he said. 'You start at the bottom and work your way up. People want to join because Henley is so different. It's much bigger than normal. Most town regattas would be two days, but this is five. And [in the enclosure] a man has to wear a blazer and a tie – you see some old boys in their eighties and nineties in wheelchairs and whatnot and they're still wearing their college blazer and cap. They look ... well, it's real memories, Henley, it really is.'

Henley is unique purely because of its geography. At Reading, the River Thames – an implacable body of water sliding over two hundred miles from Gloucestershire to the English Channel – suddenly veers north then sharply east. Henley sits on the outer edge of this curve, Remenham on the inner, and between them they possess a coveted straight stretch of water. 'It was the perfect place in God's eyes,' said Christopher Dodd, the consultant historian for Henley's timber and glass River and Rowing Museum, about five minutes upstream from the course. 'It's the longest stretch of water on the non-tidal Thames. That's why Oxford and Cambridge chose it as the site of their first Boat Race in 1829 and that's what made the good citizens of Henley realise that a regatta could attract a big crowd.'

Ten years later the town started its own regatta – or rather, a regatta became a handy excuse for a town carnival – and right from the start it attracted good rowers. In the nineteenth century the banks of the Thames were already home to a large number of rowing clubs. The sport began in the universities and public schools, anywhere that had a piece of river, some boats and some leisure, and expanded to include amateur clubs that drew members from business and the professions. Regatta races began to increase in number and become more specialised. As time went on the men managing the races – known as the Stewards – began to take over, developing the rules to suit the rowers. Gradually the event split into two: the Henley Royal Regatta and the Town & Visitors' Regatta, which still runs the week afterwards. Large crowds turned up to join the fun at both.

In 1851 Prince Albert became the Regatta's royal patron. Five years later, the Great Western Railway built a spur to Henley, with three platforms to cope with the regatta crowds, and even those had to be extended by the end of the century. I was dumbfounded to arrive at Paddington first thing in the morning to find forty-minute queues for the ticket machines, all because of Henley. The event went through its fair share of ups and downs, though, and periodically its popularity slumped. 'The regatta fell on hard times up until the 1920s,' said Christopher, 'but things got a boost when the chairman at the time, Sir Harcourt Gold, invented the Stewards' Enclosure and put a cachet on where you could watch the Regatta and who you could meet while you were there.' The double-pronged requirement of sport and exclusivity thus fulfilled, Henley officially joined the social whirl.

In the Schwarzenbach International Rowing Gallery at the River and Rowing Museum is the Oxford boat that won the 1829 Boat Race Christopher had mentioned. It's one of the oldest in Britain, a great hefty thing made of Quebec yellow pine, clinker-built, with thole pins apparently hewn by a giant. It was made by a Cornish boat builder used to ocean-going pilot gigs and is so chunky that it is usually described as a gig or a cutter. Also in the museum's collection is the 'Sydney eight', used when Britain won Olympic gold in 2000. It weighs 96 kilograms. It is slender as a punctuation mark, aerodynamic, hydrodynamic, with a tiny aerofoil rudder attached to its fin. The shell is American, the rig English and the oars have blades with special strips to reduce air resistance while 'feathering' – passing over the water between strokes. The Sydney cox was provided with a streamlined 'skirt' in case of crosswinds (he didn't need it). These tiny details make it possible to subtract the fractions of a second that are the difference between winning or losing a modern race. It has taken almost 200 years to refine that design and much of the impetus came from the intense competition at Henley.

For modern rowers, watching a race on the Henley Reach must be like modern jockeys watching a 'horse match'. Instead of the six or more boats you normally see at competitions there are two, rowing head to head. 'They race over a distance of one mile five hundred and fifty yards,' explained Daniel Grist, the Regatta Secretary – anywhere else he would be called a chief executive – when I went to see him. 'That's longer than the international distance of 2,000 metres, so rowers do sometimes run out of puff. There's no second or third place because it's a knockout competition. We have winners only at Henley.' I was rather shocked by this. It sounded rather, well, *American*. It also results in a huge number of races: there are twenty events for a range of competitors, from talented school rowers to internationals, and it has been an open regatta since the 1990s, so amateurs and professionals take part. Early in Regatta Week there can be ninety races in a day. Nobody could watch them all, even if they wanted to.

Daniel's job is complex. He has to oversee the seamless appearance and disappearance of a tented village on either side of the river each year. He has to make sure the caterers supply enough lobster lunches every day. He has to mediate between the diehard fans, the rowers themselves, around 7,000 Stewards' Enclosure members, the rowing clubs along the river, the town council and the Thames Valley Police. The latest police figures he had showed that a third of a million people had turned up to watch – or at least enjoy the party – during the five days of the last regatta. One in four of those were in the 'official facilities', the others were sitting along the riverbank, where clubs like Mahiki sponsor pop-up bars.

I said goodbye to the Herringtons and set off to walk to the start. All the action at Henley happens north of the bridge and people constantly and confusingly refer to the 'Buckinghamshire side' (west) and the 'Berkshire side' (east). To complicate things further the west bank of the river is split between Buckinghamshire and Oxfordshire. So while the Regatta Office is in Berkshire, the town is in Oxfordshire. The two enclosures – Stewards, which is open only to its members and their guests, and Regatta, which is open to anyone who buys a ticket – are in Berkshire, but the official corporate hospitality tents are in Buckinghamshire. Walk downstream on the Berkshire side and you will reach Temple Island, in Buckinghamshire. It's not county boundaries that count here, though, it's the enclosures; outside those the Regatta becomes one long, thin, noisy party, as if The Hill at Epsom had been reconfigured into a strip of fun five feet wide.

It was all so familiar. The posh bit was near the finish line, and the further away you got the more relaxed it was: hats in the Stewards' Enclosure, smart casual in the Regatta Enclosure, shorts, shades and T-shirts on the towpath. Small barricades of deck chairs and picnic hampers colonised bits of the bank, circling rugs and sarongs and jumbles of carrier bags. As I passed, feeling overdressed, I could hear the snap and hiss of ring pulls and easy ripples of conversation. Every so often a great shout of laughter would roll across the water. Whole families sat between tufts of coarse river grass or in the shade of small trees. Groups of students had college colours painted on their faces and flags tied onto their shoulders. Every so often world-class rowers shot past unnoticed, on their way to victory or defeat.

I thought about the losers a lot. When the River and Rowing Museum commissioned the artist Chris Gollon to be painter-in-residence for the Regatta a few years ago, they gave him a Silver Badge, the sort of access-all-areas status normally reserved for the Queen. He chose to paint the losers, alone and adrift at the end of the race, slumped in exhaustion and defeat, their demeanour exactly mirrored by their wives and girlfriends ashore, whose champagne glasses are wilting in sympathy. In reality, of course, you never see them because you are too busy admiring the winners. Corinthian values have had to take a stern seat.

When I came to Henley before the regatta, I walked into Leander Club by mistake. Leander – which has a distinctive salmon-pink blazer, sometimes worn with a pink rowing cap, a tie with a hippo on it and matching pink socks – is the foremost rowing club in Henley and one of the most famous in the world. Until relatively recently it was synonymous with the national rowing squad: it was Leander members who won for Britain in the 1948 'Austerity Olympics', when the rowing events were held out here, and the club's walls groan with trophies. Steve Redgrave, Matthew Pinsent and James Cracknell are Leander members. So is Debbie Flood, an Olympic silver medallist in the quadruple sculls – women have been allowed to become full members since 1998. As I walked in, four rowers walked out, carrying their kit. They were huge, perfect alpha males; the sort of athletes Olympian ideals were made for. Only later did I realise not all rowers were like this; these were heavyweights, the Usain Bolts of rowing, and they epitomised a new style of professionalism in the English sport.

Leander was originally founded on the Tideway in London in 1818, only moving to its site by Henley Bridge at the end of the century. Most of its members were University men – meaning

Oxford and Cambridge – and all were respected rowers. Its name reflected classical and amateur ideals, though Leander was famous for swimming, not rowing, and not in a good way: while crossing the Hellespont to make love to the beautiful Hero, he got lost when her guiding light blew out. He drowned. She committed suicide. Never mind. It sounds right. The only local club with an older history is the Henley Rowing Club, founded in 1830 straight after the first Boat Race, and now based south of the bridge. It focuses on the Town & Visitors' Regatta. Walking down the towpath, though, I passed two others, the Upper Thames Rowing Club (1963) and the Remenham Club (1909), where members happily put down their pints to explain what was going on. 'God, it's a boring sport to watch,' they said cheerily, 'only rowers enjoy watching rowing. That's why there's not much sponsorship.'

Sponsorship makes Henley special by its absence. The Royal Regatta, despite being one of the first events to embrace corporate hospitality during one of its periodic dips in the 1970s, is not sponsored. It may have tents awash with logos on the far side of the river – where they have novelties such as champagne fountains and ice pools to bathe their feet in while enjoying views of the boats and enclosures – but the enclosures are resolutely brand-free. The HRR remains unsullied by a company name or logo, though its own branding is dark blue and vaguely nautical in nature, with subliminal messages of Britishness, pluck and all-round reliability.

All the way down the river, lined up next to the central boom, little skiffs bobbed on the water, glowing like conkers. They were usually filled to overflowing with at least four people and a picnic basket. In Edwardian times the river was almost solid with them. Many of them come from Hobbs of Henley, whose boatyard is perfectly placed between the bridge and the railway station. 'It was set up by my great-great-grandfather in 1870,' said Jonathan

Hobbs, who now runs a fleet of over fifty river boats. 'Back then you would have seen boats fifteen abreast, moored up to the booms. There were far more boat companies then. Even my father tells me stories of big punch-ups among the boat owners on this wharf, fighting over customers.' The reason Hobbs has survived is that one of his antecedents heard the branch line from London was coming and moved the boat yard to its present spot, once the garden of the old Royal Hotel. Its skiffs and launches chunter up and down cheerily, adding to the jollity.

It's a long walk to the start at Henley – one mile five hundred and fifty yards, as I well remembered – and as I strolled along the parties thinned out and eventually disappeared. The atmosphere down there was very different. It was cool and green and dreamy, more like the Thames of Ratty and Mole or *Tales of the Riverbank* than a sporting venue. There was a Start Enclosure run by the Copas family, local turkey farmers and substantial landowners, who own Remenham Farm, where the swim started. Temple Island looked wistfully unattainable – it is in fact a highly sought-after venue – and drooped romantic tendrils in the water. Round the back you could see nervous crews practising before the start, which was a wooden jetty with two platforms parallel to the bank. On them, flat on their stomachs, were two men, each holding on to the tail of an eight.

'You come out of the Boat Tent [at the end of the course, near the bridge], which is a high-pressure environment,' explained a panting Nick Bartlett, a nineteen-year-old University of Newcastle rower who had just lost when I met him. 'It's really hot in there and you can see your opponents and how good their boats are. Some people get clapped out, cheered, if they've got supporters. You put your boat on the water, paddle all the way down by the far bank past Temple Island, do a few bursts, some practice starts and some spins. Then you paddle to the start blocks and wait, which is really nerve-racking.' The umpire, flag furled, tells the crews what to expect ('When you are straight and ready I will start you like this ... attention ... *go!*') and some people are so nervous they take off then. The coxes hold their hands up until their crew is ready. When they drop, the race begins. Nick struggled to describe the noise. 'Henley's got such a party atmosphere, you do get shouted at,' he said with a grin, 'that's why it's so exciting. It's huge. You have to keep your head in the boat. That's what I try and do. It's an event. That's why people love it.'

I stayed down there, watching boats explode out of the blocks towards the dazzle of colour and noise that awaited them. An American man from Philadelphia whose son was rowing told me that their rowers started slowly, thirty-five strokes a minute or so, while the British did forty-five or more off the starting line. He said nobody in America wore blazers and rowing caps. He'd never seen anything like it, bar the Kentucky Derby.

Later in Regatta Week I went back to Henley. A guiding colleague who had rowed for Trinity College Dublin invited me to join her family picnic in Lion Meadow, 'out of the Stewards' Enclosure, turn right, a two-minute walk'. I knew enough now to recognise a car park hierarchy when I heard one: Lion Meadow is a grassy field running alongside the Stewards' Enclosure, the equivalent of Ascot's Number One Car Park. It is here, as soon as the last race finishes around seven in the evening, that corks pop and barbecues spark to life and college ties trail lethally over the burgers. People keep the same space for decades. The most prestigious are near the enclosure entrance. My friend Jane and her husband David had a space there until they forgot to renew it in a fit of abstraction. After a one-year grace period, it is thrown to the slavering hordes in next-door Butler's Field, who are always hoping for an upgrade. Further north – *terra incognita* for the regulars, obviously – was Green's Field, the daily car park for the public.

In the Stewards' Enclosure, life went on as though two World Wars had never happened. It was very relaxing. The musicians of the Grenadier Guards played jaunty summer airs. There were simple pleasures such as visiting the trophies – plates, cups and mugs – in their tent, including the Ladies' Plate, which is not a plate and is not for ladies. It's for men and they win a solid-silver claret jug plus a medal each. Males of all ages strolled by, wearing with utter insouciance blazers of every stripe and shade, set off by matching caps. The larger the man, the smaller the cap, seemed to be a rule of thumb. Every so often the poached-salmon-pink of Leander could be discerned swimming slowly through the crowd like a predator at the top of the food chain. Sartorially speaking, though, they were outgunned by the fire-engine-red blazers of the Maggie rowers.

Lady Margaret Boat Club is Maggie's full name and it's connected to St John's College, Cambridge. It was founded in 1825 and claims to be the oldest college rowing club on the River Cam, housed in a brick-and-timber boathouse with red doors like a fire station. It also claims to have invented the blazer – the woollen, informal (for the time) jacket later adopted by sportsmen, naval types and schoolboys across the country – though there's a rival claim from the crew of HMS *Blazer.* It is said the Maggie rowing crew utterly intimidated the opposition with their show of coordinated tailoring, turning up 'in a blaze of glory' wearing sumptuous jackets, red as a fresh drop of blood. Nobody seems to know who won.

Jane and David are both Irish and both had rowed for Trinity College Dublin. David had won the Ladies' Plate – or rather, the claret jug – in 1977 and when I found him unpacking the cold box from the back of the car as various teenagers drifted in and out, I asked him to explain blazer etiquette. I'd seen them for sale in New & Lingwood on Jermyn Street. Could anyone buy one? Or would they be fingered as imposters?

'You could buy one, I suppose,' he said, 'but you'd spend your life being collared by middle-aged men asking if you read Greats in 1956.' Blazers, he added, were not as simple as they looked. 'Most oarsmen here will have a club blazer,' he explained, 'but if you rowed for your university you could have a university blazer and a college blazer too. At Trinity, the novice blazer is known rather endearingly as a "Maiden blazer" and it's black and white stripes. If you progress to junior level, you get white with black piping. Senior level is black with white piping.' He tried to order a junior blazer because it looked so jazzy but they wouldn't let him, despite the fact he had raced at Henley three times for Trinity and won the Ladies' Plate. He said he couldn't really be bothered to argue. 'What I like,' he said, 'is seeing the same people come back year after year after year with their blazers fading and fading and fading. It's reassuring, somehow.'

When I said I was going to walk back to the start, he looked at his watch and raised his eyebrows. I found out why halfway down the course. Six o'clock is the witching hour at Henley: the atmosphere changes as if someone has flicked a switch. The day was cooling and people were packing up. Crowds were jostling to get onto the towpath while others struggled to leave. Couples argued. Children wailed. There was a fight. I remembered Tony Herrington saying that two years before they cancelled the fireworks because of a fight on the bank. Every so often, it's great to be in an enclosure. I turned on my cork heel and walked back upstream.

Back in Edwardian safety, I was thinking of the only time I had been to Henley before, years ago, with friends and their parents. I thought I would ring one of the friends to tell her I remembered the day with affection. I was describing the cheery scene when I saw an elderly man bearing down on me, pop-eyed with rage. I turned, thinking somebody must be horsing around on the river-bank. Then I saw accusing glances coming from people all around me and the full horror dawned: *I was using a mobile phone.*

The man was one of the Bowler Hat Attendants – normally affable fellows, first cousins to the Greencoats, Red Collars et al. – and he was livid. Not only had I broken the rules. I clearly didn't know them. And everybody else did. They all looked away, embar-rassed. It was pure Bateman: I was 'The Woman Who Used Her Mobile Phone in the Stewards' Enclosure'.

20

HELLO, REAL WORLD

'We're too late, apparently.' Tom, aged forty-two, was sitting on a hay bale holding a plastic glass of red wine. 'The time to come was four years ago. And it's doubled in size since then.' There were four of us lazing in a row in the sun. More hay bales doubled up as a coffee table on which sat some foam cups, a magazine, some recyclable takeaway boxes and a half-full plastic wine bottle. On the far side were five people we had never met before, kicking back in old cane chairs, nodding sagely. It was weirdly like a parish coffee morning, in a suburban drawing room made of hay.

This was day three of Secret Garden Party, an East Anglian music festival of almost mythical status. My epidemiologist friend Elizabeth was lecturing in the science tent on HIV/AIDS and it seemed a good opportunity to experience what *Debrett's* called 'The Modern Season'. I'd never been to a big festival: little ones, yes, jazz festivals, yes, the Hay Festival, often, but not Glastonbury, the Isle of Wight, Bestival and so on. This was where Celestria reckoned the debby girls now went, in minis and wellies rather than taffeta and pearls, along with half the under-thirties in Britain. Our mate Lilo had flown in from Madrid to try *una fiesta inglesa*. Tom, a friend of Elizabeth's, had dropped by to hear her lecture. It was on needle sharing, prophylaxis and dry anal sex and she was handing out chocolate-flavoured condoms and genital-shaped sweets. She wouldn't let Lilo and me go in case we put her off. It all felt a very long way from Number One Car Park.

There are striking similarities between festivals and the grandest events of the season, despite the 300-year age gap. They all start off small. If they're good, they get bigger. More people want to come. The event takes its place in a circuit of similar events. People start to attend purely because they have heard of the event, rather than for whatever is on offer. All the early adopters then get huffy and say it's too big and everyone's going and it never used to be like this and now they're going to another, smaller, festival somewhere else. There is always a hierarchy of experience. There is always another, smaller, festival somewhere else.

Cambridgeshire is flat and Abbot's Ripton, where the festival is held, is very flat. It's on the edge of the Fens. Its perimeter fence, patrolled by security to avoid mass gate-crashing, made it look like an old airfield, and young marshals in fluorescent jackets were directing traffic in the parking area. One put her head into the car window to check our tickets and stop us smuggling in glass bottles. She told us where to drive in and park. We lugged our gear back as the *duf-duf-duf* of amplified music floated into the Cambridge-blue sky, found an empty field, couldn't believe our luck, half got the tents up, found it was for security personnel, took them down again and re-pitched in a tiny corner between the festival and the orange Portaloo lines. It was like getting to the beach and being unable to see a spare inch of sand. Once you get your eye in, there are gaps everywhere.

Walking into an alien environment is always a powerful experience. I felt myself bristling like a dog. Everywhere you looked there were children masquerading as adults, or adults masquerading as children, depending on which way you looked at it. People were wearing Kigu animal onesies – Japanese all-in-one suits with cartoonish stripes, spots or spines – face paint, feathers in their hair or garlands of flowers. There were teepees and pink silken-fringed umbrellas and, in the distance, huge tents. There were stands selling everything from Chilean empanadas to sashimi. Most girls were in denim cut-offs or miniskirts with opaque black tights, tiny tops and wellies. The men were in beanie hats and T-shirts from other festivals. I was taken aback at how infantilised it was. I had been expecting scary.

At the lecture tent Ben Goldacre, the *Guardian*'s 'Bad Science' writer, was talking to a rapt audience, several of them in animal suits. Some raised their paws to ask questions at the end. There was a lake with an island on which perched a helicopter-sized dragonfly, there was a bicycling pirate ship, there were mature trees hung with lanterns as round and yellow as Edams, and a grandfather clock in a huge birdcage. A man sculpted a nude woman in sand on a real sofa. She had no pubic hair, irritating Elizabeth, who feels strongly about such matters. 'What *is* it with this generation?' she muttered. There was a Psychic Mojito Fortune Teller's Tent ('mint tea leaves read here'), a Sado-Masochism Tent (they were sweet) and a fey Temple of Wanton Woodland Creatures in a rambling copse hung about with spiders' webs of blue nylon rope. Two girls with flowered hair played on swings, giggling. I hated it. And then I didn't. It took twelve hours or so: I had to slow down sufficiently to mesh my pace with theirs and stop thinking 'Oh for goodness' *sake*!' It required a complete change of gear.

Part of the reason for this dislocation, aside from everyone else being nineteen, was there were other things to worry about. Late July onwards is a car crash of social events: next up was Cartier International Polo Day – one of the glammiest dates of all – followed by Glorious Goodwood, a bona fide Edwardian racing fixture and traditional end to the season on land. Then came Cowes Week, which in the old days was either one last hurrah or the first event of the summer recess, for afterwards everyone who wasn't going shooting in Scotland stayed on their yachts for long sailing holidays. Last up would be Jennie and Patricia's Queen Charlotte's Ball, revived, Rasputin-like, to take place in early September.

An email had arrived to say I could go to the Royal Yacht Squadron Ball after all. My season was complete. I had been to Cowes to interview the Commodore and liked him. He bumped into Victoria Mather. Between them they agreed she could invite me: doubly generous as she was helping to organise it and had to persuade some friends, who had never clapped eyes on me, to give me dinner and take me on with them. Having dinner at the ball would be more expensive. Soon the invitation crashed onto the doormat. 'All the Raj!' it said in twirly letters, and the emailed instructions added helpfully 'Port Out and Starboard Home.' Oh God, *it was fancy dress*. Or was it? Perhaps it was just gently themed? This is where dress codes are really scary. How do you know? Who do you ask? I knew the Squadron was deeply formal, but there was also that mad naval streak of jolly japes and Crossing the Line. Which was it to be?

This was why debutantes needed mothers, I decided: the logistics of having fun are surprisingly draining. I found myself weeping every so often from sheer fatigue and sartorial stress, to minimal sympathy from freelance friends struggling through the recession. 'Let me get this right,' they would say, sardonically, 'you're worried about wearing the wrong thing to a boat club ball?'

'No! No! Well, not yet, no. It's the polo I'm worried about – and being thirty years too old for Secret Garden Party. You don't *understand*.'

I was worried about money, too, which I realise has its ironies. Tickets and transport alone sucked up cash as a thirsty outfield sucks up rain. And it all had to be fitted around two other jobs. Luckily I had some time to assemble a witty outfit or two. And it would be good to end ten weeks of assiduous social mountaineering on a high.

Back on the hay bales it was dawning on us that we had the only bottle of wine for miles around. Occasionally men passed with brimming pints in plastic glasses, but otherwise there was very little alcohol to be seen. 'I think it's fair to say there's *some* alcohol,' said Tom thoughtfully, 'but most people will be taking MDMA or cocaine to stay awake. Or ketamine, I suppose.' The three of us tried not to look impressed. We knew ketamine was a horse tranquilliser, the horror drug *du jour* in the newspapers, but we weren't entirely sure what its benefits were. 'I've tried it twice and I don't see it,' he sighed, 'it's very difficult to dose. If you take a tiny, tiny, tiny amount, called a bump, then you do get a small amount of energy from it. But the wrong dose is the difference between half a centimetre and a centimetre, then you kind of disappear into a world in your head.' We all nodded. A centimetre of what, I wondered, imagining some sort of giant horse suppository. But there are some things you just can't ask.

Tom was seven years younger than me. Seven years is a long

time in festivals. He said he wasn't going to anything like as many as he used to, or doing as many drugs. He had been meaning to come to Secret Garden Party for years and was enjoying it, despite being too late. He thought the landscape a bit flat, but liked the easygoing vibe. This was what SGP was known for: its innocent, anything-goes creativity. And at least Tom was from the age of digital recording and boutique drugs. We were from the age of analogue music and alcohol. It was a genuine divide: we were already in our early twenties when MDMA, we quaintly called it Ecstasy, appeared. Back then, the word 'festival' meant something more diffuse.

Ever since David Garrick organised his Shakespeare Jubilee in Stratford-upon-Avon in 1769, there have been festivals attracting national, rather than local, attention in Britain. Few last for ever: most of the ones we have today are less than a century old. Benjamin Britten and Peter Pears, with the writer Eric Crozier, started the Aldeburgh Festival on the Suffolk coast in 1948. The Cheltenham Literature Festival – the oldest in England – began a year later. The Hay Festival, started in the Welsh Borders 'book town' of Hay-on-Wye in 1988, is now a fifteen-festival, five-continent phenomenon with an annual audience of a quarter of a million, which I go to whenever I can, usually camping or sharing a B&B with friends. Thirty years of solid prosperity, in southeast England at least, had spawned a Golden Age of Festivals, but somehow, slowly, music began to dominate. If someone is off to a festival now, it's not the Nottingham Goose Fair or Apple Day at Brogdale: they're going to camp and dance their heads off for days.

Don't be fooled by the touchy-feely vibe, however: there's a hierarchy here, too. Some music festivals are old enough to qualify for a bus pass. Both Reading and the Isle of Wight – held on a farm near Godshill in 1968, when 10,000 people, most of whom looked like Jesus, rolled up to see Jefferson Airplane and T. Rex – pre-date Woodstock in America. They released a pent-up wish to hang out and hear amazingly loud music. So big and so noisy was the 1970 Isle of Wight festival, when Jimi Hendrix appeared, that Parliament passed an act banning island gatherings over 5,000 people, which had to be repealed when they revived the festival in 2002. It is now a popular annual fixture on the circuit. Sixty-five thousand people had turned up there the month before we got to Cambridgeshire.

The day after Hendrix's death in 1970 and three weeks after the Isle of Wight Festival, some musicians staged an impromptu gig at a dairy farm in Somerset. It lasted for two days and the farm's owner, Michael Eavis – apparently inspired by the Bath & West Blues Festival – managed to book Marc Bolan and Al Stewart. Fifteen hundred people paid a pound, with free milk thrown in. Forty years on, Glastonbury is to festival lovers what Stonehenge is to druids. It has transcended the festival concept to such an extent that it has become a rite of passage for anyone who can afford the price of the very expensive ticket. I, of course, have never been, mainly because it's the same price as the Summer Exhibition Preview Party but also because the tickets sell out in hours and I always forget.

'Glasto' is now so big (a staggering 135,000 people – three times the size of the Burning Man Festival in Nevada) it is like building a small city every year, with associated licensing and security issues. They have to miss a year every so often so the land, the staff, the county of Somerset and the funkiest dairy cows in Britain – their byre doubled as an early incarnation of the Pyramid Stage, built on the ley line between Glastonbury and Stonehenge – can have a rest. But in fallow years there are now dozens, possibly hundreds, of alternatives: Reading, Leeds, Isle of Wight, Big Chill,

Green Man, Latitude, the V Festival, Bestival, WOMAD, Lovebox, Wireless, Tartan Heart, Rewind, Wilderness, Cornbury and many, many more.

'I've been to quite a few, yep,' said the woman in the next-door tent, clattering pots and pans as she cooked. 'V when I was younger, Bestival, Lovebox, Glasto. I did Festibelly in the New Forest last year and it was great, only about five thousand people. I first came here when there were twelve thousand people, which was FANTASTIC.' She sat back on her heels, dripping curry onto the tent floor. 'It was what a festival should be: no sponsorship, local food, smaller bands. I think it's now about thirty thousand, maybe bigger – you've got helicopters overhead now. I suppose the festival season starts in June, really, and it goes through until the autumn. It means the summer to me.'

As festivals evolve, they seem to be meeting in the middle. Lectures and workshops at Secret Garden Party, for instance, are packed, while the Hay Festival has launched an alternative rock festival, Merthyr Rock, in the old industrial area of South Wales. Elizabeth, who speaks at everything from science conferences to TED (Technology, Entertainment, Design) talks in the US, was appearing at Hay as well. Hybrids such as Port Eliot in Cornwall 'curate' a jumble of music, poetry, writing and comedy. The main difference between these and season events, aside from the informality, is the lack of a truly self-conscious *passagiato*. Anonymity is fairly important. The chillaxed attendees of Secret Garden Party were far more suspicious of my notebook than any of the captains of industry at Chelsea, Henley or the Summer Exhibition.

As the night wore on and the sky darkened, the site lit up. There was something truly magical about it. It became an evening of wandering from tent to tent, listening and watching. The benevolent atmosphere was at least partly thanks to so little alcohol.

Though the music, we all thought, clearly needed good drugs: the musicians seemed to have turned up with chaotic backing bands made up of their mates. By the next day we wished we were staying and regretted buying only two-day tickets. What could be nicer than sitting on straw bales, watching the world go by, talking about nothing to random people you would never see again? That afternoon the news of Amy Winehouse's death ran through the site like wildfire, causing a moment of introspection. You could see faces drop as people took it in.

I packed up while it was still light and gave my space to a West Londoner who worked in TV. 'I'm a retired raver, now, that's what I am,' she said, shaking her head in disbelief as I helped her put up her tent, 'I'm thirty-five and I've got a son, but I used to work at The Eclipse in Coventry. I was so, so into music.' She said she went to Bestival with mates and this year was going to WOMAD, probably taking her boy. Some friends had just been to the Priddy Folk Festival near Bath. She was a lexicon of drug information: she matched them with different types of music for me, laughing, and agreed one often needed the other. It was oddly reassuring being with her, like being in a chaotic kitchen with a thoroughly competent cook.

Later she hailed me as I set off to see Blondie on the main stage. 'I was thinking about why people come to festivals,' she said as we ambled along. 'I think it's like a pilgrimage. For me, raving was like my kind of church, you know, take drugs, wave my hands in the air, but there's that pilgrimage concept, of setting off on a journey to go and celebrate why we're here. A festival's not like going out with your mates. You travel for a certain amount of time and you get there and everyone's there for the same reason. I know it's an industry and it must be very successful, but it's more than that. It's a celebration of music but also of life and what's good about being

a human being. You do what you like, nobody's going to say anything; they don't give a shit. In life in general you're judged in a
split second whereas here ...' – she started to laugh and nodded
at a man in a poncho, face paint and an oversize hat – '... case in
point. Who cares?'

The crowd for Blondie was huge. Lilo headed back to the main
site to find something quieter. Elizabeth disappeared like rat up a
drainpipe, threading her way through to the mosh pit. My new
friend stayed with me, clearly feeling I shouldn't be left on my
own. 'That guy just tried to sell you MDMA,' she said, pointing.

'Oh. I just apologised. I thought I'd stood on his foot.'

'I know,' she said, looking worried. She needn't have been. For
a start I was the only one in the crowd who knew the words.

Blondie were disappointing and the set was short. I got stuck
trying to get back to meet the others: there was a bottleneck over
a footbridge and big bouncers were holding everyone back. There
was a mild commotion – 'Mind your backs, ladies and gents!' – and
we split to allow the passage of a small group of adults, ten years
or so older than me, who looked as if they were going to a point-
to-point. One seemed to be in a Lord Lichfield-style Burberry
mac. Now I felt worried. Should they be out this late? Had anyone
offered them MDMA? Who were they anyway?

'Lord and Lady de Ramsey,' muttered a guard, holding us back
and nodding respectfully.

One of the founders of Secret Garden Party is Fred Fellowes
and these were his parents, who own the land. They are in good
company. Forget creating an all-white garden or building a lake:
these days anyone with land wants a festival. One of the first private estates to dip a toe in the water was Knebworth House, home
to nineteen generations of Lyttons (now Lytton-Cobbolds), which
has staged legendary rock festivals from the late 1970s. It had just

held the Sonisphere heavy metal weekend. The Big Chill is at Eastnor Castle, Herefordshire, owned by the Hervey-Bathursts. Cornbury, where the Camerons go, began at Cornbury Park, the Rotherwicks' Cotswolds home, but had moved to Great Tew after a falling-out. The Rotherwicks had a new festival, Wilderness ('music, food, theatre, literary debate and outdoor pursuits'). Tartan Heart started in Inverness-shire with a few tents at Phoineas House on the Belladrum Estate, home to Joe Gibbs and his artist wife Leonie, and now runs for five days. Some people had come to SGP from Kimberley, an invitation-only mini-festival for around 2,000, held at a small stately home in Norfolk.

Yes, the days of building a racecourse or a polo ground on land you own are long gone: today you want a festival, because every-body, in this age of electronic media, reality TV and social networking, craves live music, world food and the company of other human beings. Most racecourses were now laying on gigs after the day's sport, to keep hold of the punters. Museums and galleries across the country were doing the same. English National Opera were working with Damon Albarn from Blur and Gorillaz. And anyone under thirty going to the Cartier International would be far more likely to mention the Chinawhite after-party than Smith's Lawn.

21

CHUKKAS AND CHAVS

The South Stand at Guards Polo Club for Cartier International Day was all very well, but I was conscious of a certain feeling of lassitude. My glossy programme drooped in my hand. The sick-coloured shoes had a slightly grubby look to them, like old Elastoplasts. Even the sight of eight breeched and booted men thundering up and down on the emerald turf in front of me wasn't hitting the spot. It took a pint of Pimm's and some dogged soul-searching to realise what was wrong. I was suffering from SAD, or Seasonal Affective Disorder. In the old days they called it ennui.

Of all the places to strike, it was ironic that it was at the polo, widely considered to be the sexiest sport of all. Nice players, nice ponies, nice setting. Guards Polo Club is in the southeast corner of the 2,000-hectare Windsor Great Park, the only public park to be run by the Crown Estate. Because of its semi-royal status as a sort of giant allotment for Windsor Castle, it has a regal feel. Royal residences dot its verdant landscape. There are drifts of royal deer. Prince Philip spent much of his polo-playing heyday here and had a lot to do with the fact that the area known as Smith's Lawn, named way back for a gamekeeper who had nothing to do with horses, is now home to ten magnificent polo grounds.

On my advance visit the club was deep in monsoon. Ever since Ascot, tropical deluges had displaced the hot, dry spring and I marvelled at a circle of hardy spectators in folding chairs beside an open car boot, holding umbrellas over their sandwiches and waiting for play to resume. It did, of course. The drumming rain added to the slightly surreal sense of being in Poona, or Ooty, or some other corner of Empire. The clubhouse was a long cream bungalow with a verandah. Behind it stretched miles of faultless grass. You could almost hear the tinkle of ice in gin and bitters.

And now it was Cartier Day. The sun was high in the sky, the celebs had been decanted from the Lawn Bar and lunch tent, papped, tootled twenty yards by golf buggy and poured into their VIP seats, and the cream of British polohood was in action on beautiful, glossy ponies, swerving and ducking and twirling their sticks against Brazil in the annual Coronation Cup. Even I had heard of Mark and Luke Tomlinson, whose family owns the Beaufort Polo Club in Gloucestershire. They are British pros, with seven-goal handicaps, playing worldwide in a game that is authentically international. It's the only season sport that can't claim English origins.

Polo was the national sport of India until the sixteenth century, when its enthusiastic adopters, the Mughal emperors, began to lose power. They called it 'pulu' – after the Tibetan word for a stick – and the sport was even then known to have an ancient history, possibly going back 2,500 years. Polo, so the old saying goes, was born in Central Asia, spent its childhood in Iran and reached maturity in the northern areas of India. It makes sense: back then Central Asia was home to the most skilled horsemen in the world and it was Shah Abbas in Persia who built the polo ground now so popular with picnickers in Isfahan. It almost certainly started as some form of cavalry exercise, without many rules.

As for the northern areas of India, one was Manipur, on the far eastern border with Burma, and it was there the crossover took place between the mountain tribes and the British Empire. A young subaltern on a posting saw the game – played in Manipur for centuries, if not millennia – and with some tea planters set up a team to challenge the tribesmen. Being British, they then formed a club. The Retreat at Silchar, founded in 1859, is long gone – all that remains is a memorial plaque – but the game swiftly spread to Calcutta (where the club still exists) and throughout British India. It then crossed the Indian Ocean and the first game in England was played on Hounslow Heath. Officers at Aldershot then took it up and by 1875 new headquarters had been established at Hurlingham, then a smart pigeon-shooting ground in southwest London. There they codified the rules.

One of my favourite childhood books dates from around this time. It's *The Maltese Cat* by Rudyard Kipling and the front page says simply 'A polo game of the Nineties'. It tells of the plucky Skidars playing the sleek Archangels in the Upper India Free-for-All Cup and is written from the point of view of the ponies, particularly a flea-bitten grey called The Maltese Cat. The Skidars are a 'poor-but-honest native infantry regiment' and I was always puzzled by the fact that all the players in the pictures were white. It was only re-reading it as an adult that I realised that the white officers of the poor-but-honest native infantry regiment played the polo, while the native officers held the bundles of spare polo sticks around the edges of the ground. Still, to me, who had never been to India, it was magical; I could feel the dust and smell the sour odour of the pony lines.

Which is why, when I arrived for Cartier Day and heard they had pony lines, that's where I went. There were dozens of ponies lined up on hard standings that smelled of clean straw, waiting patiently for valet service. Young grooms moved efficiently between them. They were being prepared for the Coronation Cup that afternoon and were already sporting their team colours – yellow blankets and leg bandages for Brazil, red and white for England – and their neat little hooves were oiled and gleaming. They pricked up their ears as visitors approached. All the mounts for the Coronation Cup are borrowed from private owners, so that neither team has an advantage over the other. They looked expensive, like footballers.

However, the small-headed, smoothly muscled, athletic animals tethered under the corrugated-iron roofs were no more ponies than I'm a size zero. They were horses, and they were well bred. There was not a flea-bitten grey to be seen. It was a fine illustration of how the game of English polo has evolved: the only remnant of its colonial and military roots is a certain down-to-earth Englishness (the folding chairs and umbrellas) and this has long since been leavened by an international glamour (the sexy Argentine *polistas*) that has drawn more money into the game. With money there is always a restless quest for speed. And for speed you need thoroughbreds.

'They used to be real ponies,' explained Louise Thomas, a groom for the Brazilian team, 'originally they had to be under 14.2 hands, but it changed as they started using more thoroughbreds.' Ponies are measured in hands – a hand being four inches – from shoulder to ground and the Upper India Free-For-All ponies would have been much smaller, 13.3 or less. That wouldn't cut it in the modern game. 'Even since I began, the high-goal game has changed,' she said, 'polo is now such a professional sport.' By high-goal she meant top end. Players' handicaps range from the lowest, minus two, to the highest, ten, and must add up to a team total: in English polo a high-goal team has a maximum of twenty-two, but on International Day it may be higher as each country fields its best players. Most of the world's ten-goalers are Argentinian: I saw some once, playing at the Polo Open in Buenos Aires. They looked like centaurs in pith helmets.

Quite aside from its gigantic playing area – almost three times the length of a football pitch and substantially wider – polo has other eccentricities. It is played in four to eight seven-minute chukkas – from an Indian word *chakka* for circle, or round, as in a round of cards – and, like basketball, is so exhausting that the players, in this case the ponies, are constantly changed. Teams swap ends after every goal. Each player has a spare mount at both ends of the ground, changes ponies at half-time and brings between nine and twelve animals – owned by his/her *patron* (pronounced Argentine-style, with the stress on the second syllable and best translated as an owner-player) – to a game. Like most sports of the season, it's not cheap. And one of the privileges of being a *patron* is playing with your team, so that amateurs and professionals mix in one match. 'It's like Roman Abramovich turning out for Chelsea,' said a Guards Club member.

Today was special. It was not only the centenary of the Coronation Cup, inaugurated by King George V, and the last of three Test matches played by England each year, the others being at Cowdray and Beaufort. It was also the last Cartier International Day. The hunt was on for a new sponsor (Audi have now taken it on) to fund what is effectively the annual end-of-season jolly of the polo world. After this, the top pros would take their ponies and their sex appeal and head south, like migrating birds, leaving English polo to occupy itself until the autumn. That's why, though it was far from the last match of the year, everyone – from *patrons* to players, from journalists to grooms – was there. Too many, perhaps: rumour said that Cartier was shifting its sponsorship to the Queen's Cup in May because the event was losing its cachet. 'Too many tats and not enough A-listers' was the refrain: the same story I'd heard at Ascot, told with the same relish. After all these weeks I still couldn't think of a solution. Except possibly uniform.

Chronologically speaking, the Cartier International Day is a latecomer to the season, a good fifty years after Glyndebourne. Prince Philip and others founded Guards Polo Club in the 1950s: polo had taken a pasting during the war and needed some momentum, the Queen agreed to lease the land and as a result the club and Smith's Lawn became associated with English polo's military and colonial roots. Twenty years later Major Ronald Ferguson, Sarah Ferguson's father, founded International Day. It was low-key, discreet, not in the least suitable for *Hello!* until Cartier swooped in and transformed it into a sort of glamorous celebrity cuckoo, all teeth and tan, and the world (or rather, the press) suddenly sat up and took notice.

'It's very rare that you get an event that transcends the sport,' mused Richenda Hine, the editor of the glossy *Polo Magazine*, who was sitting behind me in the South Stand. 'Royal Ascot, or the Grand Prix, I suppose. This is the only polo event you'll read about in *Now* or *Heat*. It all began in the Liz Hurley years, I think, when Cartier really started moving it in the celebrity direction. I'd say the Gold Cup at Cowdray is where the real polo crowd goes; the parking spaces there go on sale a few months before and they sell out in minutes, like getting a ticket to Take That. You can eat and watch at the same time: line-side parking with a picnic is the thing to do there. This is a bit of a circus: lots of people don't know one end of a polo stick from another. They're here for Chinawhite and the after-party: all the grooms will head down there afterwards. It's still really good fun, though, and why not? It's like going racing if you're not into horses.'

Richenda explained that Smith's Lawn, and specifically the Queen's Ground where the match was taking place, was like Lord's. It was the Holy Grail of polo. I could see that: it had an air of belonging about it, a quiet confidence. The Royal Box was on the southern side – so the sun was not in the spectators' faces, a thoughtful colonial touch – and was flanked by raked white timber stands. The box itself had a little lawn outside hemmed in by a white picket fence with a gate onto the ground. On the other sides of the field, like two cheery parasites, were the Temples of Fun: the Cartier Tent opposite – a big pavlova of a marquee with an outside Lawn Bar for maximum paparazzi exposure – and Chinawhite's tent to the west, run by the eponymous London nightclub.

It didn't feel like a sporting fixture. It felt like a day out, or a very large, very upmarket village show. There was a morning match for up-and-coming players, to get everyone in the mood, and the club's juniors did a display game. The hounds of the local hunt arrived and foamed around the huntsman as he took them across the ground to cheers of delight. The military band of the Irish Guards struck up. A horse-drawn Red Cross van, a First World War ambulance raising money for the military charity Horses Help Heroes, appeared. In honour of the Brazilians, the London Samba Club snaked across the grass clad in bikinis and flesh-coloured tights.

Sitting by the runway leading to the Cartier tent I found two

Kiwi women, surreptitiously picnicking while assessing the pass-ing celebrities. If you weren't in a proper seat you could stand up and drink but not eat, they explained. If you sat down you couldn't do either, except in designated picnic areas. Stewards enforced this rule every so often. Meanwhile they delivered a devastating fashion commentary. 'Oh. My. God,' said one, 'I know we're not from here, but really? An orange mini on *that*?' She took a bite of sandwich and hid it in her bag. 'That driss is stunning.' They didn't recognise many British celebrities and thought A-listers were a bit thin on the ground. They thought a tanned Andrew Neil, squiring a young woman in a tiny dress, was from *Coronation Street*. 'A journalist? Rilly?' they said politely. 'His daughter looks very pretty, though. Great driss.'

In the packed South Stand the dress code was smart casual; everyone looked summery and relaxed. Over the samba it was hard to hear the commentator, who turned out to be bellow-ing: 'Could the London Samba School please be QUIET!' It's theatrical, polo. The players canter out in a virile fashion, twirling their sticks, as names and handicaps are read out to cheers – particularly from the polo crowd, who know them all. As play begins the sound of stick on ball is surprisingly light and the ball goes surprisingly far. Because they can hit it backwards, with a cunning flick of the wrist, the whole thing has a cartoon-like quality. One minute eight horses are going one way at top speed, then they all screech to a halt, realise the ball has gone the other way and gallop all the way back again.

For some reason, though, the game didn't quite take off, like a dinner party with all the right guests that never really gels. Or maybe it was the effect of my SAD. There were a few good ride-offs – when they gallop along locked saddle-to-saddle and for one heart-stopping moment you think their stirrups have got tangled and they *are* locked saddle-to-saddle – and one guy had what Richenda called 'a good crunch' when he fell off and needed minor medical help. But he didn't even need an ambulance. It never quite hit what you would call electric levels of excitement.

Not that it mattered: after three chukkas we all emptied onto the ground and an informal party began as people found friends and met people and chatted while toeing lumps of grass back into place in a vague way. In the background young men in boiler suits were doing the job for real, filling in holes that might trip unwary ponies, working at three times the speed of the rest of us. After the second half, when England won by a single goal, Prince Philip, now a slim, marginally stooped figure, stood on the Royal Box lawn to shake hands and hand over the silverware. It was courtly.

I trotted over to the North Stand afterwards, to find most of it decamping to Chinawhite's. There were groups of office mates and two hen nights – both beautifully dressed and finishing off spectacular picnics – and two more Kiwis who had come by coach on the cheapest tickets they could get and were helpless with laughter, practising their English accents. 'You've gotta say "poh-loh",' they told me, making horse faces, 'and we say "poy-loy". We were expecting it to be quite divided because it's Cartier and there are royals, so we knew we'd be in with the plebs. We thought we might be allowed to do the divots, but perhaps we've seen *Pretty Woman* too many times.' Royal Ascot, they told me, was older than New Zealand.

Millie from Guadeloupe was en route to Chinawhite's with her friend Joelle from France. Joelle lived in London and came every year. 'I love it,' she said. 'People dress up, they like to party but they still follow the rules. I love the procession and the Guards, they're magnificent.' Then she really surprised me. 'People mix here,' she added, 'you have the very wealthy and the less wealthy.

Nobody cares. Everyone's together, nobody looks up or down. In France, I think we classify people more. Here I think you can tell who's wealthy and who's not, but it all holds together.' Well, knock me down with a feather. What happened to *liberté, egalité, fraternité*?

While trying to readjust my national self-image to a startling new one of general bonhomie and easygoing classlessness, I was hit by a pang of patriotic affection. The ritualised chunks of tradition that had occupied my summer were very nearly over and I was doing them a disservice by drooping about in this fashion. Some stiff upper lip was required, I told myself, some playing up and playing the game: everyone else thought these events national treasures, even – or perhaps especially – foreigners. And to be honest, I couldn't believe it was all trundling slowly to an end.

22

THE SULTAN OF SPEED

After months of trying, I finally had an interview with a genuine mover and shaker, the Earl of March and Kinrara, the chairman of Goodwood Racecourse and founder of two of the grooviest motor racing fixtures on the planet. In season terms this was like meeting a woolly mammoth not only alive but grazing merrily on the Siberian tundra. While most events owe their provenance to some distant historical figure and take decades, maybe centuries, to ripen to maturity, Charles March had managed to add two new ones in the past fifteen years. The Festival of Speed and The Goodwood Revival both had undoubted cachet without being snotty. He also happened to have a gorgeous racecourse on the Sussex Downs and antecedents who had played a significant role in the season's history.

In a fold of what Kipling called 'the whale-backed Downs' of West Sussex, between Petworth and Chichester, lie what must be the grandest kennels in England. The architect James Wyatt built them in 1787 to house the Duke of Richmond's foxhounds. Symmetrical wings for the animals flank an elegant cube for the huntsman, with a neoclassical pediment and fan-lit front door. They have long since been converted into a clubhouse for private members, but from the windows there is a hound's-eye view of Goodwood House, the Richmonds' flint and Portland stone family seat. Now home to the Earl and his family, it is set in sloping parkland graced with cedars of Lebanon and a cricket pitch (the very one on which the rules of cricket were formulated). The fact the hounds had a Palladian kennel larger than many country houses – and central heating decades before the family did – says quite a lot about ducal priorities over the centuries.

The 1st Duke of Richmond was the natural son of King Charles II, the Merry Monarch, and his Breton mistress Louise de Keroualle, the Duchess of Portsmouth. There is a portrait of them in the Long Hall in Goodwood House: Charles gazes magisterially out of the canvas and Louise – clearly unwilling to be left out – parades across one corner attended by her ladies-in-waiting. Her Protestant English rival, Nell Gwynne, was said to refer to her rudely as 'Squintabella', but she was highly organised and apparently far shrewder than she looked. King Charles, as we know, was a polymath and a party animal. It was a sensational genetic combination that seems to have passed down the generations: their son, Charles Lennox, became Duke of Richmond and Lennox in 1675 (and later the Duke of Aubigny and Duke of Gordon) and, great entertaining genes aside, passed on a further legacy: the heir apparent to the dukedom is always called Charles.

The first duke would leave his mansion on Whitehall, a horseshoe's throw from the old Tudor royal palace, and make for the South Downs to ride to hounds with the Charlton Hunt. He rented the original house at Goodwood before buying it in 1697 and his descendants gradually enlarged it, partly to house their Grand Tour treasures after the London house burned down. The third Duke commanded the mounted Sussex Militia and set up a flat racing course called The Harroway for his officers to hold an annual race meeting. The first, in 1802, was such a success that it became a three-day meeting under Jockey Club Rules. Spectators began to turn up. So did Society. The July Meeting became a fixture of the season.

Ten generations on from the 1st Duke, Lord March, runs the Goodwood Estate, his parents having retired to the dower house. Right now he was sitting in his club in Mayfair, conducting a series of sponsors' meetings. On top of everything else he is slim and irritatingly good-looking, with well-cut grey hair and glasses. He doesn't seem aware of this, though every editorial ever written compares him breathlessly to Hugh Grant. He didn't quite wince when I mentioned the season, but a less courteous man might have rolled his eyes and banged his head on the table: Channel 4 had been doing a fly-on-the-wall documentary all year, no doubt asking similar questions, and anyway Glorious Goodwood, the event I wanted to discuss, is just one of a clutch of enterprises he runs in West Sussex. It sits alongside the Festival of Speed in June, the Revival – a retro motor race meeting – in September, a flying club, two golf courses, a hotel, a pub, a health club and a farm shop. His real passion, though, is cars.

'My first memories are of horses and cars, because we used to go to the horse racing in July and the car racing on the Easter Bank Holiday,' he explained. 'My grandparents would open the house up especially. It was shut during the war, so everything was under dustsheets. We only got the paintings out of the attic a few years ago.' His grandfather, Freddie March (not a Charles because he was a younger son), was an apprentice at Bentley Motors and converted a wartime aerodrome on the estate into a motor racing circuit in 1948. His father, the current duke, not only moved his young family into Goodwood House, which he gradually restored and opened to the public for the first time, but did a huge amount of work on the racecourse, including building its distinctive, white-pinnacled Gordon Enclosure in the 1970s, which is visible right across the South Downs.

Another childhood memory was the sheer glamour of the July races. The then viscount and his sisters would get up early and rush to the stables – which are nearly as grand as the kennels, but nearer the house – to see the horses staying, as they still do, for race week. People would arrive all the time to join the house party and Goodwood House would be bustling with staff, which it wasn't usually. There were often royal visits – the Queen sometimes came by helicopter – and they would watch them all arrive from the top of the staircase, mesmerised by the hustle and bustle.

The royal family's connection with Goodwood goes back generations. It was Bertie, Prince of Wales – later Edward VII, whose death resulted in Black Ascot – who delighted in its garden party atmosphere and relaxed dress code. He stayed every year with Queen Alexandra. This drew press interest and it was reporters who coined that happy piece of alliteration, 'Glorious Goodwood', capturing in one buoyant phrase something people still respond to today. Goodwood is fun. It's relaxed. It's in a beautiful setting. The quality of the racing, while not as sensational as that of Royal Ascot, is more than enough to draw in the buffs. Even the racecourse colours are jaunty: three scarlet horses at a flying gallop on a background of egg-yolk yellow, topped by the five-leaved ducal coronet.

This was the only press jolly I'd been invited to that summer and I was looking forward to it: I was sick of invading other people's picnics with a microphone, I wanted to be one of the gang for a change. It took about five minutes on the train down to realise that wasn't going to happen, mainly because everyone else already had a gang. Across the aisle was the model and muse Saffron Aldridge with three girlfriends. I thought I recognised one from Condé Nast days: if it was so, I'd seen her saunter into reception one morning, summoned to collect a delivery. It was a single, sumptuous lily, a creamy fold of perfection. She picked it up, read the note, went 'Oh *God*!' and left it there. I'm ashamed to say I thought she was rather cool. They nodded hello and ignored me. So I settled down to eavesdrop and ogle their clothes while pretending to read the press kit.

They had judged it to perfection. Goodwood's sartorial style is casual but chic, quietly expensive but not flashy. Somehow these women managed to look chilled and feminine at the same time. Their slender, tanned wrists were set off by slender, branded watches and their glossy hair was artfully tousled. The male race-goers around us were wearing linen suits and ties if they were over thirty-five; drainpipes, pointy shoes and slightly-too-tight single-breasted jackets if not. Panama hats sat beside empty Starbucks cups. The panamas are thanks to Edward VII: there's a famous photograph of him sitting in the Royal Box at Goodwood wearing a bizarre white top hat and surrounded by a sea of men in black. His hat really was white and I wondered what it was made of. Ermine? Polar bear? Guinea pig? It was in fact silk and it caused a sensation. The more oleaginous courtiers sent their valets to London to find albino toppers. The next year they turned up white-hatted, but the Prince was one step ahead. Determined to enjoy this most relaxed of race meetings, by 1906 he was wearing a informal suit that could be teamed with a white bowler, straw hat or panama. It's been panamas ever since.

The racecourse at Goodwood rivals Cheltenham for top setting. It occupies the flattened top of the Downs, an ancient chalk landscape striped with medieval grazing and studded with ancient hill forts ridged like Walnut Whips. The track appears on ancient maps as a 'circus', probably knew human life for millennia before that and has always been a source of fascination: the Devil is supposed to have driven his hounds across this land. It is overlooked by an Iron Age fort, The Trundle, which has its own racing subculture, and every year sprouts Portaloos and bookies' stands and offers magnificent, if distant, views of the racing below. I could see hundreds of people milling about up there, little points of colour forming queues in front of tiny lines of tiny bookies, like a 'Where's Wally?' drawing. I was coming back there with friends and a big picnic on the Saturday.

This was Thursday, Ladies' Day, and we were waiting for the start of the new celebrity ladies' race, the Magnolia Cup, possibly named for the trees seen all over the estate or possibly for the paint that, according to Lord March, covered most of the house interior when his grandparents were in charge. The celebrity ladies were wearing silks by celebrity designers, had been practising with celebrity trainers, who had lent them horses, and had a formidable back-up team of celebrity stylists, journalists and friends.

Just as I'm glad I saw Eton v. Harrow at Lord's and the Summer Exhibition at the Royal Academy because they put Test cricket and fine art into some sort of context, I'm glad I saw the celebrity ladies' race that day at Goodwood because it showed just how hard it is to be a jockey. All the women competing were experienced riders, but they weren't professional. Instead of a flowing line of doubled-up riders with knock-knees and bums in the air, a straggle of slight figures, some frankly exhausted, flew along gamely on their mounts. It was more haphazard, messier, with flapping elbows and wobbling knees, and the roar of the crowd was generous, quite different from the sound of racing fanatics bringing a winner home. Annette Mason, wife of the Pink Floyd guitarist Nick Mason, came off badly to gasps of horror and was surrounded with screens before being driven to hospital. She was fine, but it was a reminder. It's no picnic, horse racing.

Still, up on the hill or down on the course there's a fizz about Goodwood, a sort of end-of-term excitement, which seems to infect everyone. Indeed it was the end of term for politicians, just before the summer recess, and when I visited Goodwood House later, the house manager showed me some gold plaques in the Tapestry Drawing Room. 'We have quite a few of these,' she said. 'They record His Majesty George V holding Privy Council meetings at the house. The dates are all our racing dates for Glorious Goodwood.' More Privy Council meetings have been held here than at any other private house in Britain. Attendees included the Earl of Durham, Harold Macmillan, the Rt Hon. J. C. Wedgwood and the Earl of Sefton. One plaque read: 'Queen Elizabeth II held a Privy Council meeting in this room on Wednesday July 31 1957'. Even the Archbishop of Canterbury heard a report by the commission on church and state in October 1970. 'Ah, not racing, though!' I said. She looked at me. 'That's the winter meeting.'

The poshest bit of Goodwood Racecourse is the Richmond Enclosure, which is open only to Members and their guests. We were in the Gordon Enclosure, in a box, and I found myself torn between being polite to my hosts and getting out to the Parade Ring and the Horsewalk – the equine equivalent of a catwalk, leading from ring to racecourse – and the bookies' stands. I wanted to be back on Kate Fox's circuit, not eating canapés and watching the racing on a monitor inside. So I legged it and milled about with all the panamas and silk dresses, watching the winners come in and the competitors go out, and scuttling off to the track to watch each race.

People were amazingly chatty. 'I've been coming to Goodwood for at least fifteen years,' said Nicky Stafford, who runs a syndicate of around twenty horses. 'It's more relaxed than Ascot, it's more compact and friendly, you don't have to wear a hat, you can see all your friends. You've got a huge paddock and the wonderful views of the Downs. The racing is not as good, to be honest, you haven't got Group Ones every day, but you've got a few Group Ones and some Group Twos and Threes. We've had winners here; all our syndicate members just love it. Goodwood has so much cachet.' She said her nineteen-year-old daughter loved Ascot because she never knew the old setup, but she came to Goodwood too, 'with all the young'. She also said the Goodwood Ball had been revived for the first time the night before and she thought it was the best party she'd ever been to. 'That will become the new sought-after invitation of the year, I'm sure,' she said.

The issuer of that invitation was Lord March. It was intriguing to wonder what gives him the Midas touch, the ability to make things seem fun while keeping it all under control. He inherited a great hand of cards and could easily have just let things jog along: instead, it has grown and prospered and now half a million people a year turn up to the events of Goodwood's summer. It's a huge business, a big local employer. He didn't really know why. He looked slightly weary when I posited Charles II's party genes and said actually he had a great team behind him. So I decided it must be a cocktail of circumstances, one of which is his commercial background. He was an advertising photographer for some years in London – he shot the stills for Stanley Kubrick's 1975 film *Barry*

Lyndon among other things – before moving down to Sussex. He has a sharp eye for visual detail and obviously likes trying new ideas. Add that to a stately home, a racecourse and a motor racing track and you get the sort of easy style that Goodwood has.

The motor racing events have even more pizzazz, but somehow the word 'social' doesn't fit them. They are normal. Their elite is the car buffs. The friend who explained Wimbledon debentures rebuilds classic cars and goes to the Revival every year. 'To race there would be a bit like the Mille Miglia in Italy,' he said dreamily. 'It's something you have to do if you're a car enthusiast. It used to be aristocrats and horses, now it's self-made millionaires, or billionaires now, and cars. Watch the March Trophy and you'll see a line-up of cars on that grid worth well over £250m. You'll see cars you used to see only in museums racing aggressively against each other. It's theatre of the highest level, one of the most magnificent sights you'll ever see. And the Revival Ball ... to go you've got to have a car in a race, or be a guest of someone who does. For a petrolhead like me that's heaven on earth. For me, that's the new high point of the season.'

The Festival of Speed, which is a few years older, takes place in front of the house, where the Earl's mother, the Duchess of Richmond, once held international dressage competitions. Now cars scream past and up the famous Hillclimb in high gear. It's one of the few events that Formula One drivers come to for fun. 'It's a true test of a driver,' said Lord March, 'you just drive straight up the hill at top speed and it's who's fastest. It's very straightforward. When we first did it we had fifty cars and thought we might get a few hundred spectators and twenty thousand turned up. We couldn't man the gates, we didn't have anywhere to put the money. Then a driver died on the first day and I thought it was all over. It was terrible.'

What was clear, though, was that there was a huge audience looking for something Formula One just couldn't supply. Both motor racing events have become hugely successful, without damaging Glorious Goodwood. They appeal to utterly different audiences but have some key season components: *passagiato*, history, a smattering of royalty and sport pursued to an incredibly high standard. Best horses, best cars. 'We've started from scratch with the motor events,' he said, 'but we've been able to draw on all that archive, fabulous pictures, fabulous stories, fabulous drivers.'

That Saturday I met friends on The Trundle and we laid out our rugs and picnic on the hill. A friend's little boy cantered about in a cardboard box with a horse's head and tail, held on by raffia strings. 'My dad always used to say the horses were the size of bees from up here,' said the patriarch of a huge family I passed on my way down to the racecourse. 'You need binoculars, really, but you can see everything, it's a great view.' He was right. The sun blazed, toy clouds hung in the sky and the Downs rolled sublimely away in all directions. I was with friends. It was heaven. Down on the course later I spotted the guy from my gazebo at Ascot, now in his linen and panama ensemble: he told me that the day he won a grand on the first race at Goodwood, ordered a bottle of champagne and sat alone drinking it and watching the racing, was one of the best days of his life.

The last race of the last day at Glorious Goodwood is the Stewards' Cup, a six-furlong 'cavalry charge' for twenty-eight horses. As I stood watching the line of horseflesh thundering to the finish, I thought of the 3rd Duke and his militia and what they had started two centuries before. And I did wonder what the Earl would pull out of the bag next.

23

RED SAILS IN THE SUNSET

It was early August and my season was almost over. Every so often, all these months later, I wake in the night and stare into the dark sweating, thinking about the dress I nearly wore to the Royal Yacht Squadron Ball. It was one of those spur-of-the-moment purchases: a white linen and cotton shift teamed – here was the masterstroke – with one red and one green shoe. Port out, starboard home: it was summery, it was colonial, it was discreetly witty. Or so I thought. But the nearer August came, the more I worried. I tried it on for my friend Jasper, who had come to stay. He looked at me. 'I think it's a bit ...' he searched for a tactful description, '... *tennis* club. Perhaps ... not quite formal enough – but what would I know?'

There was little time to replace it. In the end I texted Victoria, trying to sound insouciant, as though I was rifling through my packed wardrobe and deciding which of my many ensembles to choose. 'Above knee OK for RYS?' I messaged. It pinged back with terrifying speed. 'Not OK,' it said, 'Is ball. Suggest Indian.' Jasper and I looked at each other in horror.

'Southall?' he said.

'Not enough time.'

'Streatham?'

'But where?'

I got a tube to Tooting Broadway, shouted 'Sari!' at everyone I met, was directed to the Lal-Kurti Saree Shop on Upper Tooting Road, galloped in, collapsed on the glass counter and gasped that I had to leave with a party outfit in twenty minutes. They didn't flicker. I was shoved in a cubicle and every so often a hand appeared holding another cloud of gossamer: silver on sea green with a satin bodice shot with blue, a hot-pink top and sunset-orange pantaloons, a scarlet tunic embroidered with gold thread. I left with a tomato-red pearl-encrusted shalwar kameez – tunic, trousers, scarf to tie around the neck and hang down the back – and blingtastic ruby and diamond drop earrings. It felt absolutely brilliant. It took fifteen minutes.

Cowes Week had already begun. It immediately hit the head-lines when a small boat failed to get out of the way of a tanker: every newspaper and news site carried images of the huge vessel ploughing over the little one, whose deflated spinnaker wrapped around the towering bow. No one was hurt and it was held to have been the small boat's fault, but it showed one of the reasons that Cowes Week is world famous. 'Solent sailing is really challenging,' said Annie Kettle, who I met on the RedJet hi-speed ferry to the island, 'the wind here is so unpredictable. I mean, it's mid-August and we've had everything from thirty-knot gusts of wind to days becalmed. Then you've got all the shipping lanes and Southampton and Portsmouth bringing in the container ships and the cross-

Channel ferries and the warships ... it's hectic out there. You really have to be good, which is why it still brings in the world-class sailors and the high-performance boats.'

The Solent is a chevron of water, no more than five miles wide, separating the Isle of Wight from England's south coast. It's always been dangerous: Henry VIII's flagship, the *Mary Rose*, sank here and James I himself was nearly shipwrecked. Once a year, at low tide, a sandbar called Bramble Bank surfaces from the water like a whale and remains for about an hour, just long enough for the Island Sailing Club (from Cowes) and the Royal Southern Yacht Club (from Southampton) to sail out for a cricket match. The apex of the island itself is split as if cloven by an axe. This is the mouth of the River Medina, flowing north from the island's centre, and its headlands are the Cowes, 'cow' once being the word for a castle. The Royal Yacht Squadron is in West Cowes; its headquarters, the Castle, was built by Henry VIII to survey the straits. The East Cowes fortification is long gone, but nearby is Queen Victoria's summer retreat at Osborne.

Annie had been catering to crews all week at her Gosport café and was now on her way to sail on one of the big boats in the Volvo Open 70 class, thanks to her sister who was in marketing. She said most crews rented rooms in private houses or took a crew house, sometimes with a cook, the same place every year if they could. There were loads of crew house parties. Then there were the yacht club dos and low-key nights in pubs and the Marina Village, which was full of beer tents and food outlets and music stages. Lots of people partied on their boats. The population of under 10,000 more than doubles during Cowes Week. I was beginning to feel really quite excited. I had a spare night after the ball.

It was mid-morning and the Marina Village was just coming to life. Wires chinked on metal masts and light bounced off blinding-white hulls and fawn decks. Girls wandered by with long tangled hair and Ugg boots. The Pimm's Bus was opening up, slowly and reluctantly, as if recovering from a huge, Bertie Wooster-sized hangover. You could smell fresh coffee. Out on the water sails of every shape – isosceles triangles, thin shark's fins, wide symmetrical ones like children's drawings – were already zipping about and a fleet of Redwings, elegant shallow-keeled Bembridge boats with tall, round-shouldered red sails, was spread across the blue horizon.

Later I got a ride on the press boat, which was full of sailing reporters and photographers who knew what was going on. They wanted to watch the X One Designs, known as the XODs, which come from all round the Solent and were celebrating their centenary by lining up practically the entire fleet of 146 boats. I didn't realise at the time how rare this was, to see a long line of yachts on the open water, identical but for their cheery keel colours, champing at the bit like horses in the Goodwood cavalry charge. It had turned cloudy so their white sails stood out against the sky. Then a gun went off and they were unleashed. It was a marvellous sight.

The history of Cowes Week is entwined with the history of the Squadron, which was formed, as so many things seem to have been, in a tavern in St James's. The year was 1815, it was two weeks before the Battle of Waterloo and the forty-two yacht owners who turned up were in buoyant mood. They formed a sea yachting club for gentlemen owners of vessels of ten tons or over. They called it the Yacht Club – although there were two in Ireland, two in England and one in Russia already – and met for two dinners a year, one in London and one in Cowes. Two years later the Prince Regent became a member and when he became king added 'Royal' to the name. When William IV ('the Sailor

King' or 'Sailor Billy') ascended the throne he consented to a name change to the Royal Yacht Squadron. At that time it operated almost as an informal offshoot of the Royal Navy. Today it has a maximum of 475 members, most of whom are sailors, and it has occupied Cowes Castle for almost 150 years.

'In the early days it was ship owners who mostly provided the fleet for the Crown,' explained Stuart Quarrie, the Regatta CEO, whose office doubles as Regatta HQ during Cowes Week, 'so as suppliers the RYS was allowed to use the white ensign, like the Royal Navy. Of course these very rich owners began to race – you know, "I wager you a thousand pounds my ship can get to that point before yours" – it was the age of the tea clippers and so on.' In fact various clubs were allowed to use the white ensign and it took years for the club to claim the exclusive right to its use, but the first race was held in 1826. As leisure sailing took off and other yacht clubs were founded in the middle of the century, they began to hold race days too. Eventually these became known collectively as 'Cowes Week' and competition was intense in the pursuit of speed. Boat builders aimed for 'celerity in sailing and beauty of construction' and the Royal Navy began to reap the benefit of the resulting advances in technology.

During the glory years, when the Prince of Wales, later King Edward VII, segued gracefully from Goodwood to Cowes (where he was Honorary Commodore), Society turned up in droves. A magazine cover shows him on the jetty, clad in a yachting suit and matching bowler, watching as Queen Alexandra is handed into a launch for their return to the Royal Yacht. A young sailor, head bowed, holds the painter. The King leans on a stick. All around is the crowd, in boaters and floral hats, frankly curious.

There are numerous images of the royal couple: Edward in full naval fig with an officer's cap and the Queen in tiny-waisted, frilled white muslin with an artfully feminine boater; with the Russian royal family aboard Edward's specially commissioned racing cutter HMY *Britannia*; with his nephew the Kaiser, whose yacht *Meteor II* later beat *Britannia*, causing a royal huff. It was just like a race meeting, but with yachts instead of horses: guests would descend for grand house parties and regatta jaunts. Until 1997, when she was decommissioned, the second *Britannia* moored at Cowes every year, as a floating palace for the Queen and Prince Philip.

It was Prince Philip who was partly responsible for the regatta as it is today. The situation had become chaotic by the mid-twentieth century: during Cowes Week the sailing instructions, start and finish lines varied from day to day, depending on the club in charge. Sailors faced different rules and entry requirements. When the Prince became Commodore in the 1962, he 'knocked everyone's heads together', as one member put it, and persuaded them to form Cowes Combined Clubs, with shared rules and responsibilities. Today Aberdeen Asset Management sponsors the regatta, which is run by Cowes Week Limited (a subsidiary of Cowes Combined Clubs) from Stuart's office on Bath Road. The RYS plays a large part in race management, not least because the onshore start and finish lines are in front of the Castle, which has the best view. Volunteers from all six Cowes clubs and two other Solent clubs act as race officers on its battlements. The Squadron's own regatta is on Tuesday and Wednesday.

'Cowes is the biggest regatta of its kind in the world,' said Stuart. 'It's multi-day and all keelboats, we don't have dinghy sailing here. Up to a thousand boats will come in for it and many of those are intending to sail every day of the week.' He explained they were divided into the Black Group – larger vessels with cabins, often with big crews and very rich, or corporate, owners –

and the White Group, open day boats, with crews of between two and four people. Here were the plucky amateurs, still holding their own in a world-class event. Here were Victoria's Corinthian values. As a result there could be up to forty races running concurrently, each for a different class of yacht. The logistics were once again extraordinary. The smooth running of races depended on numerous volunteers, from course-setters to timekeepers to race officials, some onshore and some afloat.

I had been trying to find Victoria all afternoon. I left my case at the Castle gatehouse and got permission to look for her inside. 'Get a drink on The Lawn,' said a friendly member, 'she'll be along soon.' The Lawn was once known as the Deer Park and was the only place women were allowed until they finally stormed the Castle bastions in the 1960s. Now they have their own light-filled annexe on its west side. I had another Bateman cartoon moment when I tried to pay for my drink: 'No cash,' said the barman, managing to look surprised and suspicious at the same time. Members' drinks go on their mess bills. Like the Queen, they don't need to carry cash. You have never seen so many permutations of navy and white stripes with the odd splash of red, nor so many men wearing ancient sailing trousers faded to the colour of stewed rhubarb. My black linen shirt screamed London.

In the end I found the house Victoria was staying at and made myself known to the friends she was staying with. We were going to have an Indian takeaway that night, they told me, before going to the ball. Right now it was teatime. I sat in the kitchen as people with faces flushed from the sun and wind and clad in giant waterproof trousers that came up to their chests talked sailing. I zoned out to the clink of teacups and clatter of cake tins and unintelligible bits of conversation: 'Oh, he was definitely over, no question.' 'Was he?' 'God yes.' 'Did they protest?' 'God yes.'

Johnny, Victoria's husband and one of two Rear Commodores at the Squadron that year, took me on a tour of Cowes' waterfront. 'Look at it,' he said, 'isn't it great? This just turns into one huge party in the late afternoon.' There was the thump of rock music, muted for the moment, and people were strolling or sitting in the sun to eat. Massive screens would later show the race action. It was all fleeces, tanned legs, sea-salted hair and shorts, and most of the competing boats were moored on pontoons. As we strolled around it became clear there were two Cowes Weeks: one was onshore, where the crews and the public needed to be kept entertained, and other was out at sea, where sailors were hard at it.

Sailing is a tricky spectator sport. The Solent during Cowes Week looks completely beautiful – hundreds and hundreds of sails, all in different sizes, colours and shapes, zooming back and forth – but non-sailors have little hope of understanding it all. Races usually take around three hours and apart from starts and finishes much takes place out of sight. I met a video cameraman who was developing a system of streaming the sailing direct to screens onshore so spectators could see what was going on. 'People complain they don't involve the public enough,' he said, 'but in the end it is a yachting regatta. It's for sailors to go racing and even they don't know where the course is until minutes before the start. So it's difficult to keep people really involved – and that's what we're really keen to do.'

Up on the battlements of the Castle were twenty-one brass cannons on little mounts, each thirty-nine inches long, facing out to sea. They were the start and finish guns and had once been mounted on a scaled-down warship, the *Royal Adelaide*, used by William IV on Virginia Water. Johnny silently pointed out the line officer, in a varnished chair, staring hawkishly seawards, and behind him a race officer in overall command. There was an atmosphere of deadly concentration. A flag was hoisted for each class and a cannon was fired ten minutes before the off. This was the signal for the yachts to start jostling, whizzing skittishly around to get the perfect position and cross the line with clear air ahead, rather than a rival yacht hogging their wind. Before each race the officer in charge called silence. Then: 'Five, four, three, two, one,...' BOOM! A cannon would jerk and send up a puff of smoke, and the straggling line of boats would start to pull apart.

Before the ball I got talking to Jonathan Peel. He worked in television animation for networks like Nickelodeon and Disney ('The only 1960s rock'n'roll promoter to be a Squadron member,' he said, with relish). He was certainly the only music promoter I had ever seen wearing black mess trousers and a black monkey jacket with black buttons decorated with a gold 'RYS' and an anchor, the Squadron's formal evening wear. He was also a course-setter for the White Group. The more I heard about it, the more impossible it sounded. Between 10.30 and 12.30 in the morning, he explained, races started at five-minute intervals, Black and White Groups alternating; smaller boats went from the Squadron start line, larger boats from a starting boat off shore. I tried to imagine hundreds of horses at Ascot running races of different lengths, taking place all over the course, when they only knew where they were starting minutes before, and only then if they listened to the radio or saw a flag, and I couldn't.

'First thing in the morning you have a sniff of the day to see what you think is going to happen,' he said. 'I've been sailing here since 1954 or something, so you do have an idea even before you talk to the weather forecaster. You sketch out what you think is a good way of handling the day and divide up the buoys with the Black Group setter so the big and small boats don't mix. Your first consideration is what would be a nice course from a helmsman's

point of view, say if you were in a Daring or a Swallow or whatever. Then you want all those classes to have an ideal race without
getting muddled up, though you can't avoid it at the finish.'

I looked at him in awe, amazed at how differently our brains
must be configured. But enough of sailing. We had to change. It
was party time. I put on my shalwar kameez, rubies, diamonds,
silver bindi and flat slippers with silver thread and found all the
other women in Indian clothes too. I sent up a silent prayer of
thanks to the Lal-Kurti Saree Shop. It was the most comfortable
I had felt, sartorially speaking, all season. Then the takeaway
arrived and we opened tubs of chicken korma and pilau rice,
trying not to get curry in our embroidery, and afterwards strolled
along to the Castle in the darkness. It was ablaze with light. People
were finishing dinner in the huge pavilion on the Lawn. Others
were arriving and the rooms were filled with cries of greeting and
nautical post-mortems.

It was by far the best-dressed event I had been to that summer.
The weather-beaten faces and hearty clothes of the afternoon had
gone, to be replaced by startlingly chic long dresses. When did sev-
enteen-year-olds start looking as though they were on the red
carpet at the Golden Globes? I wondered irritably, wincing anew
at the thought of my discarded fancy-dress ensemble. The only
person who looked completely mad was a former Commodore,
Lord Iliffe, in a Groucho Marx nose, moustache and glasses, baggy
shorts, a white linen shirt, tennis shoes and – did I dream this? –
a tennis racket. Victoria appeared in a sumptuously embroidered
coat from a designer in Calcutta, a shalwar kameez from the
market in Goa and a bindi. 'Good,' she said, looking me up and
down. 'Well done.'

It wasn't the easiest of nights. I never saw the Commodore.
Everyone was friendly but I felt rather like the French exchange

that people might feel they had to look after and I didn't want to spoil their evening. This was their big do of the year. I did a lot of circling and trying to look as if I had just spotted a great friend across the room. I had my hands hennaed. I had my fortune told. I admired the portraits. Then I joined the crowd around a sensationally good magician, slim and exotic, with dark hair and beautiful almond eyes. He could have flown in on a magic carpet from Samarkand. I picked up his card. It said 'Drummond Money-Coutts'. Life is sometimes very unfair, I reflected. Of all the people who didn't need to be able to magic fifty-pound notes out of top hats it was him. 'The best of the best,' murmured Victoria as she flitted past. 'Costs a fortune. Worth every penny.'

The next day I went to the Esplanade, to the west of Princes Green, a stretch of grass to the west of the Castle, bequeathed on the condition that it never be commercially exploited and always remain open for public use. Beside it runs a deep stretch of water, right up to the sea wall, and the boats sometimes finish along here with their spinnakers ballooning. It was doubly popular today because the Extreme 40s were racing. These forty-foot carbon-fibre catamarans, the F1 cars of sailing, were doing for sailing much what the Twenty20 game was doing for cricket. They were fast, they were sexy, they were crewed by superstars – Olympic gold medallists and America's Cup winners – and they had room on their double-bed-sized netting deck for a 'fifth man', usually a corporate guest. These people could be seen leaping off at the end of their fifteen-minute race, raving with excitement. One came off bleeding profusely from a gash over one eye.

These races were compered by DJs and accompanied by a throbbing bass soundtrack. It was all noise, excitement and whipping up the crowd, who sat in their shorts and fleeces and gasped as the boats tipped up on their sides, sharp little keel fins showing, and the sailors yelled instructions at each other and, every so often, intoxicatingly, there was a crash. 'BOOM! It's a crash!' the commentator would bellow, unnecessarily. 'Wow, that was big, that was bad ... let's see what's going to happen NOW-W-W-W!' It was as far removed from the elegant slow motion of the Squadron as could be. The only thing they had in common was that the Extreme 40s swirled about before the start while listening for the words: 'Five, four, three, two, one.'

I stayed for a long time, wondering if this was the future. The sun slid down in the sky and the crowd slowly began to move east, settling like sparrows into any open space they could find. It was Friday, the last night of the Regatta, and there were to be fireworks off a barge in the harbour. Victoria texted, asking if I would like to join them for supper first. On the way I stopped to sit in the graveyard of Holy Trinity Church, overlooking the Solent. It had been a long, long summer and now it was almost over I didn't know if I felt glad or sad. Around me was a cheery crowd, with their backs against the graves, waiting for the show to begin. When I got to the back of the house I could see through the window all my ball companions sitting around the dinner table, a circle of good friends, and I suddenly couldn't face invading again. I wanted to end my season on my own.

So I took my place back in the graveyard, where people were chatting and waiting. Down on the water you could just see little vessels bobbing at a safe distance from the pyro-barge. They had chugged over for the evening from around the island. Behind them loomed the big boats, the Fireworks Cruises, like elephants around a waterhole. People were hurrying by on the road below the church wall, or revolving slowly with their mobiles clamped to one ear, looking for their friends. The graves slowly filled up.

There was a long, dark silence. Then the first rocket went up, soaring high over the water and the clustered houses of the town and the boats full of pale upturned faces, to a great roar from the crowd. Then another. And another. Slow chrysanthemums of gold bloomed in the sky and fire rained down in waterfalls and scribbles of colour. After a while everyone stopped ooh-ing and aah-ing and just watched as the spectacle moved towards its crescendo. What a night, what a summer, I thought, as the last rocket went up. It arched high over its reflection in the water, to wild cheering, and exploded in a big fat dandelion of red and silver fire.

THE BUTTERFLY
SUMMER

When I got back to London in mid-August, it was blissfully quiet. The schools were on holiday, the traffic was down, you could get into theatres and restaurants and for those of us who remained there was a lovely sense of peaceful possession. I wore jeans and T-shirts and no make-up. I saw friends and spent hours walking on my own, reacquainting myself with home. It was what I needed after the hectic, variegated summer.

In the past, people didn't feel like this at all. London died at the end of the season, or it did for anyone who was still there, having, by some hideous oversight, neglected to get a berth in a shooting lodge or steam yacht for August and September. 'No one would have been seen dead in London after Goodwood,'[1] writes Fiona MacCarthy firmly in her book about her deb season – and that was in the late 1950s. The further back you look, the worse it was. In the 1920s the *Sydney Morning Herald*, 11,000 miles away in another hemisphere, warned its readers not to get caught out:

'The "season" of 1929 is drawing to its close,' it announced. 'Only one or two important events remain before society departs from London and goes north to Scotland, or to country resorts for shooting and fishing ... Soon the West End will be empty of people who matter, and overseas visitors who are wise and "know the ropes" will be missing, too.'[2]

The people who didn't matter, the other five million or so, stayed behind to clear up, or, no doubt with a sigh of relief, enjoy having the parks, the streets and the river to themselves. The grand London houses were closed like clams for the winter and their staff returned to the country. Hotels and gentlemen's clubs took the opportunity for a thorough cleaning. Chefs took holidays. Paris in August is probably the nearest you could get to this today.

The best description of the gloom, not to mention wounded pride, suffered by those who failed to escape is at the start of Erskine Childers' wonderful 1903 secret service novel *The Riddle of the Sands*. His hero, Carruthers, is slogging away in an empty office. His friends, including the girl he loves, are shooting and flirting in a Scottish lodge, '... while I – well, a young man of condition and fashion, who knows the right people, belongs to the right clubs, has a safe, possibly a brilliant, future in the Foreign Office – may be excused for a sense of complacent martyrdom, when, with his keen appreciation of the social calendar, he is doomed to the outer solitude of London in September'.[3] The analogy he uses, as he changes at his chambers, is someone alone in the colonies who still dresses for dinner.

As for me, I went back to freelancing and to shopping at Battersea Park Road Tesco and paying my TV licence and going to the pub. Soon the fizzy hues of my summer began to fade. I sat down to write just as the next season began, in Olympics year, and found myself pawing like an old warhorse, wanting to join in. I even felt a pang of nostalgia for the sick-coloured shoes, which I had put in the recycling bin at the council dump. But time constraints meant I could only get to about half of the events in person. I had to see the rest on telly or hear about them on the news.

I watched in amazement as an anti-capitalist protestor called Trenton Oldfield jumped into the Thames during the Boat Race, miraculously – many rowers felt tragically – avoiding injury as he popped up between the scything oar blades, causing a restart and ruining any thoughts of records. It was announced that Royal Ascot was stiffening its dress code, banning 'fascinators' – Alice bands with feathers – in the Royal Enclosure, lowering hems to the knee and causing much media debate on the subjects of Fascinators v. Hats and Chavs v. Toffs, which gave them the opportunity to rerun pictures of the famous bandstand fight scenes from 2011.

I went to the men's tennis final at Queen's, courtesy of a friend, but it ended abruptly when a furious player kicked out and inadvertently injured a linesman. The resulting automatic default had the whole crowd booing: not the player – though they booed him a bit, too – but the club. The tennis old guard must have been revolving in their graves: sod the rules, the crowd was saying, we've paid to see the tennis ... it was an entirely different interpretation of playing up and playing the game. And as if anarchy wasn't enough, it rained so much the Henley Classic Swim was cancelled for safety reasons and the sheer volume of water meant few Royal Regatta records were broken. The only compensation was that the men and women of Leander won twelve medals at the London Olympic Games.

As the year went on, Britain fell in love with the royal family again over the Queen's Diamond Jubilee, London fell in love with itself again over the Olympics, and Kate Reardon fell in love and got engaged, causing turmoil because she was just about to host *Tatler*'s Black Book Party for eligible singles and she was no longer single or eligible. In the end, she greeted everyone outside and went out to dinner with her fiancé. Edward Gillespie retired from Cheltenham. Frankel the wonder horse retired to stud. The Tory chief whip retired precipitately, alleged to have called the Downing Street policemen 'plebs' when they wouldn't let him bicycle through the gate. 'Plebgate' reignited Chavs v. Toffs, presenting yet another golden opportunity to rerun the fight pictures. Frankie Dettori stunned the racing world by testing positive for drugs. Ian Hislop of *Private Eye* presented a television series on the British and their stiff upper lip. And to my great pleasure, Victoria's husband Johnny won his White Group race at Cowes.

Looking back on my season, I now realise its perceived poshness is sleight of hand – maybe true for the tip of the iceberg, but not for 90 per cent of the people who go – and struggle to think of other paying events that allow large numbers in for under a tenner, or free. I now know the apparently unchanging demeanour of these events conceals an extraordinary ability to adapt. In the same way I now regard the aristocracy as a biological miracle, like a particularly resilient bacteria that mutates under pressure.

In the end, Edward Gillespie's comment about theatricality applied to all the events I attended: the set and the script remain but the cast changes, so gradually, unnoticed, the whole thing quietly evolves. In a funny way the season belongs to everyone, like a cycle of mystery plays, or the religious calendar, whether they care or not. Perhaps its greatest glory is its brevity, the fact that it blooms joyously and dies back for another year: marking the passing of another English summer.

People keep asking me which event I liked best. I'd have to say the Derby and, weirdly, the cricket, but I'll go to all of them again. How could you not? It toughened me up, too: I found all that dressing up reduced my anxiety about clothes. No one was looking at me, dear; it was liberating in the extreme. I was left with an incipient racing habit, a new respect for Englishness, in all its bizarre manifestations, and a collapsed butterfly hat.

ACKNOWLEDGEMENTS

Thank you to Graham Coster at Aurum Press for his good humour, light touch and support when this book was delayed for personal reasons, and to Stuart Cooper who commissioned it in the first place.

I would like to thank the people who so generously shared their expertise, knowledge or contacts with me. Many are mentioned in the text but others are not, particularly Stephen Wallis of Jockey Club Racecourses, Bridget Guerin, now a steward at York Racecourse, Catherine Addison (née Althaus) for debutante memories, and Victoria Pakenham, whose horse Sir Percy won the Derby in 2006.

Victoria Mather and Johnny Raymond let me gatecrash their dinner before the RYS Ball, Jennifer and Geoffrey Malone did the same with their Ascot picnic, Jane and David Hickey provided Henley hospitality and Tim and Annabel Seegar baroque partying at the Derby and Ascot despite barely knowing me. Thanks to Anthony Connell for the opening image, the Aldous family for taking me to the Fourth of June, and Philip Winston for happy visits to Glyndebourne over the years.

Alice Prier of Alice & Co made my Ascot dress and Susie Hopkins of Susie Hopkins Hats my butterfly headgear for a fraction of their normal prices. Doug McKinlay came and took photographs as a favour. The staff of the *Daily Telegraph* travel section – particularly Michael Kerr and Joanna Symons – has been unfailingly patient and supportive.

I also owe a big debt to the patient souls at each event, especially the ones who put the odd ticket my way: Judith Speller at Goodwood, Nick Smith and Karen Smith at Ascot Racecourse Holdings, Daniel Grist, Secretary of the Henley Royal Regatta, Tom Kean for letting me join the Henley Classic swim, Beth Wild at Lord's and Neil Robinson in the Lord's Library, Diana Butler at the Guards Polo Club, Dr Brent Elliott and Hayley Monckton at the Royal Horticultural Society, Mark Pomeroy at the Royal Academy library, Angela Harcombe and Harriet Collins of JSC Sport for Epsom Racecourse and Charlie Cooper for welcoming me to the Irish Travellers' campsite, Stuart Quarrie and Michelle Warner of Aberdeen Asset Management Cowes Week, Commodore Michael Campbell and Patricia Lewington at the Royal Yacht Squadron in Cowes, Johnny Perkins for help with Wimbledon and Audrey Snell at the Kenneth Ritchie Wimbledon Library in the All England Club, Julia Aries and the Press Office at Glyndebourne, Paul Mainds, the director of the River and Rowing Museum in Henley and Rosie Harkness of Rose Tinted PR. Any errors are of course mine.

To the friends who have listened so loyally, I can't thank you enough. For writing advice, Ian Belcher, my cousin Ilay Cooper, Sarah Murray, Elizabeth Pisani, Bryn Thomas of Trailblazer Guides and Jasper Winn deserve special mention, also Charles Colville, Mark Curtis, Amelia Fitzalan-Howard, Lucy Hannah,

Steven Szymanski, Toby W, Nicky and Adrian Scott-Knight and Rick and Ros Lovell.

Finally, to my brother James, my sister-in-law Arabella and family and my mother Diana, whose middle name should be Patience, I owe you.

Sophie Campbell
London
January 2013

NOTES

1. A TOE IN THE WATER

1. *Debrett's Peerage & Baronetage 2011.* (Debrett's, Nov 2010). *On Tour, Debrett's New Season from Glyndebourne to Glastonbury.* (Debrett's, March 2009).

3. THE LAST TRUCK TO CHELSEA

1. Miller, Thomas. *The Poetical Language of Flowers*, or *The Pilgrimage of Love.* (David Bogue, 1847).
2. Tyas, Robert. *The Language of Flowers*, or, *Floral Emblems of Thoughts, Feelings, and Sentiments.* (George Routledge & Sons, 1869). p.150.

4. A GARDEN GROWS BY THE RIVER

1. *A Handbook to the Royal Horticultural Gardens. A sketch of the history of the Royal Horticultural Society, and a description of the gardens at South Kensington. With illustrations.* (Published for the Royal Horticultural Society by Lacon and Ollier, 1864). p.11.
2. *Ibid.* p.27.
3. *Minutes of Horticultural Society, Volume I,* first page. (the Royal Horticultural Society, 1804–15).
4. *Gardeners' Magazine* 1827 cited by Dr Brent Elliott in *The Royal Horticultural Society, A History 1804–2004.* (2004, Philimore & Co). p.114.

5. Flanders, Judith. *Consuming Passions: Leisure & Pleasure in Victorian Britain.* (Harper Press, 2006). p.27.

5. NOT A THING TO WEAR

1. Sherwood, James and Devonshire, Duke of. *Fashion at Royal Ascot: Three Centuries of Thoroughbred Style.* (Thames & Hudson, 2011). p.12.
2. Walker, Richard. *The Savile Row Story: An Illustrated History.* (Prion, 1988). p.41.

6. THE UPS AND DOWNS OF EPSOM

1. Church, Michael. *The Derby Stakes: the complete history 1780–2006.* (Raceform Ltd, 2006).
2. Letter to the Editor from 'Bona fide'. Mounted in the 1st Minute Book. p.57. (By permission of Wenlock Olympian Society).
3. Fox, Kate. *The Racing Tribe: Watching the Horsewatchers.* (Metro, 1999).

7. AND ALL FOR A BUNCH OF STUDENTS

1. Brownlow, John. *Memoranda, or Chronicles of the Foundling Hospital, Including Memoirs of Captain Coram.* (Sampson Low, 1847). p.12.
2. Anon. *A Rap at the RA.* (London 1875).

9. THE BUTTERFLIES EMERGE

1. Campbell, Margaret. *Forget Not: The Autobiography of Margaret, Duchess of Argyll.* (W. H. Allen, 1975). p.46.
2. Trevelyan, G. *English Social History: A Survey of Six Centuries: Chaucer to Queen Victoria.* (Longmans & Co., 1944). p.15.
3. Foreman, Amanda. *Georgiana, Duchess of Devonshire.* (HarperCollins, 2008). p.331.
4. Lovell, Mary S. *A Scandalous Life: The Biography of Jane Digby el Mezrab.* (Richard Cohen, 1995). p.14.
5. Mingay, G. E. *English Landed Society in the Eighteenth Century.* (Routledge & Kegal Paul, 1963). p 19.
6. *Ibid.* p 6.
7. Davidoff, Leonore. *The Best Circles: Society Etiquette and The Season.* (Rowan and Littlefield, 1973). p 18.
8. Cannadine, David. *The Decline & Fall of the British Aristocracy.* (Papermac, 1996, c1992). p.10.

10. MUSIC ON THE MITTEL DOWNS

1. Colegate, Isabel. *The Shooting Party.* (Hamish Hamilton, 1980). p. 26.
2. 'The Summer Magic of Country-House Opera'. Moore, Charles. *Daily Telegraph*, 12 July 2011. p.34.

11. NOBODY'S LOOKING AT YOU, DEAR

1. *Hairdressers' Journal* 1963, cited by Professor Christopher Breward in a speech at the London College of Fashion, May 2002.
2. Edward VII letter to Queen Victoria in July 1869, cited by Sean Magee in *Ascot: The History*. (Methuen, 2002). p.100.

12. TOPPERS AND TAILS

1. Andra-Warner, Elle. *Hudson's Bay Company Adventures: Tales of Fur Traders.* (Heritage House, 2009). p.14.

13. THE ROYAL ENCLOSURE AT LAST

1. Magee, Sean with Aird, Sally. *Ascot: The History*. (Methuen, 2002). p.19.
2. Smith, Godfrey. *The English Season*. (Pavilion Books, 1987). p.90.

14. THE PERFECTLY PACKED BASKET

1. MacCarthy, Fiona. *Last Curtsey: The End of the Debutantes.* (Faber & Faber, 2006). p.201.
2. Beeton, Isabella. *Beeton's Book of Household Management.* (S.O. Beeton, 1861). p.915.
3. Davidson, Alan. *Oxford Companion to Food*. (Oxford University Press, 1999).

15. THE LAST OF THE GILDED YOUTH

1. 'Cricket: Eton v. Harrow'. *The Times*, 11 July 1910. p. 21.
2. *Eton Chronicle*, cited by Anne De Courcy in *1939: The Last Season*. (Thames & Hudson, 1989). p.200.
3. Taylor, D J. *On the Corinthian Spirit: The Decline of Amateurism in Sport*. (Yellow Jersey Press, 2006). p.105.

4. 'Cricket Sent Back to the Pavilion'. Boston, Anne. *Observer*, 27 June 1993. p.54.

16. THE BUTTERFLIES TAKE OFF

1. 'Obituary: Betty Kenward'. *Daily Telegraph*, 26 January 2001. p.31.

17. THE TENTED VILLAGE

1. Betjeman, J. *Collected Poems*. (Houghton Mifflin,1959). p. 97
2. Gorringe, Christopher. *Holding Court: Inside the Gates of the Wimbledon Championships*. (Random House, 2009). p.183.

18. THE CARPET OF GREEN

1. Harvey, Graham. *The Forgiveness of Nature*. (Jonathan Cape, 2001). p.267.
2. Uglow, Jenny. *A Little History of British Gardening*. (Chatto & Windus, 2004). p.32.

EPILOGUE: THE BUTTERFLY SUMMER

1. MacCarthy, Fiona. *Last Curtsey: The End of the Debutantes*. (Faber & Faber, 2006). p.142.
2. 'For Women: The London Season. Closing Events'. *Sydney Morning Herald*, August 31 1929. p.12.
3. Childers, Erskine. *The Riddle of the Sands*. (Smith, Elder & Co, 1903). p.15.

BIBLIOGRAPHY

BOOKS

A Handbook to the Royal Horticultural Gardens. A sketch of the history of the Royal Horticultural Society, and a description of the gardens at South Kensington. With illustrations. (Published for the Royal Horticultural Society by Lacon and Ollier, 1864).

Barstow, Phyllida. *The English Country House Party.* (Equation Books, 1989).

Battiscombe, Georgina. *English Picnics* (Harvill, 1949).

Bourdieu, Pierre. *Distinction: A Social Critique of the Judgement of Taste*, trans. by Richard Nice. (Harvard University Press, 1984).

Cannadine, David. *The Decline & Fall of the British Aristocracy.* (Papermac, 1996, c1992).

Church, Michael. *The Derby Stakes: The Complete History 1780–2006.* (Raceform Ltd, 2006).

Cook, Matthew and Duncan, Paul. *The British Season – A Celebration of Summertime Entertainments.* (Little, Brown, 1994).

Crookenden, Kate, Worlledge, Caroline and Willes, Margaret, compilers. *The National Trust Book of Picnics.* (National Trust, 1988).

Davidson, Alan. *Oxford Companion to Food.* (Oxford University Press, 1999).

De Courcy, Anne. *The Last Season.* (Thames & Hudson, 1989).

Egan, Pierce. *Book of Sports & Mirror of Life.* (Thomas Tegg and Son, 1836).

Elliott, Dr Brent. *The Royal Horticultural Society: A History, 1804–2004.* (Phillimore & Co Ltd, 2004).

Fenton, James. *School of Genius: A History of the Royal Academy of Arts.* (Royal Academy of Arts, 2006).

Flanders, Judith. *Consuming Passions, Leisure and Pleasure in Victorian Britain.* (Harper Press, 2006).

Foreman, Amanda. *Georgiana, Duchess of Devonshire.* (HarperCollins, 2008).

Geddes-Brown, Lesley. *Chelsea: The Greatest Flower Show on Earth.* (Dorling Kindersley, 2006).

Gorringe, Chris. *Holding Court: Inside the Gates of the Wimbledon Championships.* (Century/Random House, 2009).

Helliker, Adam. *The Debrett Season: A Light-Hearted Romp Through the Social and Sporting Year.* (Debrett's Peerage Limited, 1981).

Higgins, John (Ed). *Glyndebourne: A Celebration.* (Jonathan Cape, 1984).

Hughes, Spike. *Glyndebourne, a History of the Festival Opera Founded in 1934 by Audrey and John Christie.* (David & Charles, 1981).

Hutchison, Sidney C. *The History of the Royal Academy.* (Chapman & Hall, 1968).

Kelly, Ian. *Beau Brummel: The Ultimate Dandy.* (Hodder, 2006).

MacCarthy, Fiona. *The Last Curtsey, The End of the Debutantes.* (Faber & Faber, 2006).

Macinnes, Peter. *The Lawn: A Social History.* (Murdoch Books, 2009).

Miller, Thomas. *The Poetical Language of Flowers, or The Pilgrimage of Love.* (David Bogue, 1847).

Magee, Sean with Aird, Sally. *Ascot, The History* (Methuen, 2002)

Mingay, George Edmund. *English Landed Society in the Eighteenth Century.* (Routledge & Kegan Paul, 1963).

Mintz, Sidney. *Tasting Food, Tasting Freedom: Excursions into Eating, Culture, and the Past.* (Beacon, 1996).

Mortimer, Roger. *The History of the Derby Stakes.* Second Edition (Michael Joseph, 1973).

Nichols, R. A. and Wray, F. A. *The History of the Foundling Hospital.* (Oxford University Press, 1935).

Noel, Celestria. *Harpers & Queen's Guide to the Season.* (Headline, 1994).

Noel, Celestria. *Debrett's Guide to the Season.* (Debrett's Peerage Limited, 2000).

Pullar, Philippa. *Gilded Butterflies: The Rise and Fall of the London Season.* (Hamish Hamilton, 1978).

Plumptre, George. *The Fast Set: The World of Edwardian Racing.* (Andre Deutsch, 1985).

Randolph Spencer Churchill, Lady. *Reminiscences.* (Edward Arnold, 1908).

Seaton, Janet. *Kelways Glorious: The History of a Pioneering Somerset Nursery.* (Kelways Nursery, 2009).

Sherwood, James. *Fashion at Royal Ascot: Three Centuries of Thoroughbred Style*. (Thames & Hudson, 2011).

Simmonds, A. *The History of the Royal Horticultural Society, 1804–1954*. (RHS, 1954).

Smith, Godfrey. *The English Season*. (Pavilion Books, 1987).

Steinberg, Ted. *American Green: The Obsessive Quest for the Perfect Lawn*. (Geographical Review. Vol 98; No 4; 2008).

Titchener-Barrett, Robert. *Eton and Harrow at Lord's: Since 1805*. (published by the author, 2005).

Tyas, Robert. *The Language of Flowers, or, Floral Emblems of Thoughts, Feelings, and Sentiments*. (George Routledge & Sons, 1869).

Tyrrel, John. *Running Racing: the Jockey Club Years Since 1750*. (Quiller, 1997).

Uglow, Jenny. *A Little History of British Gardening*. (Chatto & Windus, 2004).

Wirt, E. W. *Flora's Dictionary, A Treatise on the Language of Flowers*. (Lucas, 1831).

WEBSITES

British Horseracing Authority (www.britishhorseracing.com).

The Championships, Wimbledon (www.wimbledon.com/championships).

Cheltenham Festival (www.cheltenham.co.uk).

Cowes Week (www.aamcowesweek.co.uk).

Debrett's (www.debretts.com).

Epsom Downs Racecourse (www.epsomdowns.co.uk).

Fortnum and Mason (www.fortnumandmason.com).

Glyndebourne Opera (www.glyndebourne.com).

Goodwood (www.goodwood.co.uk).

Guards Polo Club (www.guardspoloclub.com).

Henley Royal Regatta (www.hrr.co.uk).

Lord's (www.lords.org).

Meyer and Mortimer (www.meyerandmortimer.co.uk).

The National Horseracing Museum (www.nhrm.co.uk).

Newmarket Racecourses (www.newmarketracecourses.co.uk).

Royal Academy (www.royalacademy.org.uk).

Royal Ascot (www.ascot.co.uk).

Royal Horticultural Society (www.rhs.org.uk).

Royal Opera House Collections (www.rohcollections.org.uk).

The Royal Warrant Holders' Association (www.royalwarrant.org).

INDEX